TWAYNE'S WORLD AUTHORS SERIES
A Survey of the World's Literature

Sylvia E. Bowman, Indiana University

GENERAL EDITOR

SWEDEN

Leif Sjöberg
State University of New York at Stony Brook

EDITOR

August Strindberg

TWAS 410

August Strindberg

AUGUST STRINDBERG

By WALTER JOHNSON

University of Washington

TWAYNE PUBLISHERS
A DIVISION OF G. K. HALL & CO., BOSTON

Library of Congress Cataloging in Publication Data

Johnson, Walter, 1905-
   August Strindberg.

   (Twayne's world authors series: TWAS 410)
   Bibliography: p. 207-215.
   Includes index.
   1.   Strindberg, August, 1849-1912.
PT9815.J6   839.7'2'6[B]   76-17910
ISBN O-8057-6250-7

For
RUTH INGEBORG

Contents

About the Author

For over four decades the author of this book has given a major portion of his time and energy to the study of Strindberg and his works. A B.A. at Augsburg College, an M.A. at the University of Minnesota, and a Ph.D. (in Scandinavian) at the University of Illinois, Walter Johnson has served as professor of Scandinavian languages and literature at the University of Washington and spent his sabbaticals and some summers in Scandinavia, including two years (1957-1958 and 1964-1965) as a Guggenheim Fellow in Stockholm. He has received the Swedish Order of the North Star, the Distinguished Alumnus Award from Augsburg College, an honorary doctor's degree at the University of Uppsala, and the gold medal of the Swedish Academy.

Among his publications are the ongoing Washington Strindberg (ten volumes of translations of Strindberg plays and introductions to each plus a translation and edition of Strindberg's *Open Letters to the Intimate Theater*); an edition of four Hjalmar Bergman plays; the volume *Strindberg and the Historical Drama*; a volume on Swedish-English literary relations in the eighteenth century; two textbooks for students of the Swedish language; many reviews; and articles on American Swedish, recent Swedish literature, and Scandinavian drama and theater. A member of the editorial staffs of *Scandinavica, The Swedish Pioneer Historical Quarterly,* and *Scandinavian Studies,* he served the last named journal as managing editor for twelve years. At present he is continuing his Strindberg projects and doing a study of Vilhelm Moberg, the author of the tetralogy about Swedish immigrants in the Middle West.

Preface

Studying Strindberg's works, examining the literature about them, reporting on my research, translating and introducing his major dramas, teaching undergraduate Strindberg courses, and conducting graduate Strindberg seminars have led me to ever-increasing interest in him as a human being and appreciation of him as a literary artist. He has played and is playing, directly and indirectly, such an important role in modern literature, it seems to me no thoughtful reader can afford to be ignorant of him as a personal force and as the creator of seminal works of art.

Since the books in this series are intended for the general reader and not for the specialist, I have provided an introduction to the man and to those of his works which are most significant and vital, given the reader at least an idea of what else he contributed, and indicated some direction for the study of his works. Dealing even briefly with every one of them here is impossible: The bulk of his creative writing is simply too vast. The rest of his activities and achievements were so numerous, moreover, that only those that were primary have received more than passing attention.

I have provided an English equivalent for each Swedish title even when the work has not been translated into English because Strindberg's titles were carefully selected and are decidedly informative. If a particular work is, to my knowledge, not yet available in English, I have so indicated by placing an asterisk (*) after the title the first time it occurs.

The translations of brief passages from his works are my own unless I have otherwise indicated. Since most of these excerpts are from the collected works (*Samlade skrifter*) or from the ongoing edition of his letters (*August Strindbergs brev*), I have indicated the source of the original immediately after each translation as *SS* and *Brev* respectively.

Not all the translations listed in the bibliography are available in bookstores, but chances are good that a reader can obtain any of those now out of print through the services of public, college, and university libraries. Translations that will appear in the future will, hopefully, be listed in the annual bibliography published in *Scandinavian Studies*.

WALTER JOHNSON

Acknowledgments

Acknowledgments should be made to the Strindberg Society for its excellent edition of Strindberg's letters, to such helpful secondary sources as *Strindbergs systrar berätta* and *Ögonvittnen,* to those scholars who have contributed stimulating studies of Strindberg and his works, and, perhaps above all, to the late John Landquist who edited the collected works and who in many ways encouraged the present writer in his study of Strindberg and his works.

Chronology

1847   September 24: marriage of Strindberg's parents, steamship agent Carl Oscar Strindberg (1811-1883) and former waitress Ulrica Eleonora Norling (1823-1862). Their children who survived infancy: Carl Axel (1845-1927), Oscar (1847-1924), Johan August (1849-1912), Johan Olof (1853-1943), Anna Maria von Philp (1855-1937), Elisabeth Magdalena (1857-1904), Lovisa Eleonora Hartzell (1858-1927).

1849   January 22: birth of (Johan) August Strindberg. Baptized February 3.

1853   Father's bankruptcy.

1854- Pupil in turn at Klara School, Jakob's School, and the
1867   private Stockholm Lyceum.

1862   March 20: death of his mother (tuberculosis).

1863   February 13: marriage of Strindberg's father and his housekeeper Emilia Charlotta Petersson (1841-1887). Their child: Emil Zacharias (1864-1912).

1864   Confirmed, Adolf Fredrik's Church (Stockholm), Church of Sweden.

1867   May 25: passed *studenten* (the comprehensives) as number 18 in a class of 20. September 13: fall term at the University of Uppsala.

1868   Substitute teacher, Stockholm. Resident tutor for Dr. Axel Lamm's sons. Studied medicine with Dr. Lamm.

1869   Failed in tryout as actor at the Royal Theater. Failed examination in chemistry at Uppsala. Plays: *A Namesday Gift** (*En namnsdagsgåva*); *The Freethinker** (*Fritänkaren*).

1870   Spring and fall terms at Uppsala — organized Runa, a society for would-be writers. Plays: *In Rome** (*I Rom*) produced at the Royal Theater; *Hermione** given honorable mention by the Swedish Academy.

1871   First summer on Kymmendö. Fall term at Uppsala: passed examinations in English, French, German, and Italian and in modern literature. Play: *The Outlaw* (*Den fredlöse*) produced at the Royal Theater (King Charles XV impressed: granted Strindberg a stipend of 200 crowns).

1872 March 3: left Uppsala. Failed tryout as actor in Göteborg. Newspaper writer. Play: *Master Olof* (*Mäster Olof*), prose version completed August 8.

1872- With fellow artists in the Red Room at Bern's Restaurant.
1877

1873- Journalist in Stockholm. Translator. Editor. Reviewer.
1883 Creative writer.

1874- On staff of the Royal Library: became Oriental specialist
1882 (Chinese, Japanese).

1875 Met Baron (*friherre*) Carl Gustaf Wrangel, a captain of the guards, and his wife, Sigrid (Siri) Sofia Matilda Elisabeth von Essen Wrangel (1850-1912). Strindberg's appraisal: "the most beautiful woman in Sweden." Play: The "Middle" Version* of *Master Olof* (*Mellanspelet*).

1876 Attempt at suicide. Siri divorced. Siri on stage (1876-83). Plays: The "Verse" Version* of *Master Olof; The Year 48* (*Anno fyrtioåtta*).

1877 January: death of Sigrid Wrangel, Siri's daughter. December 30: marriage of Strindberg and Siri. Their infant daughter died January, 1878. Their other children: Karin Smirnoff (1880-1961), Greta von Philp (1881-1912), Hans (1884-1917). Play: *The Epilog* (*Efterspelet*) to *Master Olof.* Fiction: *From Town and Gown* (*Från Fjärdingen och Svartbäcken*).

1879 Financial bankruptcy. Fiction: *The Red Room* (*Röda rummet*), a novel which brought him breakthrough to recognition as writer.

1880 Play: *The Secret of the Guild* (*Gillets hemlighet*). Cultural history: *Old Stockholm* (*Gamla Stockholm*) with Claes Lundin.

1881 Successful initial production of prose *Master Olof.* Verse and prose: *Poems and Realities* (*Dikter och verkligheter*).

1882 Resignation from the staff of the Royal Library. Plays: *Lord Bengt's Wife* (*Herr Bengts hustru*), *The Journey of Lucky Peter* (*Lycko-Pers resa*). Cultural history: *The Swedish People on Holy Day and Everyday, in War and Peace, at Home and Abroad or A Thousand Years of the History of Swedish Culture and Manners* (*Svenska folket i helg och söcken, krig och fred, hemma och ute eller Ett tusen år av svenska bildningens och sedernas historia*); social and political satire: *The New Nation* (*Nya riket*).

Chronology

1882- Fiction: *Swedish Destinies and Adventures* (*Svenska öden*
1892 *och äventyr*),* four volumes.

1883 Death of father. Fall: self-exile to France (Grez, Paris) and
      Switzerland (Ouchy, Chexbres). *Poems in Verse and Prose*
      (*Dikter på vers och prosa*).

1884 Moved to Geneva. Verse: *Nights of Sleepwalking* (*Sömn-
      gångarnätter*). Fiction: *Married* (*Giftas*, I). Tried for
      blasphemy. November 17: Acquitted.

1884- Increasingly serious marital difficulties: Attempts at
1891 determining Siri's unfaithfulness.

1885 Fiction: *Actual Utopias* (*Utopier i verkligheten*);
      Autobiography: *Journey into Detention* (*Kvarstadsresan*,
      account of the 1884 trial in letter form).

1886- Strindberg's "naturalistic" period.
1892

1886 Fiction: *Married* II (*Giftas*, II). Autobiographical novels:
      The Son of a Servant, The Development of a Human Being
      (*Tjänstekvinnans son, En själs utvecklingshistoria*, I); *Time
      of Ferment* (*Jäsningstiden = Tjänstekvinnans son*, II); *In
      the Red Room* (*I röda rummet = Tjänstekvinnans son*,
      III); *The Author* (*Författaren = Tjänstekvinnans son*, IV
      published 1909).

1887 Moved to Bavaria. Plays: *Marauders* (*Marodörer*); *The
      Comrades* (*Kamraterna*); *The Father* (*Fadren*). Novel: *The
      People of Hemsö* (*Hemsöborna*). J.W. Personne's *The
      Strindberg Literature and Immorality among Pupils in the
      Schools* (*Strindbergs-litteraturen och osedligheten bland
      skolungdom*).

1887- Psychological narrative essays: *Vivisections* (*Vivisektioner*):
1890 "The Little Ones"* ("De små"), "The Great Ones"* ("De
      stora"), "The Battle of the Brains"* ("Hjärnornas
      kamp"), "Hallucinations"* ("Hallucinationer"), "Divine
      Nemesis"* ("Nemesis divina"), "Mysticism — for the Time
      Being"* ("Mystik — tills vidare!"), "Psychic Murder"
      ("Själamord").

1888 Completion of autobiographical novel: *A Madman's
      Defence* (*Le plaidoyer d'un fou*, written in French;
      published in German, 1893; in Swedish translation, 1893-94;
      in French, 1895). Plays: *Lady Julie* (*Fröken Julie*), *Creditors*
      (*Fordringsägare*). Fiction: *Life in the Skerries*
      (*Skärkarlsliv*). Popular science: *Flowers and Animals*

(*Blomstermålningar och djurstycken*).

1889 Attempt at establishing an experimental theater in Copenhagen. April: return to Sweden. Plays: *The Stronger* (*Den starkare*), *Pariah* (*Paria*), *Simoom* (*Samum*), *The People of Hemsö** (*Hemsöborna*). Cultural history: *Among French Farmers** (*Bland franska bönder*).

1890 Novel: *At the Edge of the Sea* (*I havsbandet*).

1891 March 21: Strindberg and Siri granted separation.

1892 March: divorce from Siri final. September: moved to Berlin (The Cloister, a tavern he called Zum Schwarzen Ferkel — association with Christian Krohg, Edvard Munch, L. Schleich, etc.). Plays: *The First Warning* (*Första varningen*), *The Keys to Heaven** (*Himmelrikets nycklar*), *Debit and Credit* (*Debet och kredit*), *Facing Death* (*Inför döden*), *Mother Love* (*Moderskärlek*), *Playing with Fire* (*Leka med elden*), *The Bond* (*Bandet*). Exhibition of eight Strindberg paintings, Stockholm. Strindberg's turning from creative writing to science and alchemy.

1893 January 16: première of *Lady Julie* (Thèâtre libre, Paris). Organization of the Swedish Writers' Society (*Sveriges författarförening*). May 2: marriage of Strindberg and Maria Friederike (Frida) Cornelia Uhl (1872-1943). Their child: Christine (Kerstin) Sulzbach (1894-1956). Stays in Heligoland, in England, in Austria (with Frida's relatives), in Paris.

1894 October: parting from Frida. Staying on in Paris. December 13: première of *The Father* (Thèâtre nouveau).

1894- The Inferno Crisis (*Infernokrisen*). "Scientific" studies and
1897 experiments, including attempts at gold making. Illnesses, including psoriasis. Occult experiences. Keeping records of what was happening to him. Conversion to Strindbergian syncretism.

1895 Collections for Strindberg (Knut Hamsun, Nathan Söderblom), scientific and pseudoscientific work: *Sylva Sylvarum**.

1896 Scientific works: *Antibarbarus**; *Botanical Garden** (*Jardin des Plantes*). Autobiography: *The Occult Diary* (*Ockulta dagboken,* February 21, 1896 - July 11, 1908.

1897 Resumption of primarily creative writing. October 19: divorced by Frida. December: settled in Lund. Autobiographical novel: *Inferno.* Popular science: *Swedish*

1908 Marriage of Harriet Bosse and actor Gunnar Wingård. July: Strindberg moved into the Blue Tower (Blå tornet, Drottninggatan 85). Brief engagement to Fanny Falkner. Drama and theater: *Open Letters to the Intimate Theater* (*Öppna brev till Intima teatern*). Plays: *The Last of the Knights* (*Siste riddaren*), *Abu Casem's Slippers** (*Abu Casems tofflor*), *The Regent* (*Riksföreståndaren*), *Earl Birger of Bjälbo* (*Bjälbojarlen*).

1909 Plays: *The Black Glove** (*Svarta handsken*), *The Great Highway* (*Stora landsvägen*).

1910 August: Strindberg's withdrawal from the Swedish Writers' Society. December 11: closing of the Intimate Theater. Philological speculation: *The Origins of Our Mother Tongue** (*Modersmålets anor*), *The Roots of World Languages** (*Världsspråkens rötter*). Religious speculation: *Religious Renaissance** (*Religiös renässans*).

1910- The Strindberg Controversy (*Strindbergsfejden*): *Addresses*
1911 *to the Swedish Nation** (*Tal till svenska nationen*), *The People's State** (*Folkstaten*).

1911- John Landquist's edition of *Strindbergs Samlade skrifter*
1920 (the collected works in 55 volumes).

1912 January 22: public celebration of his birthday. March 2: received the Anti-Nobel Prize (ca. 50,000 crowns through public subscription). April 21: death of Siri von Essen Strindberg. May 14: death of August Strindberg (stomach cancer). May 19: buried at Solna (Norra Kyrkogården). Inscription on cross of dark oak: AVE CRUX SPES UNICA.

1945 June 1: founding of the Strindberg Society (*Strindbergssällskapet*).

1962 International exhibition of Strindberg paintings (Ulm, Paris, London, Stockholm).

* Not available in English translation.

Nature* (*Svensk natur*).

1898 Autobiography: *Legends* (*Legender*). Plays: *To Damascus* I and II (*Till Damaskus,* I, II), *Advent.*

1899 Final return to Stockholm. Plays: *There Are Crimes and Crimes* (*Brott och brott*), *The Saga of the Folkungs* (*Folkungasagan*), *Gustav Vasa, Erik XIV.*

1900 Plays: *Gustav Adolf, Midsummer** (*Midsommar*), *Casper's Shrove Tuesday** (*Kaspers fet-tisdag*), *Easter* (*Påsk*), *The Dance of Death* I and II (*Dödsdansen* I, II).

1901 May 6: marriage of Strindberg and Harriet Bosse (1878-1961). Their child: Anne-Marie Wyller (1902-   ). Plays: *The Crown Bride* (*Kronbruden*), *Swanwhite* (*Svanevit*), *Charles XII* (*Karl XII*), *To Damascus* III (*Till Damaskus,* III), *Engelbrekt, Queen Christina* (*Kristina*), *A Dream Play* (*Ett drömspel*).

1902 Fiction and verse: *Fairhaven and Foulstrand** (*Fagervik och Skamsund*). Play: *Gustav III.*

1903 Autobiography: *Alone* (*Ensam*). History: *The Hidden Meaning of World History** (*Världshistoriens mystik*). Plays: *The Nightingale of Wittenberg* (*Näktergalen i Wittenberg*), *Through the Wilderness to the Promised Land or Moses* (*Genom öknar till arvland eller Moses*), *Greece or Socrates* (*Hellas eller Sokrates*), *The Lamb and the Beast or Christ* (*Lammet och vilddjuret eller Kristus*). Fiction: *Tales* (*Sagor*).

1904 Novels: *The Gothic Rooms** (*Götiska rummen*), *Black Banners** (*Svarta fanor,* published, 1907). November: divorced from Harriet Bosse.

1905 Novel: *The Roofing Celebration** (*Taklagsöl,* published 1907). Stories: *Historical Miniatures** (*Historiska miniatyrer*).

1906 Novel: *The Scapegoat* (*Syndabocken,* published, 1907).

1907 Plays: *Stormy Weather* (*Oväder*), *The House That Burned* (*Brända tomten*), *The Ghost Sonata* (*Spöksonaten*), *The Pelican* (*Pelikanen*), *The Island of the Dead** (*Toten-Insel,* a fragment). November 26: opening of the Intimate Theater (*Intima teatern*).

1907- Essays: *A Blue Book: Delivered to Those Concerned and*
1912 *Comprising a Commentary on "Black Banners"* (*En blå bok. Avlämnad till vederbörande och utgörande kommentar till "Svarta fanor"*). I, II, III, IV.

CHAPTER 1

The Human Being

I have depicted my characters as modern characters living in a time of transition, more hysterically in a hurry than during the preceding period at least. I have presented them as vacillating, tattered mixtures of old and new ...

My souls (characters) are conglomerations of past and present cultures, bits out of books and newspapers, pieces of human beings, torn-off shreds of holiday clothes that have become rags, exactly as the human soul is put together. — Preface to *Lady Julie*.

W HAT Strindberg had to say in the 1888 preface about human beings as characterless characters applies very well to Strindberg himself. By *characterless* he did not mean lacking in mental and/or moral qualities implicit in such testimonials as "a person of good character" and "a person with a bad character." He did *not* believe in the permanent or lasting validity of any testimonial designed to state the traits of an individual. He did believe that human beings are complex and dynamic, that it is impossible to understand anyone *fully* at any point, and that, unless circumstances have made them "vegetables," they are constantly changing, and consequently hard to catch and take hold of.

Strindberg nevertheless considered the study of man, his world, and whatever force or forces may be back of it fascinating, proper, and necessary. From very early in life he was keenly aware of both his heredity and his environment and the factors of chance and time. The older he became, the more aware he became that human beings are jumbles of contradictions, highly complex and highly dynamic creatures.

Strindberg was born to parents who were not socially equal, who had been living together for several years without benefit of clergy, who had brought two older boys into a society that labelled them bastards, and who had made their relationship legal only a relatively short time before August Strindberg was brought into the world, possibly Strindberg thought, an unwelcome addition to the burdens of a couple hoping for social acceptance and struggling for economic security.

During his early years his father's fortunes fluctuated between bankruptcy and economic well-being, the family usually lived comfortably enough in rented homes even though they rarely stayed long in any one of them, the parents tried to maintain within the family strict standards of child behavior, and they apparently were so keenly aware of social disapproval they made August and his brothers and sisters intensely aware of "what people will say."

The gifted little egotist that August Strindberg was had to be kept under control so as "to be seen and not heard" by means of discipline expressed in countless ways from reprimands to beatings. His countermoves such as sulking, pretence, and deception in order to get attention, and even open rebellion all had to do with the seemingly never-ending problems of adjustment to his parents, his siblings, his other relatives, the servants, everyone else in his environment, and, perhaps hardest of all, to himself.

August Strindberg was not only a troubled child but a very difficult one, a fact that was more or less obvious to the members of his family and others who saw or had to deal with him then. He needed affection but did not get it from the mother whose favor he tried to win but whose preference went to an older brother. He needed attention but was put down by all his immediate elders except, usually, his maternal grandmother. He needed to express himself in both word and deed but was discouraged from doing either. He resented authority in every form; that resentment may well explain why, except for brief intervals, he resented and even hated his father, the very epitome of the Oscarian [1] (or Victorian) head of the family. He did not receive needed companionship, moreover, from any of his brothers until later in life.

The family was the first human group to attract his attention and was to remain one of his major concerns throughout his lifetime. Among those who have testified about the family while August was still at home are two of his younger sisters who wrote a pleasant little book in the 1920s and apparently designed it to correct Strindberg's published accounts:

Order, industry, and good habits put their stamp on our childhood home. Within some families there is such harmony and agreement in likes and points of view one is inclined to think they have "a soul in common." That was not how it was in our family. Even as children we revealed differing temperaments and characteristics. Those who were endowed with a lively imagination had both the joy of life and a lively sense of humor, while others were melancholy and serious minded and liked serious discussions or reading books. There wasn't any decided degree of closeness or intimacy among the members of the family either. Most of us did have a common interest in music, however. Father isolated himself pretty much, and our stepmother was inexperienced and didn't understand the children, so each of them was pretty much forced in upon himself and had to solve his own problems.

The center and unifying force in this somewhat heterogeneous family was Father. ... We might say in this connection that the thoroughly concentrated power which so to speak emanated from Father often felt oppressive and frustrating for us as we were growing up. This was undoubtedly so for our brother August who was even then yearning for freedom. Father's power and dignity undoubtedly often seemed difficult to submit to.[2]

An authoritarian father albeit with good intentions, a gentle, obedient but exhausted and "nervous" mother, a young pietistic stepmother (acquired less than a year after the mother's death), and a goodly number of withdrawn siblings were the human beings who were to give Strindberg not only his concept of the family as a prison but also his dream of the happy state the ideal family might be.

If any of his brothers was in a position to speak about August Strindberg as a child, a boy, and an adult, it was his oldest brother Axel:

The image I have of my brother August as a child is the image of a very blond, perfectly golden-haired, shy and bashful boy, who always was in opposition to everything. ... He was extremely shy. And in every way. I have just been thinking that [Carl Eldh's statue] represents him naked. He was even so shy with us brothers that he changed his underwear in a closet! ... In general he must have been inwardly most like Father who was reserved and melancholy and reticent. Outwardly he resembled Mother most. ... We never suspected he was a genius. God knows we understood he had a good mind, but we never grasped what his calling was. He was now going to be this, now that. [Axel mentions these: pastor, teacher, officer, doctor, actor.] He was always anxious to show, Brother August, that there are two sides to everything. But he himself was often one-sided,

if he had gained a notion of something. If we really admired something —
well, then he always wanted to turn it about and demonstrate its reverse. ...
And he was just as stubborn as his father. But also likely to change his
mind and not stick to anything, a trait that he was unjustly blamed for even
at home. He couldn't help it.[3]

If the family was the first institution to affect his development,
church and school were surely the next. Throughout his lifetime
Strindberg was exposed to and affected by religious groups and,
during fairly extended periods, by antireligious forces. Registered
at birth in the Church of Sweden, a state church with Lutheran
doctrines and in more than its preservation of the apostolic succession similar to the Church of England; christened, and, in 1864
confirmed at Adolf Fredrik's Church in Stockholm, Strindberg was
directly exposed to state-church traditions and articles of faith
through his father's preference for and reading at home of the
sermons of the Romantic rationalist poet and liberal high-church
archbishop Johan Olof Wallin (1779-1839)[4] and through church
attendance and, most particularly, training for confirmation under
the direction of a pastor he called "strict, merciless, unfeeling,
without a word of comfort or pity" [SS, XVIII, 145].

The church's insistence on moral discipline, unquestioning
acceptance of the articles of faith, and the individual's duty to
scrutinize himself and his behavior at all times were reinforced for
Strindberg by a pietistic Puritanism favored by his mother and
especially his stepmother.[5] The constant emphasis on self-
examination, self-judgment, self-condemnation at home, in
church, and in school was probably the primary cause of Strindberg's lifelong guilt feelings. There was a curious and extremely
disturbing contradiction between his elders' and the community's
insistence that he *believe* blindly in the doctrines of the church and
yet otherwise function as a thinking human being.

What he was taught at home and in church was reinforced by the
schools' strict discipline. In his time, teachers had the duty of
serving as authoritarians in and out of school. For the most part,
Strindberg's school days were anything but pleasant periods of
acquisition of knowledge and understanding of himself, his fellow
human beings, and the world about him. A youngster with intense
curiosity, he found the schoolroom a place in which the wealthy,
the well-dressed, the socially and economically fortunate, and the
meekly obedient and *not* the intellectually alert and assertive boys

were the ones who won the teachers' approval and escaped their frequently brutal discipline.

Yet Strindberg did pass the critical tests applied by the church and the schools respectively: confirmation in 1864 (the act culminating in Christian communion and, for all practical purposes, admitting him socially to adulthood) and passing in 1867 *studenten,* the comprehensive examinations admitting him to the university and permitting him to wear the white student cap, a mark of superiority in a country that has for centuries given more than lip service to the values of superior education.

Strindberg did not become a well-adjusted young adult: Both his body and his mind presented him with problems that were never fully resolved. One of the most difficult was his sexuality, which fascinated but disturbed him. The Church and even school and home had taught him that the flesh (the body) is evil, at least as far as sexual desires go. Pastors and teachers had emphasized the notion that masturbation, sexual dreams, and premarital sexual intercourse led to horrible consequences. Yet Strindberg masturbated, and, when he succeeded in refraining, had wet dreams. Exposed to what his elders had to say and to what Dr. Kaptt's *En ungdomsväns varning for ungdomens farligaste fiende* (*Warning against Young People's Most Dangerous Enemy from a Friend of Youth*) asserted in terrifying detail, Strindberg felt guilty and suffered agony of remorse which perhaps was somewhat relieved by his later getting hold of a copy of a more sensible treatment of the matter *Farbror Palles råd till unga syndare* (*Uncle Palle's Advice to Young Sinners*).

At eighteen he began to find relief through women belonging to the oldest of professions and, surprisingly, did so without feeling guilty. Idealistic as he essentially was, he was to speak and write frankly and bluntly about his sexuality and about human sexuality in general, even making it clear what disturbed him: "I've never understood how a kiss, which is an unborn word, speech without sound, the silent speech of souls, can through a sacred act be exchanged for — — — a surgical operation! which always ends with weeping and gnashing of teeth. I've never grasped how the sacred night, the first one, when two souls should kiss each other in love, why that night should end with shedding of blood, quarreling, hatred, mutual contempt — and bandages."[6] Written much later in life (1900 or 1901), the passage clearly enough implies, too, sensitivity to the double functions of the sexual organs and to related matters. Only on very rare occasions was Strindberg able to look upon sex with any measure of humor.

From very early Strindberg was attracted to members of the opposite sex, but his own inclinations were affected by what the authorities in and out of the home had to say to him about the differences between the sexes and by what he observed. Uppvall may well have been right in insisting that Strindberg developed a fixation on his mother who did not give him the attention and affection he craved; all the available evidence indicates that he tended to glorify the madonna, the mother with her child.[7] His relations with his three sisters — all of them younger — were for the most part positive. Within his own family the only feminine being who became the object of his thorough disapproval was his mother's successor:

Even as a child he was difficult to get along with. Shy and sensitive he was at the same time very much inclined to contradiction and wanted to dispute everything, big and little. With his defiant spirit and his deeply rooted suspiciousness of everything and everyone, he was from the very first on strained terms with his stepmother and came gradually to consider her his sworn enemy. That led to Father's becoming upset with him so that constant conflicts resulted. He often turned to his oldest sister for comfort.[8]

His observations at home and in both the city and the country frequently contradicted what the church and the community as a whole had to say about sexual differences and sexual roles.

In spite of decades of efforts [9] to give Swedish women greater social, economic, and political advantages and an increasingly active struggle for Swedish women's equality and liberation, the authorities still insisted on maintaining the traditional views and practices: woman as the weaker vessel subservient to man; as the mother and the homemaker; as the primary servant of the family; as its moral guide; as a person, nevertheless, in need of guidance and protection by a male.

In the city homes Strindberg observed and noted a wide spectrum of women ranging from motherly women devoted to and caring for their husbands and children and single women eking out existence in a community providing them with few socially acceptable employment opportunities to, on the one hand, well-to-do married women who spent their time in pursuit of pleasure and, on the other, a small number of women leading the struggle for liberation and equality, sometimes sensibly, sometimes not. Very often, he noted, the terrifying results were the setting of women and men against each other, the setting up of what has become known as the battle of the sexes.

But Sweden at that time was primarily rural rather than urban, and Strindberg in his stays in rural areas during summer vacations had ample opportunities to observe rural men and women working together as partners, not as adversaries, sharing the labor of farming as well as its rewards. It seemed to Strindberg that the rural pattern of marriage, of family life, of working *with* each other and *with* the children for the common good was infinitely superior to the frequently artificial city patterns.

Much of what the leaders of the women's liberation movement advocated appealed to Strindberg.[10] He was always opposed to the segregation of the sexes in separate schools; he believed that association with each other in the classroom from the beginning would result in a happier and less artificial relationship between boys and girls, between men and women. As he matured, he came more and more to the conclusion that what was needed was the removal of unnecessary artificial barriers between the sexes, the revamping of the educational system to give both sexes training for making a living as well as for living, and, in brief, securing human liberation from the bonds of false and enervating traditions, doctrines, and practices.

Among Strindberg's many disciples and admirers, no one else has come closer to identifying Strindberg's view of women than Ingmar Bergman: "Strindberg's way of experiencing women is ambivalent. While he's an obsessive worshipper of women, he also persecutes them obsessively. He does both things at once. His psyche is fifty percent woman and fifty percent man."[11] Strindberg *was* both a woman worshipper and a woman hater, but what Bergman might very well have added is that Strindberg was as able to see flaws in men as in women. He applied his concept of love-hate, moreover, to all human relationships.

Young Strindberg developed a romantic and ideal dream of marriage which, in spite of three personal disappointments and keen observation of many other marriages, persisted throughout his life. His term is "reconciliation through woman," and, if he meant by that coming to terms with life and finding fulfillment and completion through another and perhaps better half, his choices of marital partners are somewhat startling: a beautiful Swedish aristocrat and would-be actress from Swedish Finland, a practicing Austrian journalist, and an ambitious and talented actress of mixed origins from Norway.

Innumerable people have speculated about Strindberg's selections of wives and even about what sort of woman he should have married so that the "madonna, friend, and ideal" woman before physical union would not have become for him more and more after union "the man-eater, the enemy, the destroyer." His sister Anna who knew him as well as any other woman except for his three wives made this interesting comment: "She [Siri Wrangel, born von Essen] was a stately woman with an aristocratic appearance. She had wonderful blond hair, beautiful blue eyes and lovely tiny hands. Intelligent in the highest degree this exquisite figure became in August's eyes his ideal woman."[12] Not one of the three was particularly trained for or interested in homemaking, every one of them had ambitions to make careers for themselves, all of them had clear opinions about equality and liberation, not one of them was seriously interested in playing the role of madonna — except, for two of them, on the stage. In the third of his autobiographical novels, Strindberg said, among many other things about selecting a wife: "Instead of looking for a strong mother, he looked for a woman higher on the social scale. ... He could not fall in love with a coarsely shaped woman, with dirty nails or big feet. He wanted to look up to the woman he would love. ... Socially." [SS, XIX, 124-125].

Strindberg's well-nigh uncontrollable obsession for blurting out what he thought and felt was the truth at any given point in time has been confusing for many who would like to generalize neatly about his attitude toward and presentation of women. His statements during periods of depression, disappointment, or downright anger have been an important reason for classifying him as a misogynist, a woman hater. Such statements outweigh numerically his equally important confessions of adoration for women as well as his realistic appreciation of them in his tranquil states. But the latter are there in black and white, an extremely important indication of his ambivalence and, if you will, his very human tendency to change his mind, to contradict himself.

His frank discussion of his own sexual experiences shocked many contemporaries. His works reveal that he believed "normal" human beings, women as well as men, are sexual creatures who should have sexual expression, that trying to force human beings to repress their sexuality is extremely dangerous, that women so inclined have every right to devote themselves to prostitution, and that men have the right to seek their services without having to feel guilty. Long before the sexual revolution of the 1960s and 1970s and the women's liberation movement of our time he suggested and even advocated many of the goals implicit in each. But he paid the price in widespread disapproval in Sweden, a disapproval expressed by attacks such as Personne's *The Strindberg Literature and Immorality among Pupils in the Schools* and by a generally silent but not universal boycott of his plays and his other books for substantial periods of time.[13]

Strindberg needed friends and companions very much and was thoroughly capable of getting along with other members of his own sex as long as they did not intrude too closely into his privacy, upset his personal dignity, or offer him unsolicited advice with even the slightest hint of feeling superior.

His pressing need for airing his thoughts and discussing them with other people was very great. Fortunately for him, he did get welcome opportunities in his teens from both young men and women, in his days at the University of Uppsala from some of his fellow students; in the 1870s from young men interested in the arts and in life in general who gathered informally in the Red Room at Bern's Restaurant [14] in Stockholm; in the Royal Library with fellow workers and scholars; in artists' colonies and among fellow writers during his stays abroad; and with his Beethoven group [15] in the closing years of his life.

But even in this area of living he was ambivalent. He could, on the one hand, remain a faithful friend who deserved a testimonial such as Axel Jäderin's:

He was even-tempered and sincere toward his friends; he valued our friendship. We didn't spoil him by any [particular] admiration, we thought he was an interesting personality with great gifts, but we didn't notice any lion's claw. He was cheerful and pleasant, a handy and alert observer, but hardly practical. He became depressed very easily and doubted his own abilities. ...

Strindberg was a favorite with the women back in those days. His figure was nicely put together, his head interesting, and there was a certain elegance in his bearing, which helped. But what appealed to them most was his manner toward them. He was always respectful, charming, and sincere without ever stooping to fawning.

But, as Jäderin adds, Strindberg was not the sort of person who did not consider the reverse, too:

His thoughts about friendship were free. He wanted to give and take freely. And I remember he told me later on during the Red-Room period: "Friends, no, a person shouldn't have friends, they're only a handicap. They encroach too much on one's independence." [16]

Strindberg kept a watchful eye on the slightest (real or imagined) hint of encroachment as many of his friends and acquaintances were to discover. The result ranged all the way from merely eliminating all communication with the offender to brutal and devastating attack in print, in letters, and in spoken words. The Norwegian writer and Nobel-Prize winner Björnstjerne Björnson made the mistake of offering him advice in a fatherly and, it seemed to Strindberg, condescending way, for example, before and during the trial of 1884. One of Strindberg's mildest comments — in a letter (December 2, 1884) to his friend the Norwegian novelist Jonas Lie — after telling Björnson to go to hell, reads in part: "If I were courageous or not is a matter of detail B.B. ought not to waste time speculating about. That I accomplished some good is sure, so B.B. ought to forgive me for my having been lionized. If he knew how I had been abused and libelled, he'd be satisfied. Tell him to keep still now. He has tested me as a friend; he's going to fear me as an enemy. I won't attack, but I'll defend myself, and I do that well!" [Brev. IV, 993] Many discovered the accuracy of that admission. Yet Strindberg could be the gentlest and most considerate of friends, but no one could count on his constancy or objectivity.

In one area of human relations he was constant — his sympathy for the very young. While he never went so far as his brilliant disciple Hjalmar Bergman in contrasting the very young and the adult and therefore aging ("We are born human beings, we age into trolls" [17]) there are numerous indications in his writings that he had a romantic notion of children as the helpless innocents. Yet being Strindberg, he was keenly aware of the need for civilizing them in the family, the schoolroom, and in the community.

Strindberg was fascinated by the larger communities as well as by the family and the circle of intimate friends, but the very core of that interest was his fascination with people, past and present. Through generally sharp observation and frequently imaginative interpretation, he considered his contemporaries within his sphere of direct sensual perception and, through available sources, those beyond it. Through extensive and creative reading, he extended his study of man into history of the past of mankind. In a very real sense he practiced what Alexander Pope had said, "the proper study of mankind is man,"[18] but, unlike Pope, he did "presume to scan God," too.

Conditioned at home, in church, and in school to accepting the idea that man is by nature sinful, he rarely looked upon any adult sentimentally except when he was emotionally involved with a woman and then only in the early stages of that involvement. His observations of clergymen, educators and professors, doctors, lawyers, merchants and other business men, politicians, military men, writers and other artists, newspapermen, employers, employees, farmers, and members of every other segment of society were searching. He had little if any lasting regard for rank or status enjoyed by others. His inclination, carefully nurtured and developed, was to look, as far as possible, behind masks, concealing garments, manner, and name to get at the vulnerable, stripped, pitiful, despicable, or, at best, admirable human being without artificial protection.

Most of the people he scrutinized closely at hand or as closely as possible at a distance did not fare well in his judgment. The men he considered his enemies fared worst of all in the frank, sometimes brutal, and appreciably distorted accounts he gave of them in black and white, usually without suffering severe pangs of conscience.

Since he was interested in every phase of human activity, he considered both the leaders and the followers, the employers and the employees, the people in power and the people under their control. In his examination of the political system, the class system, the church, the schools and universities, the theaters, other cultural institutions, and many other human activities not implicit in these, he studied them firsthand when he could and through both oral and written sources when he could not.

His very wide interest in human beings had a strong base in his power of observation but an equally important one in his very great reading in all kinds of literature, not least that of psychology and of history.

History was particularly important because of his very early conviction that the historic dead were just as complex and dynamic as any living person. He read history creatively; that is, he did not accept some predecessors' tendency to glorify the great ones of the past and others' to denigrate them. He compared the accounts, weighed and judged them by his own sense at the particular time for what might well have approached the realistic truth, and came to conclusions that he felt threw a great deal of light on the living as well as the dead.

Many psychiatrists and psychologists have found Strindberg and his writings highly suitable for study, primarily because Strindberg knew psychology as presented by the experts in his day and went beyond them in his study of himself and his fellow human beings to foreshadow what the great psychiatrists and psychologists were to propose and advocate in our century.

For Strindberg had a habit that shocked many of his fellow countrymen during his lifetime and continues to distress some of his readers today: the habit of revealing what he considered the truth about himself and others, about his country and its civilization, about, in other words, many matters about which there is still among certain groups a very real conspiracy of silence. Sex, for example. Or, to take a less obvious example, ways and means for committing murder without being held accountable before any human bar of justice.[19] Perhaps as shocking as anything else in Strindberg was his obsession to know himself and his eagerness in using every available device for reaching that knowledge, and revealing in published forms his objective, his methods for trying to reach it, and whatever results he found, a procedure many thought, and some still do think, hardly suitable for publication.

Although he did not find himself or other human beings flawless, he had very great sympathy for the unfortunate and the underprivileged. Even though his views on social and political matters did not remain static for extended periods, he nevertheless not only remained aware of social injustices at all times and proposed remedies for them whether, say, he was in a state of enthusiasm for socialism or in one of sincere conviction that only an aristocratic system could provide solutions to social and political problems.

Few other great writers have been as enthusiastic about external nature as Strindberg was. Born in one of the most beautiful of capitals, Strindberg loved Stockholm even while he was acutely conscious of many of its artificially created flaws. The archipelago with its thousands of islands and skerries beginning in Stockholm and extending far out into the Baltic was the object of his enthusiastic approval and admiration. The inner tranquillity and happiness he got directly for many years — and indirectly for many more — from his "own" island, Kymmendö, is one indication of his love of nature. His journeys into the Swedish and the French countrysides and his travels in Denmark, Germany, England, France, Italy, and Switzerland were for him voyages of discovery of the natural and the artificial — with his overwhelming sympathy going to the preservation whenever possible of every aspect of nature which could enrich human life.

Even though he found nature essentially beautiful and satisfying, he was aware of flaws even in external nature. The initial impulse for that awareness probably came from his early religious training which emphasized the imperfections of this world and the perfection of a lost Paradise and the omnipotent, omnipresent, and omniscient Jehovah and His host of supporting powers as rivals of Satan and his fellow fallen angels for the souls of human beings.

Throughout his lifetime Strindberg was profoundly engaged in the consideration of whatever force or forces may have set the universe going and still were in control. His speculation led through many stages of faith and doubt, from pietism through free-thinking, through agnosticism, through would-be atheism, through conversion and backsliding, and, perhaps hardest of all for him to accept, through faith in Christ, the gentle forgiving practitioner of self-negation, an act that he found beyond his understanding even at the end. But then he had discovered that there were many matters beyond human understanding and was finally resigned to asking that the Latin words for "In the cross is my only hope" be inscribed on a wooden cross on his grave.

In writing about Lady Julie and Jean as characterless characters Strindberg himself has given us the key to himself as a human being. The masses of evidence provided by Strindberg himself and the masses of testimony provided by those who knew him personally underscore the facts that he was complex and that he was dynamic. In other words, he was decidedly human in his complexity and in his capacity to change and develop. It is a fascinating activity to pursue the study of August Strindberg as he reveals himself in many of his works, primarily the autobiographical volumes but even to some degree in works that were not designed as autobiography. The pursuit is rewarding, especially if the reader remembers not only the finite nature of language but the finite nature of both Strindberg and reader. The rewards include remarkable insights into human nature, the human experience, and human possibilities.

John Landquist, who as the editor of Strindberg's complete works had probably done as much for the study of Strindberg's works as anyone could, recalled a visit to him a few months before his death in 1912: "His face, although now aged, was more virile in its expression, more sensitive and at the same time more dignified [than in Carl Larsson's famous portrait]. ... The ... impression Strindberg's whole figure gave me was that of an older man of the world, not to say a *grandseigneur*. He had a figure of medium height, well proportioned, a noble bearing and something masterful in his expression. He carried himself with the elegance and self-confidence of an actor. His glance, his highly expressive face, his gestures, and his voice, all of them gave me an impression of alert precision. It was a joy to watch and listen to him when he walked back and forth talking. He expressed himself with absolute ease and accuracy precisely in the language he wrote: I understood his language was not polished book language but his own living words." [20]

His physical endowment was very good in spite of inherited "nervousness" but it had been affected by recurring sudden bouts of fever and chill (*frossan*), painful psoriasis affecting most of all his hands, and, in the final years of his life, cancer of the stomach.

The late Märta Fröding, Strindberg's niece, spoke on several occasions to this writer about the charm and the warmth that her uncle had for the people he liked and trusted but she spoke, too, of the suspicion and coldness with which he met people he disliked and said that he did not trust strangers for whom he had not been prepared. Among the many others who have testified to his ambivalence as a human being is Fanny Falkner, the last woman he thought of marrying but who, having thought more than twice, broke the engagement. She has paid tribute to him as a lovable and admirable person but has also said, among other things: "With all his great qualities he could fix his attention on minor matters in an amazing fashion. Everything about him became very easily confused, outlawed, pure trouble, absolutely unpredictable. So one never knew what was going to happen when he called on the telephone or when one walked in through his door. Anything called sacrifice did not exist for him. There was always the overhanging danger that one day he would ruin everyone about him."[21] He was indeed a jumble of contradictions.

As one reads the many available judgments of Strindberg, one is likely to get the impression that the reaction to him as a human being and as an artist is either highly enthusiastic or uncomfortably disturbed. During his lifetime Strindberg never failed to "get under the skin" of everyone exposed to him. The reaction of those who see and hear his plays performed on stage, on TV or film, or merely read them, or study them in depth can vary in the same fashion. He was a fascinating human being, a person quite able to see into the darkest and the brightest corners of the human heart and to expose their every detail in literary art of the highest quality. He himself threw a great deal of light on himself when he wrote in 1886: "As a transitional figure he kept the specific qualities of both romantic and naturalist, as the blindworm, which has the rudimentary feet of the lizard inside its skin. This double nature was the key to his personality and to his writing" [*SS*, XIX, 140].[22]

CHAPTER 2

The Autobiographer

"Creative writing will gradually come to an end. The future ought to set up bureaus, where every human being would deposit an honest autobiography at a specific age; that could be the material for a genuine science of man if such were needed." — Birger Mörner's *Den Strindberg jag känt*, p. 168

SOME scholars and students have concluded that Strindberg's whole literary production always, directly or indirectly, revolves about *himself, his* perception of *his* world, and *his* changing concept of whoever or whatever set *his* universe going. While there is more than an element of truth in such a conclusion, some works were designed as autobiography and the rest were designed to deal primarily with other people or other matters, real or imagined. The first are frankly subjective in his effort to be objective during his pre-Inferno years and appreciably objective in his effort to be subjective in his pursuit of truth in the post-Inferno years (1897-1912).

I *The Letters*

The thousands of extant letters that he wrote, with as we shall see the exception of two sets, do not belong either with the works he thought of as autobiography or with those he did not label autobiographical. (The latter include most of his dramas, novels, short stories, essays, poems, and contributions to journalism, social history and criticism, dramatic and literary criticism, philology, science and pseudoscience, and travel literature). The letters that have been published by the Strindberg Society[1] and those that are available to the public in their original form at the Royal Library and elsewhere obviously vary in content and literary quality; they· range all the way from brief business letters or extremely brief personal notes to remarkably arresting revelations of

Strindberg as a human being in one or more of his many roles.

It could be argued rather successfully that a thorough study of his letters would reveal the writer even when they, say, attempt to conceal, as many of them do, his real intentions, thoughts, and feelings and when they, on the other hand, attempt, through deliberate candor, to make a certain impression and have a certain effect. A study of the letters in depth has not yet been made; the completion of the series by the Strindberg Society will provide excellent leads and other support and a wealth of information as the carefully edited volumes already available demonstrate.

One set of so-called letters, *Journey into Detention** (*Kvarstadsresan*), is Strindberg's account of the difficult period before, during, and immediately after his trial for blasphemy based on certain statements about communion and Christ in the story "The Reward of Virtue" (*Giftas,* I, i.e., *Married,* 1884). Following is Strindberg's comment:

I depict ... typical marriages. They all end with children, as a marriage ought to end. The child, who first justifies the union, the child who is the objective of the union, the child who replaces the illusions, the child, against whom all attempts at emancipation fail — under present conditions. In the future, when the state, the community, or an association takes charge of the children and marriages are entered more freely, then woman will be set free and the man as well. So I end the book with an interview and a foreword, in which I hint at the future. ... The book begins with a moralistic story about The Reward of Virtue! By virtue I mean the crime against nature, which under the name of abstinence is preached by married fifty-year olds [*SS,* XVII, 27-28].[2]

The letters contain pleas for sanity in women's emancipation, for human liberation, and for reforms in thinking about the relations between the sexes. They contain some highly interesting comments on the nature of art criticism, the meaning of morality, and the imperfections of human laws, but most pertinent to Strindberg's thinking during those crucial days is the plea for human liberation from stupid regulations and practices, a plea that runs through the whole account.

This set of letters supposedly addressed to a compatriot abroad does reveal that Strindberg expected trouble when *Married* appeared. It relates in some detail the confiscation of copies in Sweden, the publisher Bonnier's [3] appeal for Strindberg's immediate return to face charges, and the latter's inner confusion and disturbance: an inner response compounded of fear and guilt, self-justification and whistling in the dark, an outer response composed of consultations with friends and acquaintances and an examination of the Swedish law, particularly that portion concerning freedom of speech. Frightened by the possibility of going to prison, yet wanting to do the right thing by the publisher, Strindberg sent unacceptable documents (taking full responsibility for the book) to the authorities in Stockholm. Only when a son of the publisher came to Switzerland to bring him home did Strindberg leave for Sweden. In the letters he admitted he was nervous, upset, and afraid; attacks in the papers, a storm of rumors, anonymous letters, a host of tactless visitors, and his own suspicions were not adequately offset by generally friendly and frequently enthusiastic treatment while he stayed as he says "a prisoner" for five weeks at the Grand Hotel until he was acquitted.

What the particular set of "letters" little more than hints at are the horrible effects of the whole episode on Strindberg: Pressure in almost every conceivable form had been brought to bear on him. That pressure was to help bring into being self-scrutiny of a quality rarely indulged in by other creative writers, cruel changes in his closest personal relationships, an enormously productive period in the immediately following years, and increasing emotional, mental, and even physical difficulties.

His correspondence with his first wife became, as we shall see, part of his first extensive autobiographical project.

II   The Son of a Servant

Valuable as thousands of the letters actually composed to be sent to recipients are as sources of biographical detail and as interesting examples of the art of letter writing, they do not begin to compare with the importance of the volumes that Strindberg labelled autobiographical: The four-volume *Son of a Servant: The Development of a Human Being; A Madman's Defence; Inferno; Legends; Jacob Wrestles; Alone; The Occult Diary;* and four plays, the Damascus trilogy and *The Great Highway.*

No other human being could ever have been more conditioned to self-scrutiny and self-analysis to a point approaching obsession than Strindberg. Such factors as the pietistic emphasis on constant self-examination, self-condemnation, self-denial, self-control, and the individual's duty to be concerned about others and their behavior were undoubtedly among the most important determinants for Strindberg's lifelong extremely sensitive and lasting concern with self. In this, romantic emphasis on the individual and the naturalistic emphasis on the scientific study of man and his environment were undoubtedly complementary.

His first major study of himself came significantly during the 1880s when he was directly under the influence of naturalism and determinism. *The Son of a Servant: The Development of A Human Being* (1886-87) consists of four volumes: *The Son of a Servant* (*Tjänstekvinnans son*, 1849-1867); *Time of Ferment* (*Jäsningstiden*, 1868-1872); *In the Red Room** (*I Röda rummet*, 1872-1875); *The Author**(*Författaren*, 1877-1887). The gap between 1875 and 1877 was filled with *He and She** (*Han och hon*), a volume of letters exchanged with Siri between July 1, 1875, and some time in 1876.

How closely related his whole background and his devotion to dominant ways of thinking about the individual and his world in the 1880s were Strindberg states very definitely:

After having worked his way out of the old concept of the universe and after having given up the doctrine of Heaven and God, he had logically been directed to himself alone as the bearer of his destiny. When he tried to get to know himself, he found a chaotic confusion, which lacked body, which changed form in keeping with the observer's point of view and which probably does not have more reality than the rainbow, which can be seen but which is not there. To be able to continue his earthly existence in a more rational way than he had before, he decided to close the books on the past, to go through the events in his life from the beginning to the present, examine the history of his origins and development, as it had come about through all the combined factors of heredity, bringing up, disposition, temperament, under the pressure and influence of the external events and cultural movements of the given historical period. This was the major objective of the book, *The Son of a Servant,* and [he intended] not at all to write any confessions, to excuse himself, or any memoirs to entertain [*SS,* XIX, 277].

Strindberg insisted that he did not intend *The Son of a Servant* to be either conventional memoirs for public entertainment or an apologia or justification of himself and the life he had led.

Many readers have been disturbed about discrepancies between Strindberg's accounts and those of others. But Strindberg was aware of the tricks his memory could play on him, and, as a writer and literary artist, he had to select and to arrange his materials. His autobiography was therefore designed to be an analysis of his development because of heredity, environment, time, and chance *as* he remembered the details and interpreted them in 1886-1887 as a *finite* human being, albeit an exceptionally gifted and articulate one. The result is an autobiography that can justly be labelled naturalistic in a Strindbergian way or, if you will, supernaturalistic in decidedly subtle ways.

In a remarkable "Interview" submitted (as a foreword) to the publisher while the first volume was in press, Strindberg not only denied that the book was a defence or a confession but insisted that it was a psychological analysis of the one person he could come close to interpreting:

How is a person going to know what goes on in other people's minds, how is one to know the complex motives for someone else's action, how can one know what they said in an intimate moment? Well, one imagines. But up until now homology, the science of man, has been cultivated very little by writers, who with their slight knowledge of psychology have indulged in depicting thoroughly concealed inner [emotional and mental] life. One does not know more than one life — one's own. The advantage of depicting one's own is this: one has to do with a congenial person, doesn't one, and then, too, one always looks for the motives for one's acts. Fine! Searching out the motives was the ultimate object of this book [*SS*, XVIII, 456].

And, in the preface to the second through sixth editions:

The books are quite honestly written, not completely naturally, because that is impossible. ... Relatively truthful are the accounts, but I could not be absolutely exact. ... I have thus forgotten certain details from my childhood during the last twenty years, but am almost sure I remembered them at forty. And a story can be told in many ways, be illuminated from different sides, be intensified or decreased in color [*SS*, XVIII, 450-451].

Strindberg quite obviously was trying to be as honest as he could be about what he intended, about his procedure and method, and about the impossibility of arriving at the absolutely complete truth.

Strindberg knew very well that he had gained insight into himself and others and into the world, not only through his own observations and thinking but through wide-ranging reading in the works of predecessors and contemporaries who in varying degrees had stimulated his observations and affected his thinking. One of the remarkable facts about his autobiography is the apparent frankness with which he reveals the extent of his reading and suggests what he in 1886 and 1887 thought the impact of each book or author had had on him. Even a partial list of major foreign writers he mentions and in varying degrees discusses — Björnson, Boccaccio, Georg Brandes, Buckle, Byron, Chateaubriand, Francois Coppée, Dante, Darwin, Dickens, Dumas, Fichte, Fourier, Henry George, Goethe, Hartmann, Hegel, Heiberg, Heine, Homer, Hugo, Ibsen, Ingersoll, Jacobsen, Kant, à Kempis, Kierkegaard, Lassalle, Lessing, Jonas Lie, Locke, Marx, Mills, Max Nordau, Oehlenschläger, Ossian, Ovid, Parker, Pestalozzi, Plato, Prévost-Paradol, Ribot, Rousseau, Saint-Simon, George Sand, Schiller, Walter Scott, Shakespeare, Sophocles, Spencer, Eugéne Sue, Thackeray, de Tocqueville, Tolstoy, Jules Vallès, Virgil, Voltaire, and Zola — suggests quite properly that he was a voracious reader of all sorts of writing, literary and nonliterary. While he made no effort to present a complete record of his reading, he did emphasize what he thought was important in his pursuit of self-knowledge. In that pursuit, Swedish writers and other intellectuals from Linné and Swedenborg to his own contemporaries were pertinent, as he indicates throughout the autobiography.

Probably as typical and certainly as interesting as any illustration of his treatment of his exposure to another writer and its effect on him is what he has to say about Ibsen, the dramatist generally considered Strindberg's arch-rival. His fairly numerous references to Ibsen, and on occasion extended comments on the man and his plays, range from outright expressions of enthusiastic approval to direct and blunt attacks. Take, for example, these brief comments:

Then *Brand* appeared. It had been published as early as 1866, but did not get into Johan's [Strindberg's] and his contemporaries' hands before 1869. ... Brand was a pietist, a fanatic, who dared to believe he was right in direct opposition to the whole world, and Johan felt himself related to this horrible egoist, who what's more was wrong. No halfness, just plunging ahead, breaking and bending down everything that was in the way, because he alone was right. His highly sensitive conscience, which suffered from every step he took because it would hurt his father or his friends, was silenced by Brand. All bonds of consideration, of love, were to be broken for the sake of "the cause". ... Brand gave him faith in his conscience purer than his upbringing had [*SS*, XVIII, 355-356].

And [in 1870]

Why it [a student society he helped organize] was called Runa [song] was, I suppose, because of the dominant NeoNordic renaissance, that had accompanied Scandinavianism ... and which recently had been beautifully revived in Björnson's and Ibsen's dramas about Old Scandinavian life [*SS,* XVIII, 360].

But [in 1881]

After having considered his own time realistically, he was overwhelmed by an inexplicable longing to forget it and immerse himself in an imagined world of the past and at the same time say farewell to romanticism. In the play *Lord Bengt's Wife,* he gently ridicules woman's opinionated notions of marriage as absolute bliss and tries to put down the unreasonable demands on the married man that Ibsen has set in *A Doll House* [1879] [*SS,* XIX, 192].

And [in 1886]

How didn't *A Doll House* rage epidemically for many years so that every careless and untruthful wife was a Nora, and every married man a Helmer. People saw only oppressed noble women and tyrannic despicable men. The rest weren't seen [*SS,* XIX, 255].

Strindberg was keenly aware of Ibsen, read and considered what he wrote, and did not hesitate to take occasional exception to his views and art. An examination of all the references and discussions of Ibsen in the autobiography reveals, moreover, that Strindberg was rightly convinced that the awareness and impact was mutual.

Of the writers listed above those that had the greatest impact on the approach to the contents of the autobiography and the form it took were the psychologists and the philosophers, not least Hartmann, Jules Vallès, and Th. Ribot [4] ; for Strindberg intended his autobiography to be psychological analysis of his own evolution as an intellectual, emotional, moral, and physical human being.

Here, for example, are Strindberg's own statements in letters written in 1886 to Albert Bonnier, the publisher, and Gustaf af Geijerstam, then his friend and literary agent: "What would you say if I wrote my autobiography now that I'm dead physically, morally and economically? It would interest me if I wrote it subjectively-objectively as Jules Vallès did in *Jacques Vingtras*" [*Brev,* V, 1194] [5] ; and "Now I sit down to write myself to death in a large novel in four, five parts: 'My Novel.' Type: *Jacques Vingtras* by

Jules Vallès. A 'developed' form of the naturalistic novel, including historic, psychic, social environment, along with the author's opinions on the matter, which are the most important of all, for he is to rise above his subject and like God (in history) teach the readers to understand what they read" [*Brev*, V, 1207].

He was suffering from emotional and financial difficulties stemming to a large extent from his trial for blasphemy in 1884. The quotations account for Strindberg's decision to write his autobiography in keeping with his conviction that that was the form of writing of the future and to do it as the Frenchman Vallès (1832-1885) had in an autobiography which had just received much public attention.

That Strindberg read widely in the writings of professional psychologists is known, of course, but that he digested what he read, considered it, developed a remarkable knowledge of psychology in depth, and used it superbly in his writing has not been particularly emphasized. But these facts help explain why not only lay readers but professional psychologists and psychiatrists, be they Freudian, Adlerian, Jungian, or whatever else in their preference, find Strindberg's autobiographical volumes and many of his other works fascinating.

What Strindberg had made his own included his conviction that he could achieve only a partial understanding of *self* when he had as thoroughly as possible sought out the motives for his actions and the causes of everything about him, his awareness of the unconscious as sources of both good and evil, the extremely important roles of sexuality and of the instinct for power, the bewildering and extremely complex and dynamic makeup of the human individual, the physiological causes for many psychic effects, the very great actuality and variety of persona, and awareness of both masculine and feminine elements in the composition of any person. Those who speak of Strindberg's search for identity are correct, of course; he was to search for self-knowledge and self-understanding throughout his lifetime.

It is with such an approach that Strindberg in *The Son of a Servant* considers almost every conceivable matter that affected his development, directly or indirectly. His report on his findings is based, as he admits, on careful selection and arrangement of material designed to communicate them to his readers in direct language combining narration and exposition. The whole tetralogy is a treatment of the psychology of personal adjustment startlingly pertinent even today: The process of adjustment, the need for analysis, making and breaking habits, attention to the body, coming to terms with sexuality, selecting a vocation, adjustment to others within the family and beyond, understanding the social conventions, development of affections, acquiring emotional stability, acquisition of self-confidence, marital adjustment, the elimination of fears, the pursuit of emotional maturity, seeking motivation, and the goal of becoming an adjusted personality are all there.

Strindberg did indeed try to present an honest autobiography. The best proof of the validity of that statement lies in the fact that he did not try to make the reader like him as many an author of memoirs has tried to do or to make the reader pity him as a writer of a confession might or acquit him of blame if he had written an apologia or defence. Instead he has given us an account that is as likely to repel the reader at one time as to attract him at others.

III   He and She*

But *He and She* is decidedly different from the other four volumes. It is, for the most part, a highly entertaining exchange between two human beings very much drawn to each other, anxious to realize their dreams of happiness, and indulging in excessive enthusiasm and diction typical of their emotional condition and perhaps even of the time, not completely removed from the Romantic period. It is an important volume, however: It reveals one of the most important writers in the intimacy of man-woman relationship as a very vulnerable human being, vulnerable particularly because of his dreams of perfect happiness. It is important, too, for those who seek to understand Strindberg through its revelation of Siri von Essen Wrangel, interesting and attractive in her own right but important primarily as the most important woman in Strindberg's life.

In one of the letters in *He and She* (March 13, 1876) Strindberg in a very long declaration of love wrote, among other things:

The princess, my princess, the most beautiful woman in Sweden, the one with the bluest eyes, the smallest feet, the most golden blond hair, the most beautiful forehead, the loveliest hands...the one with the noblest heart, the proudest spirit, the noblest feelings, the most beautiful thoughts! ... I love you so that my whole being is shaken to its very foundations! ... If you are afraid of becoming my wife, you're afraid of prose — don't you know I can pluck poetry out of dirt if it comes to that[?] [*SS, LV*, 105]

Years later (1886) he recalled what he had at first thought was a chance meeting:

... she [6] stopped in front of a young woman, nicely dressed, elegantly in fact, charming and distinguished ...
What struck me about the baroness was her girlish appearance. Even though she could be about twenty-five years old, her appearance was a youngster's. She had a schoolgirl's head, a neat head completely framed by unruly locks, blond as the ears of golden grain, the shoulders of a princess, a waist as supple as a willow, a way of inclining her head toward one, open, respectful, and superior at the same time. Imagine this charming virgin mother having read without injury my tragedy [*Master Olof*]! Married to a captain of the guards, mother of a little three-year-old girl, she was crazy about the theater without having the possibility of ever appearing on stage because of the high positions of her husband and of her father-in-law, who had just been appointed chamberlain at the royal court [*SS*, XXVI, 43-44].

Out of his union with Siri Wrangel was to come much happiness and much unhappiness and an inexhaustible well of inspiration and material for his creative writing.

Strindberg's first wife came from a background and an environment quite different from his own. By birth a member of an aristocratic family in Swedish Finland with very good claims to distinction, by rearing a social being at home in circles at the top of society in Finland and Sweden, and by marriage to a Swedish baron (*friherre*) beyond the need for social climbing, the woman who became Siri Strindberg in 1877 had not been disciplined to feel ill at ease about giving expression to her feelings by showing affection openly or to hesitate about using her considerable charm in dealing with others, whatever their rank or social status might be. As one reads Strindberg's early accounts and the testimony of others, including that of her oldest daughter, one is left with the impression that Siri Strindberg was an essentially admirable human being who was interested in having a pleasant and, if possible, exciting life, who was intelligent but not intellectual, who was kind and considerate to those about her, who probably did indulge in teasing him about his virility, who probably never quite understood why Strindberg was so difficult to live with, and who certainly never fully understood why some of her behavior both at home and in public distressed him beyond words. Strindberg could reveal himself as fully as humanly possible — in writing; Siri's friendliness toward others expressed in impulsive acts, words, looks, gestures, and touch in the presence of others on occasion embarrassed and shocked him.

IV   A Madman's Defence

Their marriage, which lasted from 1877 to 1892, is probably the marriage above all others best known to Swedes, aside, of course, from their own, largely because Strindberg felt impelled in 1887-1888 to write in French a volume he called *Le plaidoyer d'un fou.* Unlike *The Son of a Servant,* the book was deliberately designed, he insisted, as an apologia or defence of himself as a married man:

This is a terrible book. I admit that without qualifications for I regret bitterly having written it.
    What made me write it?
    The obvious necessity for washing my corpse before it is shut up in the coffin forever [*SS,* XXVI, 5].

He wrote it, he insists, because a fellow author [Gustaf af Geijerstam] had said Strindberg's marital difficulties were just the right material for a novel for him [Geijerstam] to write. Strindberg believed he had better tell his own story.

The person who suffered most because of the "terrible" book was undoubtedly Siri Strindberg, the wife suspected of unfaithfulness, lesbianism, and attempts at psychic murder, not to mention perhaps less serious charges such as inadequacy in homemaking, child rearing, and housekeeping; not keeping sensible hours; consuming too much beer; keeping a dog as a pet more favored than her husband; and, in summary, not fulfilling his demands for being an "ideal" bed-partner, companion, and mother.

While Siri Strindberg never stooped to defend herself against any of these charges, her oldest child, Karin Smirnoff, did defend her mother in two books. The passage most pertinent here reads in translation:

The only judgment I have heard Siri make about *The Confession of a Fool,* as she called the book in keeping with the first translation [the German *Die Beichte eines Toren,* 1893], is literally as follows:

"Well-l! There's hardly an episode which doesn't have some basis — only everything is so horribly twisted and distorted."[7]

The daughter herself in speaking about various scholars' emphasis on autobiographical details in the plays written in the late 1880s says:

They are right to the extent certain episodes and minor elements correspond to [contents in] *A Madman's Defence* but — as I have already said: *A Madman's Defence* does not equate with reality and it is dangerous to regard it as autobiographical even if Strindberg did.[8]

What Karin Smirnoff might have concluded, however, is that Strindberg justifiably might have considered it thoroughly autobiographical in an unusual way that was to delight him as an artist and give him almost unbearable pangs of conscience as a human being.

The earliest records by and about Strindberg testify to the fact that he was, by nature, a human being suspicious of other people and the motives for their behavior, and they testify, too, to his having a very active and rich imagination. As a creative artist, he deliberately exploited both his imagination and his bent for suspecting others and their motives. While these traits are, humanly speaking, understandable enough, it is hardly typical of most creative artists to do what Strindberg has done in *A Madman's Defence*: deliberately using vague suspicions as points of departure into an inner journey by way of imaginative distortion of external events leading him to the brink of madness, injuring irreparably the woman he loved, and destroying a marriage that had brought him, as he admits time and again, much happiness.

If, as he said, his purpose was to get at the truth about his first marriage, his method, on one level at least, was that of the detective:

... I want the truth. The truth! ... For the sake of revenge? What nonsense! Revenge on whom? On my favored rivals? They have only made use of their rights as males! On the woman? One ought not to be small-minded really! And to hurt the mother of my darlings? How could I?

But I had to know; to know everything. So I want to examine my life, carefully, tactfully, scientifically; I want to make use of all the resources of psychology: suggestion, thought-reading, the methods of psychic torture — I will not neglect even the old tried tricks of burglary, theft, interception of letters, lying, forged signatures; in a word investigate everything. Is that monomania, the expression of a lunatic's evil rage? It is not for me to say.

The enlightened reader should judge after a careful study of this honest book. Perhaps he will find in it elements of the physiology of love, some light on the pathology of the psyche, as well as a fragment of the philosophy of crime illustrated by a peculiar case [SS, XXVI, 28].

To an extent, that is what Strindberg has done in this book: conducted an investigation stemming from uncertainties that have taken the form of suspicions and not carried on in ways that can be considered even approaching scientific objectivity. The results are uncertainties: a novel that makes fascinating reading for anyone who is interested, say, in the psychology of marriage or the psychology of jealousy or in such interesting matters as psychic murder, psychic suicide, and unconscious little crimes.

The fact that he had created an artistically admirable work of art was to be a source of cold comfort to Strindberg. At the time he wrote it, it may have had some therapeutic value as well as satisfaction stemming from his performance in the role of investigator. Unfortunately for him and his immediate family, the material was too intimate for public scrutiny, the charges too brutal, the evidence too vague and shadowy, and the effects on the principals highly unfortunate.

By examining his letters written to friends and acquaintances, anyone who reads Swedish can easily understand how very complex Strindberg's emotional states were during the period when he was deliberately indulging in distortion for purposes of creative writing. Some of the letters are startling revelations of feelings of personal inadequacies as well as methods he pursued in attempting to overcome them. Take, for example, these brief excerpts from letters to Pehr Staaff:

You don't need to be embarrassed!

I have even with exemplary avoidance of emotional involvement applied psychic torture on the delinquent [Siri] and will soon have sure leads.

The one I'm after now is the actor [Mauritz] Svedberg. ...

This is my analysis!

Back from Finland Siri filled my ears with his praise. Shortly thereafter he was engaged by the New Theater in Stockholm. Silent as the grave! He did not pay any visit to our home! At the same time: increasing coldness on Siri's part, developing into hate and absolute persecution: extending to my being persuaded I was insane. ...

At the dress rehearsal in the evening I went up into Siri's dressing room. Found food and drink for two. Siri was there. From outside the door we heard: Psst! Are you there?

Mr. Svedberg was received in my presence and was treated to food and drink — and — I did not kick him out — but when we got home I dared to remark it was improper for an actress to receive a man in her dressing room. ...

Siri's hatred of me grew! My never exhausted passion led naturally to compromise and I had to beg or buy sex! [*Brev,* VI, 1433]

And:

All this written down in self-defence. Siri has built up the opinion I am not a man and has insulted me publicly, where I've taken the liberty of answering: the screw doesn't need to be too little because the nut is too big [*Brev,* VI, 1435].

The letter contains unbelievably personal information about his genitals and about the couple's sexual performances that might well explain to the most up-to-date psychiatrist some of the reasons for the marital disharmony — and why *A Madman's Defence* became a major source of ammunition for attacking him and a major reason for his feeling an overwhelming guilt for many years to come.

V   Inferno

During the late 1880s Strindberg created some of his greatest plays — *The Father* (1887), *Lady Julie* (1888), and *Creditors* (1888) — and some of his finest works of prose fiction — *The People of Hemsö* (1887), *Tschandala* (1888), and *Life in the Skerries* (1888) — yet the aftereffects of his trial in 1884, the publication of the first three parts of his autobiographical tetralogy, and a flood of rumors charging him with such matters as moral turpitude, extremely bad taste, and mental unbalance, were probably the major reasons for widespread unpopularity and frequently the boycotting of his works by many of the people that counted most in the Swedish establishment for him as a creative artist: the theater people, the publishers, and the critics.

Take, as a far from exceptional example, John Personne's comments:

Mr. Strindberg in order to get bread and butter writes up his hallucinations and fantasies, produced by his sickly feverish brain, and he supports himself, his wife, and his children by publicly denigrating his wife in print. ... [9]

And, if that were not bad enough:

and, since we have got into the matter of Mr. Strindberg's originality, it must be noted that his views on sex are taken over lock, stock, and barrel from the Jewish doctor, Max Nordau; so they are not original either. And still less original is the bad temper he shows toward his wife and marriage; that [sort of thing] has existed as long as there have been weaklings who have been henpecked, consequently for a long time. But to trumpet his whole miserable wretchedness out to the whole world, to write stories about it, and to support himself, his wife, and his children with that [sort of] writing — that is original.[10]

Keenly sensitive to disapproval and appreciably unjustified criticism of himself as a person and as an artist, Strindberg had a burden of anguish and frustration compounded by an increasingly difficult marriage and unfortunately extreme difficulties in making ends meet in spite of well-nigh feverish literary and journalistic production.

The years between the writing of his first series of autobiographical volumes — the four with the covering title *The Son of a Servant* (1886-1887) and *A Madman's Defence* (1888) — and the next series — *Inferno* (1897), *Legends* (1898), *Jacob Wrestles* (1898), *Alone* (1903), and *The Occult Diary* (written, 1896 ff.) — were increasingly difficult for him, emotionally, physically, and even mentally. His divorce from Siri led to his separation from his children; a stay in Berlin led to association with fellow artists, to indulging in a bohemian life at The Cloister (a tavern he labelled *Zum schwarzen Ferkel* or The Little Black Pig), a turning away from literature to pseudoscience and natural science, and, perhaps most important of all, to marriage — probably "on the rebound" — to Frida Uhl on May 2, 1893.[11] The next year he was alone in Paris seriously ill, well into what he himself called his Inferno.

But he was never so ill that he was not able to record what was happening and what he imagined was happening to him. Out of those recordings were to come the second series of autobiographical works.

Strindberg wrote on August 23, 1896:

You said recently people are looking for:
                    The Zola of Occultism.
I feel called to that [role]: But in an expansive elevated tone. A poem in prose: called

Inferno

The same theme as in *At the Edge of the Sea.* The ruination of the individual when he isolates himself. Rescue (salvation) through: his work without honor and financial reward, duty, his family, consequently woman — the mother and child! Resignation through the discovery of each and every person's mission assigned [him] by Providence [*Brev,* XI, 3359].

If one adds an excerpt from his March 1, 1897, letter to his mother-in-law, Marie Uhl, one will have a fair introduction to his intention and to his method:

My "Inferno" is planned, I have found the form, and will write it now. To the great glory of God! [*Brev,* XII, 3537]

Inferno is then the personal record of a very badly disturbed human being deliberately withdrawn at times into isolation. That record is based on notes and particularly on a daybook kept faithfully throughout his period of suffering as a means of preserving fascinating material for later use and as a means of purging himself of torments, real, imagined, and, frequently, self-induced. It is, moreover, a book that had been planned and given form through his selection and arrangement of material, fortunately, one might well add, in view of the bulk of detail and confusion of material available to him.

Strindberg was an extremely troubled man during the early and middle 1890s. Physically, he was suffering from psoriasis, emphysema, intermittent fever, nervousness, and being on the ragged edge of exhaustion; emotionally, he was tormented by feelings of guilt about his first wife, about his children by her, about various other people he felt he had injured intentionally or unintentionally, about earlier works such as *A Madman's Defence;* mentally, he was suffering perhaps most of all because of fear that he might lose his power to work and create and certainly because of an old fear that he might lose his mind. The evidence indicates he was fascinated by all this and deliberately extended his suffering in order, I suspect, to gain more insight into himself and to secure more material for his workshop as a creative artist.

The period from his divorce from Siri in 1892 to his writing *Inferno* in 1897 is filled with other disturbing facts and experiences: his exile in Berlin in 1892 and 1893 with its emphasis on sex, art, and alcohol in the company of bohemian writers and artists; his marriage to Frida, who apparently wanted to manage him and his life, who never played the central role in his life that Siri did but who opened up a world of exploitable experience by bringing him into her mother's and grandparents' home, who provided him with yet another daughter, and from whom he separated conveniently. His parting from Frida in 1894 — the start of *Inferno* — was followed in Paris by association with various groups, by experimenting in pseudoscience and alchemy, by withdrawal into isolation, marked by illness (physical, emotional, and mental), poverty, and humiliation (rumors that he was insane, and collections of funds admirers raised, some tactfully by word of mouth, others tactlessly in newspaper appeals). But through all this suffering, Strindberg remained well enough to be keenly aware of what was happening in the world about him, to be concerned with what he was doing, and to be fascinated by what his consciousness as well as his unconscious had to present under the effects of self-stimulation.

The first major result was substantial recovery and the most productive and important period in his literary career. The first major result for literature was *Inferno,* one of the most seminal books in world literature. Even a listing of chapter titles and a brief indication of the content of each will suggest as much: I: "The Hand of the Invisible One": the "atheist's" troubles; II: "St. Louis Introduces Me to Orfila": chemical experiments; awareness of Powers; symbols everywhere; III: "The Demon Tempts": guilt, poverty, insecurity; IV: "Paradise Regained": a ray of hope through religion; V: "The Fall and Paradise Lost": telepathy and black magic, attempts at performing miracles; VI: "Purgatory": Excrement Hell, gold making, delirium, hallucinations, recognition of sin; VII: "Hell": penitential pilgrimage; VIII: "Beatrice": the Child (Kerstin); IX: "Swedenborg": Swedenborgian hell = this life; X: "Excerpts from the Diary of a Damned Soul": theosophy and black magic; XI: "The Eternal One has Spoken"; XII: "Hell Set Loose"; XIII: "Pilgrimage and reconciliation"; XIV: "The Redeemer": Visions, intuitions, inspirations; XV: "Difficulties"; XVI: "Where Does Our Road Point?"

Inferno is, among other things, an account of a conversion, and, if we mean by that term depression and self-reproach or self-conviction of sin, giving up attempts at atheism, accepting faith in divinity (God and the Powers), sensing divine presence, special attention, and even favor, then Strindberg was indeed converted from what he called atheism to a kind of religion that may be called Strindbergian Christianity.

The importance of *Inferno* lies in two areas: the nature of the contents and its implications for their exploitation in literary forms besides the lyric. In his search for self-knowledge, Strindberg had certainly opened up possibilities for self-examination going far beyond what the five senses could present and the mind deal with. Without disregarding what these could offer him, he deliberately grasped and used what his unconscious had to offer as well. Visions, intuitions, hallucinations, delirium, dreams, perhaps all manifestations not acceptable as evidence in the cold light of the scientific laboratory he then considered valid means of getting at the truth about himself, his fellows, and his world. In a century when increasing emphasis on self-knowledge and understanding has led to increasing use of the services of psychiatrists, psychologists, and other counsellors it is no wonder that *Inferno* has appealed to innumerable readers, all of them "conditioned" to pursuing knowledge of the self and adjustment to the environment so that the individual's life may be meaningful.

Inferno is important, too, for its influence on literary forms: Thought of by Strindberg himself as a prose poem, an autobiographical volume, and a novel, it was shortly to lead to his use of the material in very personal dramas, and with that achievement Strindberg was to lay firmly the foundations of important developments in both drama and theater.

For Strindberg himself *Inferno* was important in various ways: It was substantial proof of the fact that he need no longer fear he was losing his power to *work,* to create literary masterpieces; it served as a useful means for ordering the chaos and vast bulk of materials encountered in the Inferno years; and it provided him with excellent therapy leading to renewed interest and zeal for interpreting himself and others in light of new insights.

VI Legends

Legends, originally conceived as a second volume or continuation of *Inferno* and partly written in French (*Légendes*), has this dedication:

To my brothers in misfortune
I dedicate this book and at the same time request their forebearance with

the sins of indiscretion I have committed in it with honest intent and praiseworthy purpose.

It will be your task to acquit or condemn me, and I can only beg for your forgiveness if I have done wrong [*SS,* XXVIII, 210].

He had good reason for writing this dedication to a volume, about which he said, "It is up to me to build a bridge between naturalism and supranaturalism by explaining how the latter is only a development of the former" [*SS,* XXVIII, 214]. For *Legends* is as much concerned with the alleged experiences of others as with his own.

When he was living in Lund, several of his regular companions were students at the university, younger men who were undoubtedly eager to associate with what many Swedes then considered the most notorious of Swedes and to supply him with testimony, actual and probably on occasion concocted, that would parallel his own experiences during the Inferno years. The title of the book suggests as much: Strindberg may very well have looked upon his young friends and acquaintances as men being driven by higher powers to sanctification or salvation through the discipline of suffering. Strindberg probably considered himself their mentor, certainly an assistant to the Powers in making the young men understand what was or what they said was happening to them.

The recollection of parallel experiences of his own and retelling them in the form of instructive tales or legends throw light on the roles such matters as bodily pains, signs, telepathy, doubles, dreams, visions, inexplicable noises, voices, fragrances, odors, and appearances had played for him in his Inferno and he thought were playing for his young friends.

The chapter titles suggest what *Legends* offers: 1) "The Possessed Devilinvoker"; 2) "The Spread of Hopelessness"; 3) "Upbringing [and Training]"; 4) "Miracles"; 5) "The Difficulties of My Skeptical Friend"; 6) "Miscellany"; 7) "Studies in Swedenborg"; 8) "Canossa"; 9) "The Spirit of Contradicting"; 10) "Excerpts from My Daybook, 1887"; 11) "In Paris." These are all instructive as fragments of autobiography, not least perhaps in Strindberg's revelation of his very human tendency to seek in others confirmation of his own conclusions.

What he has to say about his studies in Swedenborg and their importance to him at this stage in his search for self-knowledge is a tribute to the great eighteenth-century Swede. Taking Swedenborg as his Virgil conducting him through Hell (this life), he concluded that Swedenborg's works are infinitely inclusive, that they answered all his [Strindberg's] questions, and that they provided him with much comfort because of the correspondence between Swedenborg's visions and Strindberg's and his friends' experiences. In other words, Swedenborg was at this time the comforter, guide, and disciplinarian who led Strindberg to renewed faith in the validity of "Love thy neighbor as thyself" and "Do unto others as you would have others do unto you" and to active Christian participation rather than withdrawal.

As moving as anything in *Legends* is Strindberg's account of his final visit to the places in Paris that had been the settings for his Inferno experiences — the Luxembourg gardens, Hotel Orfila, the Montparnasse Churchyard, Jardin des Plantes, Notre Dame, among them.

VII   Jacob Wrestles

Strindberg knew the Bible exceptionally well, so it should be no surprise to anyone that there are biblical references and allusions in almost every one of his works. In *Jacob Wrestles,* at times thought of by Strindberg as the third part of *Inferno* or the concluding section of *Legends* but finally allowed to stand incomplete by itself, the biblical elements are extremely important.

The key passage is Genesis 32:24 ff.:

> And Jacob was left alone; and there wrestled a man with him until the breaking of the day.
> And when he saw that he prevailed not against him, he touched the hollow of his thigh; and the hollow of Jacob's thigh was out of joint, as he wrestled with him.
> And he said, Let me go, for the day breaketh. And he said, I will not let thee go, except thou bless me. ...
> ... And he blessed him there.
> And Jacob called the name of the place Peniel; for I have seen God face to face, and my life is preserved. [Verse 28 in the Swedish can be translated: He said: "You shall no more be called Jacob, but Israel, for you have fought with God and with men and won."]

Strindberg's use of the passage is representative of his use of biblical matters throughout his vast production: It is interpreted with care and applied personally.

On his return to Lund in early 1898 after spending several months in Paris, Strindberg composed a postscript to *Jacob Wrestles,* which says in part:

As the reader has surely detected, this second part, called *Jacob Wrestles,* is an attempt to depict figuratively the author's religious struggle, and as such is a failure. For that reason it remains a fragment and like all religious crises has dissolved into chaos. From this may apparently be concluded that searching into the secrets of Providence along with all storming of Heaven is struck with confusion, and every attempt to approach religion through reasoning leads to absurdities. The cause is, I suppose, that religion like the sciences begins with axioms, which have the peculiarity of not needing to be demonstrated, and that *can* not be demonstrated, so that if one tries to demonstrate obvious necessary assumptions, one gets into what is preposterous.

When the author in 1894 in principle gave up his skepticism, which had threatened to destroy his intellectual life, and began to put himself experimentally on a believer's point of view, the new inner life depicted in *Inferno* and *Legends* opened up. In the process, when the author had given up all opposition, he found himself attacked by influences, forces that threatened to tear him to pieces; and on the way to going under he finally grabbed some lighter objects which could keep him afloat; but even these began to give way, and it was only a matter of time when he would go to the bottom. It is moments like that that the straw becomes a log in the eyes of the terrified person, and it is then that the extorted faith lifts the sinking person out of the waves so he can walk on the water. *Credo quia absurdum,* I believe because the preposterous sprung from reasoning shows me I was in the process of demonstrating an axiom [*SS,* XXVIII, 399-400].

Though Strindberg may have believed *Jacob Wrestles* to be a failure as an exposition of his religious conflict, it is highly enlightening in terms of his search for self-knowledge, the meaning of life and the individual's struggles, and the force or forces beyond the natural who care about what happens to each human being.

Strindberg spent much of his 1897-1898 stay in Paris visiting churches, observing services, observing what was happening to him, and, in solitude, contemplating his relationship to Deity, and seeking guidance from Swedenborg, the Bible, *The Imitation of Christ,* and Chateaubriand's *Le Génie du Christianisme.* It is an account of a struggle that led ultimately to his espousal of a largely creedless Christianity based on the convictions that an invisible hand had taken charge of his education and that Christ on the cross symbolized patiently borne sufferings rather than the atoner sacrificed for mankind.

"I have become used to talking to the Lord, to confiding only in Him," Strindberg wrote [*SS,* XXVIII, 325] and then proceeded to explain the nature of the dialog figuratively between the Unknown (the Lord) and himself, a dialog concerned with the implications of two basic questions: 1) You are the one who has persecuted me for two years. What do you want of me? 2) What do you want of me? Why do you torture me with your Christ? Figuratively, the Unknown does materialize and "without opening his mouth the Unknown answers with a sort of smile full of superhuman goodness, forbearance, and courtesy, "Why do you ask me when you know the answer yourself?" And a moment later as if within Strindberg himself: "I want to raise you to a higher life, to pull you up out of filth!" [*SS,* XXVIII, 342]

Jacob Wrestles deals with Paris as the City of Light, with the glories of the Middle Ages, with the pleasures and vicissitudes of solitude, and, above all, with one man's attempts to achieve a religious faith that would help explain the meaning of his suffering, his struggle, life itself. The work is, moreover, along with *Inferno* and *Legends,* parallel in illuminating ways to the most personal of all Strindberg plays, the Damascus trilogy.

VIII Alone

Alone (1903) is a lightly camouflaged synthetic self-portrait as Strindberg saw himself in 1902 and 1903 when it must have become increasingly clear to him that his marriage to the ambitious and gifted young actress Harriet Sofie Bosse was not going to lead to established family life. The book places primary emphasis on insight into his life and work and only secondarily presents analysis of the sort he had emphasized in his pre-Inferno autobiographies.

Everything in the book has something to do with solitude, isolation, and loneliness:

This is ... solitude: spinning oneself into the silk of one's own soul, becoming a cocoon, and waiting for the metamorphosis, for *that* will come. In the meanwhile one lives on his experiences, and one lives other people's lives through telepathy. Death and resurrection: a new education for something unknown and new.

One finally possesses one's own person. No one else's thoughts control mine, no one's likes, whims oppress me. Now my soul begins to grow in a newly acquired freedom, and I experience an infinite inner peace and quiet joy and a feeling of security and self-responsibility! [*SS*, XXXVIII, 145]

His attitude toward his highly appreciated solitude is ambivalent: It shifts from nuances of quiet enthusiasm to those of quiet regret.

Solitude is no longer an inferno for him, for he had sources of very warm comfort: his own spiritual diet (the Bible, books of meditation, Balzac, Goethe) for self-discipline; Beethoven and other music for inspiration; freedom from external interference from others; and the freedom to work creatively in tranquillity.

His statement, "My habit of transforming my experiences into poetry serves as the safety valve for an oversupply of impressions and replaces my need for talking" [*SS*, XXXVIII, 192], is amply explained in his accounts of his experiences in and out of doors. On his walks in the mornings and on occasion at night, he acquires nonintimate "friends," observes others and their activities, and goes now and then on his *via dolorosa* through his beloved Stockholm for flashbacks to his past. Indoors, he writes, reads, rests: a pattern of usually marvelously pleasant morning walks; of highly satisfactory work; rest; reading; difficult lonely evenings; and welcome sleep.

Alone is not merely an account of his moods and attitudes and habits. It contains his clearest statements about his creative writing. For example: "When I get home and sit down at my desk, I really live; and the energies I have acquired on my walk either of the currents of disharmony or the currents of harmony serve me now for my various purposes. I live and I live the many lives of the human beings I depict; am happy with the happy; evil with the evil, good with the good; I steal out of my own being, and speak through the mouth of children, of women, of old men; I am king and beggar; I am the highest of the high, the tyrant and the most despised of the despised, the oppressed hater of tyrants. I have all points of view and confess all religions; I live in all periods and have ceased to exist myself. This is a state that gives me indescribable joy" [*SS*, XXXVIII, 155-156].

This passage acknowledging his joy in creative work is amply explained in his many comments on his use of the world about him as a source for material. *Alone* is indeed a superb treatment of the artist at work and at rest.

As interesting as anything in *Alone* is, however, his emphasis on his primary interest: "I have never hated human beings, rather the very opposite, but I have been afraid of them, ever since I was born" [*SS*, XXXVIII, 152]. And immediately before those assertions: "For three weeks I had not talked with a human being...I became uneasy; experienced solitude as excommunication; the thought occurred to me that people did not want to associate with me because I had rejected them. And so I went out in the evening. Sat down in a streetcar, just to feel as if I were in the same room as others. I tried to detect in their eyes if they hated me, but I detected only indifference. I listened to their conversations, as if I were at a party and had the right to take part in the conversation, at least as a listener. When it got crowded, it was a pleasure for me to feel my elbow touching a human being" [*SS*, XXXVIII, 152].

Strindberg was fairly well reconciled to struggle and work in solitude, but his interest in his fellow human beings was not limited to using them for material and distraction. He needed human contact and, in spite of his fear and his insight into what he considered animal weaknesses in them, was drawn to other people. *Alone* is indeed a moving self-portrait.

IX   *"The Quarantine Master's Second Story"*

A very important complement to *Inferno, Legends, Jacob Wrestles,* and the most personal of all the plays — the Damascus trilogy — appeared in the volume called *Fairhaven and Foulstrand** (*Fagervik och Skamsund,* 1902), a collection of prose fiction and poetry. "The Quarantine Master's Second Story" ("Karantänmästarens andra berättelse") is, above everything else, an autobiographical account of his second marriage with detailed information about such related matters as the difficulties of dealing with in-laws, the joys and sorrows of being a father, and his candid and pessimistic opinion of the future of the institution of marriage.

The marriage of Strindberg and the young Austrian journalist Frida Uhl, two strong-minded individuals, was, according to this story, a textbook illustration of one of Strindberg's favorite concepts: love-hate. In his analysis of Frida and her behavior, he pays every whit as much attention to himself and his own behavior. The result is a detailed account of fluctuations between marital bliss and marital hell, between kindness and malice, between suspicion and acceptance, between cooperation and competition, between delight and resentment. There apparently was very little of the quiet tranquillity both needed for their professional work, Strindberg for his literary work and "scientific" experiments, she for her writing for newspapers and magazines. He probably meant what he wrote to his friend Richard Bergh on November 24, 1894: "I don't really know much about my marriage. As I suppose you noticed in Berlin, we never took it very seriously, and it is probably going to dissolution — I'm not quite sure yet. Sometimes it was a lot of fun, and good, but language, race, concepts of right and wrong, bad habits made it hard going sometimes" [*Brev*, X, 3010].

The portrait of Frida is that of a highly complex young woman who had no intention of resigning herself to the quiet life of making a home for a difficult genius and their child. Again there is ambivalence: beauty and ugliness, self-assertion and self-denial, approval and disapproval, kindness and cruelty. Strindberg makes it quite clear that his second wife who did want to manage him and his affairs was doing pretty much what he was up to — playing a game — and, in the process, having as difficult a time as he: "How disunity can arise between husband and wife is still unexplained, I suppose. They love each other, are comfortable only in each other's company, do not have differences of opinion, suffer when they are apart, and their whole united egotism suggests they keep the peace, because warfare between them is what causes their suffering most of all. And just the same: a bit of a cloud comes up, they don't know from where, all their good points are transformed into faults, beauty becomes ugliness, and they stand there like snakes hissing at each other; wish each other far, far away, in spite of the fact they know they need only be apart for a moment to have the suffering of missing each other begin, suffering greater than the greatest which life can offer them" [*SS,* XXXVII, 186-187].

This brief passage is only a slight part of a searching analysis of Frida and himself as wife and husband and of inner and outer factors that made their marriage extremely difficult, a marriage that both were to end when it was convenient for them and both were to use in their writing.

Parts of their difficulties certainly stemmed from Frida's family. For the first time Strindberg was substantially involved with in-laws — Frida's well-to-do, conservative, Roman Catholic, maternal grandparents and her separated but not divorced, Roman Catholic, fanatically religious mother and sophisticated father, a Vienna editor of prominence and distinction:

Prepared for everything, even the worst, he began this part of running the gauntlet, during which he had to look forward to the most curious of all his metamorphoses. From being father and husband he was to become a child again, be grafted unto a family, and get a father and a mother again, what he had lost many years ago. What made this mess worse was that his father-in-law and mother-in-law had been separated for seven years, but were to meet again because of their daughter's marriage. So he [Strindberg] had become the hyphen, the link, but since the daughter, his wife, was at odds with her father, they could therefore see in the family get-together a multiple feast of reconciliation [*SS*, XXXVI, 161].

Strindberg's stays with his in-laws in Austria led to rewarding experiences: humiliation and inspiration, rejection and acceptance, kindness and unkindness, in fact, perhaps the whole gamut of conceivable experiences with and because of in-laws, all of which were potential grist for his speculation and imagination and much of which in one form or another was to appear in the Damascus trilogy and later plays. There is even detailed analysis of the joys and sorrows of parenting. More than echoes of his experiences as a father in a new marriage were to appear in future works.

X   The Occult Diary

From February 21, 1896, when he was in the midst of his Inferno crisis, until July 11, 1908, when his third wife's remarriage to another man had ended his direct relationship with her, Strindberg faithfully kept a daybook that he called *The Occult Diary* (*Ockulta dagboken*). Its early entries provided him with much of the raw material for *Inferno, Legends,* and *Jacob Wrestles,* and its later entries are a major source of information about his post-Inferno years up to July, 1908, and particularly about his third marriage.

Like many of his contemporaries in the 1890s, Strindberg was fascinated by the occult, that is, by alchemy, magic, manifestations of supernatural forces in general, clairvoyance, visions, and the like. In his generally disturbed state, he suffered intensely from anxiety about what most people would probably regard as more or less trivial natural phenomena such as not readily explained noises, sudden pains in the body, upsetting dreams, and odd little "symbols" that his active imagination could transform into messages, especially warnings from forces beyond what was visible. He was both disturbed and fascinated by these very real or highly imagined phenomena, recorded them with enthusiasm, within a relatively short time began to try to interpret them, yet never was certain whether the actual phenomena (the noises he heard, for example) or the sources of most if not all of them were supernatural or not.

The Occult Diary does note the progress of his conversion from free-thinking or, as he called it, atheism to a confessionless Christianity. The evidence of his self-conviction of sin (intensified guilt feelings about many people and about many things), his struggle to come to some sort of terms with life and forces (the Invisible or Unknown One and His Powers) that control the in-dividual human being's life, and his ultimate acceptance of Christ — within personal Strindbergian limits, to be sure — were all recorded.

But even after his conversion when he had written the volumes dealing with his Inferno and had dramatized his Inferno ex-periences in the Damascus trilogy, he kept up the diary. Probably the most interesting of all the matters dealt with is his account of his marriage to Harriet Sofie Bosse, the gifted Danish-German actress born in Oslo and educated in both Stockholm and Oslo (then Christiania). The evidence in the diary supports the generally accepted opinion that neither husband nor wife could be considered an ideal, even adequate, marital mate. She was a gifted and am-bitious, not too kind and tactful young woman, determined not to be a "mere" homemaker but to carve out a professional career for herself; and he was an aging man in search of "reconciliation with life" in a domestic shelter from the external world and the people in it.

The marriage — begun by her "Yes, thank you" to his unusual proposal, "Miss Bosse, do you want to have a little child by me?" — led to apparently extremely enjoyable intervals, violent quarrels, partings, reconciliations, and, in 1904, divorce, but not to complete and final separation until 1908 when she became engaged to a fellow actor. The following excerpt from a May 28, 1908, entry indicates how the whole relationship affected Strindberg, who was undoubtedly attracted sexually and otherwise by his third wife and who was delighted by her bringing him yet another daughter even though she may have accused him of inadequate virility:

Woke with the idea: that H--t has only entered into an agreement with W. [Wingård] "to get companionship" (that's what she wrote to me in her first letter); he has rented a room from her in her new apartment. He gets engaged [betrothed], and the following night she is with me; he gets married, goes away, and during the night she celebrates a wedding with me. Is their relationship platonic? Spiritual marriage without rapport? *Pactum turpe* (a shameful agreement)? A eunuch-marriage? — — — Perhaps? Perhaps that's the answer. But I have even got the hint that she *did not get married* (at Pastor Fries' home) but was "bound" in some way by betrothal, or that nothing at all happened! I met Fries a bit ago, and he looked very sly.

Wept all forenoon! Resisted H--t's attacks! But after dinner I took her into my arms, instead of burning up! — No reproaches, only happiness, and freedom from melancholy and thoughts of suicide. — Abstinence has formerly led to serious thoughts of suicide, always has! (August, September 1910?)

Now I believe this is as it should be! We'll see! — — —

The evening ghastly, though H--t was with me in eros — [12]

The biggest problem in *The Occult Diary* is the nature and significance of his numerous entries stating that Harriet has sought him erotically without being present physically. For example, part of the entry for April 23, 1908: "I went to bed, became calmer. No contact with H--t during the night. I sought her, but first at about five o'clock I found her. XX " [13]

The Xs obviously have sexual implications. Strindberg apparently believed on occasion that they were actually together even though their two bodies were far apart. Were these largely nocturnal experiences in some way related to his physical illness? Were they emissions stimulated by dreams? The reader will have the opportunity to form his own opinion: No medical authority has presented a definitive answer.

As we shall see later, at least four of his plays — the Damascus trilogy and *The Great Highway* — are without question dramatized autobiography. In addition it should be emphasized that practically everything he wrote has autobiographical elements or autobiographical implications. But the volumes presented in this chapter are the ones he considered the components of his autobiography.

As an autobiographer, Strindberg was a remarkably and essentially honest recorder, reporter, and analyst about himself, his fellow human beings, and his world. His accounts are on occasion admittedly lightly camouflaged but never misleading. Even in the most defensive of all these volumes, *A Madman's Defence*, he does not falsify the evidence in order to whitewash himself or his behavior. His distortions are almost always due to his unavoidable finite perceptions or to his deliberate extension of personal experience: "And to verify the accuracy of his observations he used himself as a psychological specimen, cut himself up alive, experimented with himself, ... submitted to unnatural, often repulsive intellectual and spiritual diet" [*SS,* XXIV, 65].

In his very subtle fashion Strindberg has gone beyond the naturalists in giving an essentially honest account of himself and his world.

CHAPTER 3

The Appraiser

...the laws are so imperfect, the system of trial so uncertain, and human
nature so full of lies and pretense that I have often wondered how a judge
can have the courage to express a definite opinion. —*The Bond*

S TRINDBERG'S search for self-knowledge involved not only a
continuing study of himself but also a never-ending scrutiny of
other people, the condition all human beings share, and human
institutions and practices. His search was spurred by great intellectual curiosity, an active imagination, keen powers of observation, remarkable sensitivity, and a gift for putting his findings
at every stage into effective written words. His search was hin-
dered, on the other hand, by finite senses.

He supplemented what he could learn about himself and others
through observation, sensing and thinking, by reading widely and
sensitively in world literature, religious books, history, science,
philosophy, and psychology. At no point was he fully satisfied,
however, that he had achieved final answers to the questions he
could ask about himself, his fellows, the community, the world,
and whatever force or forces there may be beyond human perception.

I *Human Beings*

One small group of important essays filled with narrative
material under the general heading *Vivisections* (*Vivisektioner*,
written in the 1880s) can serve as an indication of his uncanny
ability at seeing into human beings, analyzing them: "The Little
People" * ("De små"); "The Great Ones"* ("De stora"); "The
Battle of the Brains"* ("Hjärnornas kamp"); "Hallucinations"*
("Hallucinationer"); "Divine Nemesis"* ("Nemesis divina");
"Mysticism — for the Time Being"* ("Mystik — tills vidare");

"Psychic Murder" ("Själamord"). His approach was realistic, not sentimental; he perceived rich possibilities and great variety in individual endowment, a dual capacity for good and evil, and at least some freedom of choice ("the margin of responsibility" as he put it in *Creditors*); he emphasized his conclusion that human beings are complex, dynamic, highly vulnerable creatures.

The first two essay-narratives, "The Little People" and "The Great Ones," illustrate Strindberg's insight into inequalities not only in endowment but also in opportunity. The first tells the story of Emil, a humpbacked dwarf with modest talents and a great capacity for exploiting every opportunity to forward his own interests at the expense of others:

People felt that Nature had been unjust to him and got the desire to do more for him than he was worth, so he got a good life and a pleasant death as his lot.

Well, he was just as small as the rest of us, just as nasty, just as tyrannical, and if he had been permitted to live longer his little feet would have trampled down still more people, for he was not in the habit of getting out of anyone's way, of being generous, of loving, of forgiving — he was that small [*SS*, XXII, 112-113].

Strindberg's concept of human beings is strikingly similar to the one stated in the Christian confession of sin, the confession that emphasizes the human capacity for evil but does not deny man's capacity for good.

"The Great Ones" is an analytical narrative about Peter, big in body and great in endowment as a human being and an artist, with the capacity to sacrifice and work for others but who becomes the victim of envy and malice, yet retains both decency and integrity in his lifelong struggle for honest self-expression and genuine achievement.

"The Battle of the Brains" presents one of Strindberg's dominant ideas in the late 1880s, the possibilities of using suggestion as a means for influencing other people in the struggle for power, and the idea is illustrated in a story based on Strindberg's own experiences on what was supposed to be a cooperative scientific journey into Italy with Gustaf Steffen (Schilf) in 1886.[1] Suspecting Steffen of trying to use him for his own purposes, Strindberg deliberately analyzed his companion-competitor in order to discover his points of vulnerability and then through suggestion defeat him. It is the very sort of situation that Strindberg exploited in *The Father, Lady Julie, Creditors, The Stronger,* and *The Bond,* all of them written after "The Battle of the Brains."

"Divine Nemesis" questions the validity of Carl von Linné's belief that God interferes directly in the destiny of individuals, punishes and rewards, protects and destroys. Strindberg speculated on the possibility that there were natural reasons why he himself seemed favored above siblings and peers, parents and relatives, friends and enemies, but speculated, too, on the reasons why a different point of view might well lead to different conclusions: "Life is just as black as the pessimists are said to depict it, and life is just as bright as optimists depict it. To put an either-or, an either black or white is only a blunder in logic, for life is both" [*SS,* XXII, 167].

Citing many personal experiences and observations, he concludes: "As a direct causal connection between the misfortune and the previously committed act could not be discovered, the illogical process received the name Nemesis divina — divine vengeance! Divine, like everything illogical" [*SS,* XXII, 175].

"Mysticism — for the Time Being" deals with a would-be atheist's speculation about possible natural explanations of the seeming efficacy of prayer in saving a sick child's life.

"Psychic Murder (Apropos Rosmersholm)" is, along with "The Battle of the Brains," by far the most important for an understanding of Strindberg's major literary works. It deals with the destruction of a human being through murder or suicide, both of which, in Strindbergian terms, may very well be unconscious little crimes. As Strindberg says in a footnote [*SS,* XXII, 188], "Ibsen's *Rosmersholm* is thus not understandable for theatergoers, mysterious for half-educated people, but absolutely clear to the person who knows modern psychology."

The techniques for destroying another person, consciously or unconsciously, are suggested in these summarizing terms:

Now one creates a majority against him, puts him in the wrong, exposes his ideas, attributes ideas to him other than his own, robs him of his means of existence, denies him social standing, makes him ridiculous — in a word, tortures and lies him to death or makes him go crazy instead of killing him.

The expressions "tortured to death," "driven him crazy," "kill him with silence," "boycott," "utterly ruin" more and more become everyday terms, and the little innocent words conceal or reveal just as many major crimes as the dungeons in feudal castles [*Tulane Drama Review,* 13:2 (1968), 115].

In the essay itself are illustrations of psychic murders and psychic suicides, illustrated beautifully — Strindberg rightly insists, for example, that Rebecca West went to work on Beate Rosmer of Rosmersholm, and he demonstrates the techniques time and again in his own dramas and prose fiction both before and after *Rosmersholm* (1886).

Strindberg's fascination with himself and with other people and his efforts to understand how to get at an understanding of people through the use of his own endowment and through the study of what others have said and written about the physiology and psychology of man and the study of other nonliterary as well as literary accounts of the human experience resulted in an amazingly large number of excellent plays and works of prose fiction.

II   *External Nature*

Strindberg's fascination with the physical world found expression in almost all his works and, as we shall see later, through his paintings and his photography. The references to nature as the setting for human beings, the effects of the natural environment on them, their attempts to adjust to it, and their far-from-occasional mistreatment of it are numerous. But besides all these secondary treatments of nature, entire works are devoted to it. Among the most important are *Flowers and Animals: Essays Dedicated to the Young** (1888), *Among French Farmers** (1889), and *Swedish Nature** (1897 and 1901). This list excludes the volumes which may be classified as scientific and experimental or which are in the borderland of natural science.

Influences on Strindberg's perception, appreciation, and judgment of external nature can be traced primarily to Carl von Linné (1707-1778), Jean Jacques Rousseau (1712-1778), and the Swedish Romantics. More than all others combined the great eighteenth-century Swedish botanist Linné had made educated Swedes keenly aware of the physical nature of their country, explored its economic possibilities, and opened his countrymen's eyes to its beauty and uses through reports and a series of provincial "journeys."[2] As a result Swedish pupils and students botanized, a fact which helps explain Strindberg's amazing knowledge of flora and fauna. Rousseau's influence reinforced Linné's and went beyond it to affect Strindberg's thinking about society. Swedish Romantics such as Tegnér, Geijer, Atterbom, Stagnelius, and Almqvist were all lovers of nature whose poetry and prose Strindberg knew very well.[3] Helpful as all these predecessors' contributions had been, however, Strindberg's own intellectual curiosity, his gift for observation, and his ability to put into telling words what he thought and felt prevented imitation and guaranteed originality.

Flowers and Animals: Essays Dedicated to the Young* consists of seven essays: "Pessimism in the Art of Modern Gardening" ("Om pessimismen i den moderna trädgårdskonsten"); "The Nightingale" ("Näktergalen"), "The Art of Fishing" ("Konsten att meta"), "Memories of Hunting" ("Jaktminnen"), "The Intelligence of Animals and Plants" ("Djurens och växternas förstånd"), "The Secrets of Flowers" ("Blomstrens hemligheter"), and "My Garden" ("Min trädgård"). All of them testify to what might well be said to be the summation of Strindberg's view of external nature: "Nature can be very charming, but when it becomes threatening, deadly, insensitive, it is terrifying. And ... I felt the horror, which has been labelled panic for Pan, god of nature" [*SS*, XXII, 234].

For Strindberg nature was fascinating in all its phases from the tranquillity of his garden to the sea in storm but hardly to be interpreted sentimentally as an ever kindly mother.

Readers of such literary works as *The People of Hemsö* have been amazed by the extent of Strindberg's knowledge of plants. They would be even more amazed if they were to read *Flowers and Animals,* a volume that shows that Strindberg had a knowledge of botany far beyond that of the highly educated layman, that he speculated about and even experimented with theories of plant fertilization, that he tried to get at the truth about behavior patterns and "reasoning" powers of plants and animals, that he considered hunting a noble and manly sport; and although he was not much of a hunter, he was on an amateur level an enthusiastic fisherman in the Stockholm skerries. It shows also that he was keenly interested in bird watching, that he feared and disliked dogs intensely, and, perhaps above all, was a dedicated and knowledgeable gardener.

"My Garden" is a gem based on practical experience in caring for his eighteen-by-eighteen-paces garden out on his beloved Kymmendö[4] whenever he could spend his summers there and in caring for his indoor "winter garden" in town. The extensive scrutiny of books and magazines on gardening; the planting of such vegetables as lettuce, cauliflower, cabbage, and cucumbers well ahead of time in boxes in town; bringing these out to the island when danger of frost was over; preparing the soil properly ("never cultivate more soil than you can take care of yourself"); using liquid manure as the major fertilizer; the never-ending struggle with noxious weeds, insects, and worms; the irritating effects of neighbors' chickens, dog, and uncontrolled thistles; planting mutually protective plants together (Strindberg suggests dill among cabbage plants, for example); and the joys of seeing the plants grow and flourish and of eating the delicious products of one's own efforts — all make sense and have value for any other enthusiastic gardener who, like Strindberg, considers gardening an art with very real possibilities for creative activity good for human beings and good for external nature as well.

On April 6, 1889, Strindberg wrote to Karl Otto Bonnier[5] proposing that he prepare a major work about Sweden:

In May I'll settle in Småland [Carl von Linné's native province] to lay the foundation for my work *About Sweden*! That I'm able to write objectively and picturesquely without politics, socialism, agrarianism, and the woman question you have seen in my introduction to *Life in the Skerries*. ...

I'd prefer doing a classic work with lasting value, but readable [*Brev*, VII, 1824].

He speculated on the possibility of doing an up-to-date version of Linné's provincial journeys; with the financial aid of friends and acquaintances, he travelled through several of the provinces in 1890 observing their "nature" and gathering material for what he thought could be used as a reader, as he wrote on October 16, 1890, to Albert Bonnier, father of Karl Otto: "A single book of about two hundred pages octavo *Sweden's Nature*, ready next spring (and possible as a reader!)" [*Brev*, VIII, 2049].

Although Strindberg never completed the ambitious treatment of one Swedish province after the other and was to see Selma Lagerlöf produce in *The Wonderful Journey of Nils Holgersson through Sweden* (1906-7) the classic literary "geography" of Sweden of a sort he had visualized, he did produce a forty-page survey of all of

Sweden and a twenty-page account of his journeys through the southern province of Skåne; both were published under the title of *Swedish Nature** after having appeared separately in 1895 and 1897.

Aside from the fact that the two travel accounts make good reading, they are important because they demonstrate Strindberg's awareness of nature as it affects human beings. While his eyes were open to both beauty and ugliness in nature, his major interest was in physical nature as the home for man; in this he shared with Linné a basic interest in the wise use of land and the preservation of natural resources. Strindberg's appreciation of nature is at once practical and esthetic. His interest in nature was not limited to its manifestations in Sweden but extended to every country in which he lived and travelled. The most significant of his nonSwedish "nature" works is *Among French Farmers: Town and Country** (1889). Environmentalists would probably find his most memorable "literary" condemnation of human misuse of external nature, however, in *A Dream Play* (1901) in the coalheaver scene which demonstrates vividly not only what man can do to injure his fellow human beings but what man can do to make nature valueless for people.

III   *The Community*

Little that Strindberg wrote does not somehow concern the communities man has set up. All of his plays, for example, deal directly with social matters; his historical dramas not only reveal his central interest in people but also his conviction that people of the past were human beings like his contemporaries and the communities in which they lived quite comparable to those of his own day. His prose fiction such as *The Red Room* (1879), *Swedish Destinies* (1882-1892), and *Historical Miniatures* (1905) examines society, past and contemporary, as much as it examines individual people.

Out of all his nondramatic and nonfictional works there are at the very least six that the student of Strindberg should know about: *The Hidden Meaning of World History* (1903); *The Swedish People on Holy Day and Every Day* (1882); *The New Nation* (1882); *Actual Utopias* (1885); *Addresses to the Swedish Nation* (1910); and *The People's State* (1910). Although no one has made a sustained effort to assess the impact of such works on the striking development of modern Sweden, the men and women who have helped change Sweden from a primarily stagnant agricultural country with no great claims to a voice in world affairs to "a model for the world" either knew Strindberg personally and read his major works or have read them.[6] At the very least Strindberg's examination of society at home and abroad has served as a stimulant and a challenge in one social area after the other: human relations, the church, education on all levels, government and politics, the economy, capital and labor, social problems, national defense (war and peace), the environment and its protection.

Except perhaps for the period in the later 1880s and early 1890s when he insisted he was a free-thinker and atheist, Strindberg read, thought, and wrote much about the past, a subject as fascinating for him as fiction. His interest in history probably had two major objectives: to discover meaning in world history and to set straight the history of Sweden and its people.

The final synthesis of his thinking about the significance of world history is stated in his *The Mysticism of World History* or *The Hidden Meaning of World History** (*Världshistoriens mystik,* 1903). He came to the conclusion, that even if human beings cannot grasp it fully, there is a definite plan for historical development, a plan set up, kept going, and watched over by a force that is both creator and guide. In this development, there is a continuing drive toward monotheism and human enlightenment with nations and individuals having definite roles or missions assigned to them. In the process of unification racially and culturally — the goal apparently — history becomes a series of recurring events and situations, alternating disintegration and integration:

People have undoubtedly for a long time thought they could detect laws governing the march of history resembling those which control nature. In history men have detected traces of the physical law of balance (European balance), the power of attraction (larger nations' inclination to assimilate smaller ones), elective affinity, substitution and so on. And from the organic world men have borrowed the concepts of the splitting of cells, segmentation, struggle and selection and the like. But the march of history shows such a union of freedom and necessity that on the one hand *one has to admit freedom of the human will to a certain degree,* on the other *admit the existence of a necessity, which in keeping with circumstances limits the efforts of the individual and brings about the synthesis.* The great synthesist who unites antitheses, resolves incompatibles, maintains the balance, is no human being and can be no one but the invisible lawgiver, who in freedom changes the laws according to changed conditions: the creator, the solver, and the preserver he may then be called — whatever you like [*SS,* LIV, 398].

His conclusions were both pessimistic and optimistic.

If Strindberg's concept of love-hate is examined, it becomes clear that he believed the individual expects and demands more of the object of his love than of any other. Applicable as this belief is to the relationship between human beings, it is equally so between a human being and his country. Certainly that was true for Strindberg many of whose essays, articles, dramas, novels, stories, and other works have Sweden and the Swedes as the subject. He loved Sweden and what he considered good in its past and present; he hated its human imperfections and weaknesses and was convinced that it was his duty to point out its flaws and in so doing help materially to get rid of them.

Strindberg rightly believed that his country was rich in beauty and resources in spite of its relatively harsh climate, that it was a good place in which to live out one's days. Of the many works in which he deals with the human beings who live or have lived there, *The Swedish People** (1882) is particularly useful in indicating what Strindberg has to say about the evolution of the Swedish community. That work is by no means the only contribution Strindberg made to the cultural and social history of the Swedes, but it is the one that, while it was cruelly attacked when it appeared, is now finally becoming appreciated and recognized as a major achievement.

The ambitious coverage Strindberg undertook can be partly suggested by the unusually long title, *The Swedish People on Holy Day and Every Day, in War and Peace, at Home and Abroad or A Thousand Years of the History of Swedish Culture and Manners* and by its length — 993 pages in Volumes VII and VIII of the Landquist edition. In dealing with the Middle Ages, for example, he considers the people and their way of life in terms of their appearance, customs, and forms of address; the king; knights; clergy; monks and nuns; craftsmen; merchants and seamen; farmers; fishermen; the poor and the unfortunate; foreigners in Sweden; Swedes abroad; homes and furniture; clothing and ornaments; food and drink; amusements, celebrations, and solemn occasions. That approach permitted him to deal with the Swedes and their life styles from pagan days until his own time.

His cultural and social history is an impressive achievement in spite of its necessarily brief treatments of many topics and, as his critics were quick to point out, its occasional inaccuracies in details. The two volumes are delightfully entertaining and informative accounts of the past approached from the points of view of all the people, not just the few who attained position and power. It is not chauvinistic history: Strindberg did not believe that any nation could develop in freedom from foreign influence, that any nation was "racially" pure. In an essay, "Sweden, Inc."* ("Aktiebolaget Sverige"), Strindberg wrote, "Being Swedish is not worse than being anything else, but not better either" [*SS,* LIV, 243].

IV   The New Nation*

A very angry young man, Strindberg attacked the Swedish establishment (*överhetsstaten*) in the brilliant satire *The New Nation** in 1882. His approach, as he said in "Realism"* [*SS,* XVII, 191ff.], was realistic — his definition of a realist is one who loves nature and the natural, who hates artifice and the artificial, and who hates contemporary social conditions, the incipient police state, and the incipient military state.

Back in December, 1865, the four estates (Lords, Clergy, Burghers, and Yeomen) had given way to a two-chamber parliament with promise of a new day for the Swedish people, politically and socially. But the years that followed, Strindberg thought, had really brought little if any good for the Swedish people, "the modest, considerate and decent Swedish people," then, as always, he thought, the victims of the establishment.

Written for the most part with sustained humor and as sober reporting, *The New Nation* examines with biting irony the big talk and promises from 1865, their retrogression into character assassination and jubileums, ritualistic shows put on to delude "the Swedish people," and their exploitation by the powerful:

The community consists of relatives, friends, and acquaintances; the community is a coterie, or rather a collection of coteries, which are all ruled by the royal coterie. You think the caste system belongs to India. It belongs to the Old World. People have the crazy notion progress consists of learning what is useless, that education is knowing what others do not know, no matter what it may be. An educated person, i.e., someone who knows when Charles XIII died, cannot let his children associate with children whose parents do not know when Charles XIII died. A bureaucrat's children cannot become craftsmen; they would waste away and die of sorrow because of blocked development, degeneration or retrogression, whatever it is called. So, my son, I want you to become a craftsman and die an honorable man without knowing when Charles XIII died [*SS,* X, 40].

The change in 1865 had brought little more than a shift in power: The bureaucrats, the new aristocracy, says Strindberg, were the people in power who protected their interests by carefully screening admission to the establishment of the selected few from "established" families; by indulging in festival talks (rhetorical nonsense); repeating big lies; by glorifying (canonizing) not only historic dead such as kings, historians, and poets of varying competence but also living servants of the establishment such as Strindberg's bitter enemy Carl David af Wirsén,[7] "official" poet and patriot; by rewarding such people by election to the Swedish Academy and/or awards of the Orders of Vasa and the North Star; by permitting nonSwedish exploiters to move into one area after the other; by neglecting to make national institutions such as the Royal Dramatic Theater and the Swedish Academy serve national purposes; and in general, by neglecting the interests of the common man. A brilliant satire comparable in quality to Jonathan Swift's *A Modest Proposal, The New Nation* made members of the establishment furious in 1882.

Strindberg did make positive suggestions.[8] His critics have objected to the fact that while he made innumerable suggestions for change, he inevitably changed his mind and made still other suggestions some of which contradicted earlier ones. What his critics have not emphasized is the fact that Strindberg provided them and his admirers as well with continuing material for debate in all areas of social life and with the very sort of stimulant needed to prevent stagnation in the status quo.

V   Actual Utopias*

Take, for example, *Actual Utopias,* the volume published in 1885 when Strindberg was in his free-thinking period and believed that socialism provided the answers to social problems:

The new society, which does not take into account any more illusions or ideals, builds on the only reality on which it can be built: egotism. Egotism is an ugly name for a human being's most glorious gift: his instinct for self-preservation. Up to now people have not understood their own interests and have been partly fooled by the controlling class' fundamental doctrine: working for your neighbor. By uniting the interests of all people's individual interests the individual's interests will be better served than before, and with that all people's [*SS, XV, 9*].

A few lines farther on Strindberg concludes his statement of intention:

This book deals with the work for improving society and with attempts at reform already achieved successfully, ... abroad, of course, for in Sweden progress goes at a snail's pace. ... And still the wise man thinks it goes too fast.

While Strindberg changed his mind about means, he always dreamed and wrote about improving the community and the human individual's lot.

Actual Utopias consists of a brief foreword and four long stories: "New Construction" ("Nybyggnad"), "Relapse" ("Återfall"), "Above the Clouds" ("Över molnen"), and "Pangs of Conscience" ("Samvetskval"). All of them attack overcivilization and advocate either directly or implicitly socialism as the solution of social ills:

Without hate, without bitterness, in spite of all persecution, all petty revenge, he set out with continued use of the method of love to figure out the social question and the woman question, which thus belongs to the gentle book *Utopias*. But, before he wrote it, he had gathered and read what all the sharpest minds had thought about these questions and he was up to his shoulders in socialism, without, however, letting himself be trapped by the Berlin program of industrialism [*SS, XIX, 232-33*].

The settings are Swiss, the individuals involved Swiss, French, Russian, and English.

At the core of these "Utopian" tales is Strindberg's concern for setting right the relationship between man and woman through the reform of marriage and the family. Equality between husband and wife, professionally and maritally, achieved by the elimination of artificial traditions and the communal care of offspring is the major answer for the scientifically trained and disciplined major characters in these stories. The chemical engineer (male) and the medical doctor (female) in "New Construction," for example, do ultimately achieve happiness based on human equality in a man-woman relationship within an appreciably ideal community. In that story, the community has been reorganized to provide for collective ownership, "democratic" management of production and distribution and the right to work and to participate in its fruits; class distinction and private property rights have been eliminated. While "Pangs of Conscience" presents a vision of a future in which the world is at peace, "Above the Clouds" suggests that among complex and dynamic human beings ideals may be beyond attainment. Human egotism may effectively block the setting up of successful cooperative socialistic societies. Even with this qualification, *Actual Utopias* served a positive purpose: It provided a challenging stimulus to the growing debate about what society should be and what could be done to realize a community in which the human individual could achieve security and dignity.

VI Addresses to the Swedish Nation

The Swedes had been very much aware of Strindberg since his trial for blasphemy in 1884; he and his enemies had given them no opportunity to disregard him completely. The awareness became acute in 1910-1911 when the so-called Strindberg controversy raged: His critics had belittled and denigrated him, he had received no official encouragement and recognition from the establishment, and he had not helped matters by writing devastating attacks on prominent Swedes in such works as the novel *Black Banners* (*Svarta fanor,* 1904, published 1907). From April 29, 1910, through 1911, Strindberg contributed one article after the other to the Stockholm dailies, *Aftonbladet* and *Social-Demokraten.* These were later assembled in four collections: *Addresses to the Swedish Nation** (24 articles), *The People's State** (14 articles), *Religious Renaissance** (11 articles), and *The Czar's Courier or the Saw Filer's Secret** (8 articles). Of these, the first two are particularly pertinent to an understanding of Strindberg's involvement with society.

Addresses to the Swedish Nation is primarily concerned with the establishment's misuse of cultural institutions such as the Swedish Academy and the false evaluation of past and present heroes such as Charles XII (Strindberg called him "Sweden's destroyer"); Verner von Heidenstam (1859-1940) as the contemporary glorifier of Charles XII and at one time Strindberg's close friend; and Sven Hedin (1865-1952), the lionized and decorated explorer and the last person to be ennobled (1904) by a Swedish king. Strindberg's articles are tinged with the effects of outrage, anger, irritation, and perhaps envy; yet they contain enough accuracy in the charges and more than enough provocation to cause not only Hedin and Heidenstam but many others on all social levels to respond acrimoniously or favorably in articles and in oral protest or approval. The controversy concerned Strindberg as a person, as a literary man, as a critic of society: If it accomplished nothing else it aroused attention throughout the whole nation to Strindberg, its greatest living author; to the role of literature in a society rapidly becoming democratic; and to the proper functioning of cultural institutions such as the theaters and the Swedish Academy.

VII   The People's State

The People's State suggests Strindberg's role in the modernization and democratization of Sweden.

The articles in it are attacks on royal power, bureaucracy, the established church, the Swedish Academy, and other forms in the power structure which, Strindberg charged, had the power and the technique for shutting out anyone likely to upset the status quo and therefore were cooperating enemies of the common people. In spite of exaggerations and even inaccuracies, Strindberg's support of proposals for limiting royal power, revising the national constitution, initiating universal suffrage, protecting the rights of the people, simplifying and democratizing the governmental and judiciary processes, and providing for a basic education program are all matters that have been substantially achieved since Strindberg's day.

Laboring men, younger writers, university students, and many liberals responded with approval to Strindberg's final efforts to bring about reforms. These were the groups that had long been aware of his achievements and his contributions to national life. They were the ones most keenly aware of his never having received "official" forms of encouragement and recognition: He had not been elected to the Swedish Academy, had not received a poet's stipend or any other form of government support, and had not been awarded the Nobel Prize in literature. On his last birthday — January 22, 1912 — thousands of his supporters marched by torchlight to the Blue Tower to award him what he called the Anti-Nobel Prize, a nationwide collection initiated by working men and presenting the people's tribute (*folkets hyllning*). On May 19, 1912, eight laborers serving as his pallbearers bore him through crowds of mourners to his final resting place where his friend and admirer Nathan Söderblom, later to become one of the greatest archbishops the Church of Sweden has had, spoke, taking as his theme, "Blessed *are* they which do hunger and thirst after righteousness."

VIII   *Strindberg and Religion*

Any mention of Strindberg's appraisal of human beings and their world must, I think, include some consideration of his life-long concern with the possible force or forces behind creation. None of his major works is free of the implications of that concern, direct and indirect. Throughout his lifetime in struggling for an-swers to questions about divinity and its role in creation and particularly about its human creatures, he was exposed directly to the teachings of the Church of Sweden and of pietism. His studies and his avid curiosity exposed him to contemporary scientific discoveries and theories that were directly contrary to what his church had taught him; these led him to avow atheism in the 1880s and early 1890s. His Inferno years ended with his conversion to a type of creedless Christianity, a great interest in the Roman Catholic Church, extensive reading in religious writings from Swedenborg and Kierkegaard to books involving oriental faiths and practices, and, in the closing years of his life, to a fairly firm faith in a benevolent deity, actual meaningfulness in earthly life, and a life beyond the grave. Not that he became a blind believer: faith alternated with doubt, believing with backsliding — for Strindberg.

The Church of Sweden in which he was christened and confirmed had taught him that human beings are fearfully and wonderfully made in the image of God; that man, unlike God, is by nature and by deed a sinner in need of salvation; and that he must accept the articles of the creed (many, if not all, of its provisions, he felt, are beyond human understanding), recite the confession of sins with sincerity, and attempt to lead the Christlike life (self-negation ideally, self-restraint at least). The pietists emphasized acceptance of Christ as one's savior, conversion, personal testimony in public, reading of and using the Bible as one's guide in living, serving as one's fellow human beings' keeper, and, in general, exercising one's freedom of will.

Strindberg himself has discussed his religious development in detail in his autobiographical volumes and supplemented those accounts in various articles and essays including the late brief summary with the French title, "Assistons-Nous à une dissolution ou à une évolution de l'idée religieuse et du sentiment religieux,"* in which he says, among other things, that through the influence of economic and technical advances and of Strauss, Renan, and others:

We were soon done with Christianity and right after that religion was a "thing of the past," which one did not even bother to argue about. At the same time the Ape was discovered; and when the Darwinists found their image in him, the image of their god, the twilight of the gods had come.

But at the end of the 1880s ... the religious impulse returned, but under new forms. Ancient wisdom was dug up; Vedantism, Buddhism made their way into Europe under the names of Theosophy and occultism. ...

At the end of the 1890s, we could hail religious congresses, where all the people of the world knelt together (Chicago, Paris, Stockholm). ...

This certainly seems to be the way of religious development toward the goal — a monistic confession, "without dogmas, without theology" [*Samlade otryckta skrifter,* II, 260-262].

Strindberg's final conclusions about religious and moral matters included the leap into faith in a benevolent deity and supporting powers, a universe with meaning and order, acceptance of the Judaic-Christian code of ethics, and hope for a more perfect life after death.[9]

CHAPTER 4

The Scholar and the Scientist

He had ... found out that there was something that could put him on a level with the highest people in the community, something he could get: that was knowledge. ...

To find out about everything, to know everything was a mania for him. ...

But he did not want to do the experiments in the textbook; he wanted to make discoveries [*SS*, XVIII, 84, 95, 97].

I *Strindberg and Scholarship*

STRINDBERG apparently would have liked to take all knowledge as his province, and there is ample evidence that he tried to be well informed on practically every subject. He was, moreover, not satisfied to be a layman far better informed than most of his educated contemporaries but aspired to genuine scholarly achievements within both the humanities and the natural sciences. His motivations were a mixture of personal ambition and idealistic desire to benefit humanity.

Although he found both the lower schools and the university imperfect, they helped give him a good basic discipline in both the arts and the sciences. What he says about the flaws in the curricula and the teaching suggests that those very flaws may have impelled him to get partly on his own an impressive knowledge of literature, history, religion, government, mathematics, biology, chemistry, geology, and physics. By the time he was in his twenties, he had, moreover, acquired, in addition to the Scandinavian languages, an adequate control of German and French and, of course, Latin and some knowledge of English, Italian, and what he called comparative linguistics, knowledge of language great enough to permit him to learn Chinese and to catalog the holdings in Chinese at the Royal Library. In time he was to acquire a working knowledge of still more languages. [1]

The schools and his own boyhood enthusiasm for plants and animals, for chemistry, physics, and even anatomy made his herbarium, insect collection, and mineral collection meaningful. Encouraged in this sort of activity by his father, he not only read the available books about the sciences but also performed experiments at home. The natural science that was perhaps to give him not only breadth of knowledge but also lifelong satisfaction was botany, the science in which his favorite natural scientist, Carl von Linné, had achieved "discoveries" Strindberg admired: the classification of plants and appreciation of their beauty and usefulness.

When Dr. Axel Lamm proposed that Strindberg become the resident tutor for the Lamm boys and study medicine under the doctor's direction, Strindberg leaped at the chance but with curiously typical motivations:

Becoming a wise man who understood the secrets of life was his dream for the time being. For the time being, because he did not really want to get into a career which made him a set part of the community, not out of fear of work, for he worked enthusiastically and suffered when he had nothing to do, but out of dread of being classified. He didn't want to be bound as a set part of the community, become a number, a cog in the wheel, a screw. He couldn't be tamed. He wanted to stand aloof and look on, teach and instruct. To a certain extent a doctor's profession was free. He wasn't a bureaucrat, had no bosses, no office, no definite hours [SS, XVIII, 287-88].

Strindberg says nothing about dedication to medicine.

Dr. Lamm apparently did a great deal to forward Strindberg's study of medicine: He arranged to have him use a chemistry laboratory at the Technological Institute; he guided his studies in zoology, anatomy, botany, and physics; he encouraged him in his preparation for required examinations in Latin and chemistry at the University of Uppsala; he took him along on calls and allowed him to assist in minor operations and observe major ones. Dr. Lamm gave Strindberg above all else two things he needed very much: thoughtful support and the chance to talk about anything that interested him.

Strindberg's interest in becoming a medical doctor was not great enough, however, to bear a reverse. He did pass the Uppsala examination in Latin but failed in chemistry. He used that failure as one excuse for giving up the study of medicine. Years later he wrote: "And slave away for such a long time [eight years] to get into this nasty profession finally! To analyze samples of urine, poke about in vomit, dig in the crevices of the human body. No thanks!" [*SS,* XVIII, 309]

Strindberg had many of the qualifications for becoming a productive scholar: He had a very good mind, intellectual curiosity, the gift for observation, and the ability to analyze and to come to conclusions on his own. There were, moreover, such factors as extensive experience in the Royal Library with ready access to pertinent material and practical training in how to obtain it, some discipline in the chemistry laboratory with its attendant emphasis on the values of accurate observation and honest reporting, and exposure to contemporary and earlier scholarly literature within the humanities, the social sciences, and the natural sciences.

Both his literary and nonliterary works on Sweden and its history can be taken as illustrations of his ability to use not only his own observations but also those made by predecessors and contemporaries. Yet these works are not scholarly in a professional sense; they are rather usually brilliant popular works based on observation and thought but hardly the results of painstaking research in depth. That what he has to say strikes the sympathetic and informed reader as essentially correct is probably the result of insight rather than of patient study and careful coming to conclusions on the basis of established facts.

At the Royal Library he deliberately set out to become a specialist by seizing the opportunity to classify and to catalog the Chinese collection. He learned Chinese well enough to do the job, he searched out the facts about Swedish-Chinese relations by getting at the pertinent references in the two literatures and coming to substantiated conclusions about Chinese and Swedes' knowledge of each other; he reaped rewards for his scholarly efforts:

After a year's headsplitting studies he handed in the catalog and not without a certain satisfaction. He was a "sinolog" and had exclusive rights on the Chinese language.

He then developed the subject and tried to relate it in many ways to Sweden, looking for references to Sweden and Swedes in Chinese literature, and to China and Chinese in Swedish literature. The results were a memoir, which was presented in the French Institute, correspondence with sinologs over the whole world, a medal and memberships in learned societies. In that way he gradually succeeded in acquiring a healthy idiotism, which seriously was on the verge of extinguishing all intelligence [*SS,* XVIII, 122].

While Strindberg's fears of sinking into the healthy idiocy of excessive and pedantic concentration may partly explain his resignation from the staff at the Royal Library, they were not deterrents in any way to his desire to be informed on what was happening in the social and the natural sciences. In his letters and in his autobiography, he considers in some detail his readings in and other exposure to thinkers and scientists such as Buckle, Darwin, Henry George, Hartmann, Ingersoll, Linné, Marx, Mill, Max Nordau, Parker, Th. Ribot, Rousseau, Swedenborg, Voltaire, to mention only a few.[2] Strindberg was interested in knowing what had been said and written about people and their world, hence his extensive reading in literature about people as physical, as social, and as spiritual beings and about the nature of their world. He became well informed in psychology and physiology, in plant and animal life, and in the various branches of the physical sciences.

By the middle 1880s, Strindberg was not only well informed about contemporary scholarly research and scientific methods but he was also under the direct influence of naturalism and what that *ism* implied. For Strindberg, naturalism apparently had a primary source in Darwin's theory of the origin of species and had to do with evolution, the struggle for existence, and the key factors in the individual's life (heredity, environment, time, and chance). Under the influence of Schopenhauer, Nietzsche,[3] and others, Strindberg for a good number of years placed emphasis on man as a biological being limited to making this life as meaningful for himself as possible. That objective involved then the study of man and the study of his environment, hence Strindberg's concern with psychology, the social sciences, physiology, and, in general, all the natural sciences in the late 1880s and into the 1890s. The results of this shift in primary concern can be seen not only in Strindberg's plays and nondramatic literary works of that time but also in his decision to pursue scientific study rather than belles lettres after 1892.

He had, to be sure, been an alert observer of man and his environment from the beginning, had reported his observations and his insight into their significance in one impressive work after the other, had even admitted on occasion his human limitations of senses and understanding, and had produced what one might justifiably call case reports. On the basis of those reports he had made recommendations for change; that these recommendations frequently contradicted each other he generally ascribed to personal intellectual development based on greater experience and greater insight into human beings and their world. In none of these studies with the exception of the memoir on Chinese-Swedish relations had he ever carried his research and studies to the point of "healthy idiotism."

In two areas he did hope his contributions were likely to be definitive: natural science and philology.

II   *Strindberg and Science*

On July 6, 1889, he wrote to his fellow writer Ola Hansson (1860-1925):

... Am reading an unbelievable lot about science, collecting [material] for my future *Antibarbarus*. ...
Belles lettres nauseate me and I'm gradually going to transfer to science. It's an incomparable joy to pursue that [*Brev,* VII: 1867].

On July 12, 1889, he wrote to Hansson:

I probably can yet live for thirty years more, a whole lifetime and belles lettres should be produced when one's young, but my youth was ruined by wicked people, and now I've lost my illusions about it.
Science is superior, of course, and I should certainly grow and develop and not sink into becoming an exhausted literary man [*Brev,* VII: 1870].

During the next few years there was a gradual decrease in the number of his literary works and a decided increase in his devotion to science and, one must add, to the borderlands of science.

His concept of scholarship and his understanding of the way to achieve recognition as a scholar are interesting:

... the shortest way to a scholarly position and reputation is this: that I complete in detail a French article I have in outline form and notes, and will send to the French Academy through my professor and marquis [d'Hervey de Saint Denys], who has read an article of mine for me there already. Since the topic concerns French educational and political history, I think I can count on a grant from the French government for the printing. With this work [*Les relations de la France et la Suède*] I'll have a scholarly reputation right away and can become a member of the French

Academy, obtain grants for further research, etc. [*Brev,* VII, 1876]

But the primary emphasis was to be on "discoveries," not on painstaking research. That might lead to "healthy idiotism."

Strindberg took his speculations about science and his chemical experiments very seriously. He did become well informed about the natural sciences. His references to them in his literary works are based on broad and even detailed knowledge and original speculation about scientific matters. Scientists have found his "discoveries" interesting.

Take *Antibarbarus** (1893), for example. It has the subtitle *An Extensive Investigation of the Nature of the Basic Elements and a New Way of Looking at Chemical Processes according to the Prevalent Monistic Theory of the Unity and Oneness of Nature as It was Applied to the Other Natural Sciences by Darwin and Haeckel* and consists of four papers on Strindberg's speculations about the nature of sulphur, the transmutation of carbon, the structure of air and water, and the transmutation of metals. The nonchemist who is able to wade through *Antibarbarus* is likely to be impressed by Strindberg's apparently wide reading in literature about chemistry, his obvious tendency to take issue with authorities, and his decided self-confidence.

For the layman, two short articles — "Contemporary Gold-making" ("Nutidens guldmakeri") and "The Synthesis of Gold" ("Guldets syntes") — can serve as reminders that probably above everything else in his studies and other pursuits in natural science and the borderland of science Strindberg wanted to make gold and that he experimented over an extended period with no firm results scientifically but with great benefit to his autobiographical and literary production as both *Inferno* and the Damascus trilogy demonstrate.

His concurrent study of chemistry and involvement in occultism may have helped lead to his engagement with alchemy, "the medieval chemical science, the great objects of which were to transmute base metals into gold and to discover the universal cure for diseases and means of indefinitely prolonging life," as *Webster's Collegiate Dictionary* [4] succinctly puts it. Well into the Inferno period Strindberg apparently made no effort to distinguish strictly between alchemy and modern chemistry as less and more factually based science; he contributed articles on the two to Paris journals and devoted much of his time and energy during several years to them.

But after his conversion, his faith in science as the means of solving human problems changed:

Swedenborg never found any contradiction between science and religion, for he saw the harmony in the universe, the correspondence between the lower and the higher, the unity in the contradictions, and like Pythagoras observed the lawgiver in the laws, the creator in the creation, God in Nature, history, and human life. Modern decadent science, which though it has been given the microscope and the telescope, sees nothing, but observes only bubbles and cracks, spots and streaks, and when it draws conclusions, they are merely stupid or false.

Newton, Leibniz, Kepler, Swedenborg, Linné, the greatest [scientists] were devout Godfearing men; Newton wrote an exposition of the Apocalypse, and Kepler was a mystic in the truest meaning of the word. His mysticism led to his discovery of the laws governing the orbit of the planets. Humble and purehearted they were allowed to see God, while our decadent [scientists] only were allowed to see an ape attended by microscopic vermin [*SS,* XLVI, 30].

The change in attitude toward science remained dominant.

III   *Strindberg as a Philologian*

The renewal of faith involved not only religion but every other area of human interest as well. Take, for example, his renewed interest in languages and philology. The fifty-second volume of Strindberg's collected works, *Philological Studies** (*Språk-vetenskapliga studier*), represents the extent of his philological studies: *Biblical Given Names and Their Relatives in Classic and Living Languages* (1910); *The Ancestry of Our Mother Tongue* (1910); *The Roots of World Languages* (1911); *China and Japan* (1911); and *The Origin of the Chinese Language* (1912). These works demonstrate at least an almost unbelievable capacity for work. His interest in languages may very well have helped him become the greatest contributor to the vocabulary of Swedish and its greatest stylistic innovator.[5]

Strindberg did not rate his contributions to philology too high: "So it is not my discovery, but I am only the pupil, who has, however, worked on in the master's [Gesenius'] footsteps" [*SS,* LII, 14]. He is frank about the nature of his "discoveries": "My attention was fixed on the Hebrew language because I discovered it was the most perfect of all, a living thing developing from a seed, in which all others lie hidden. For, without the common sound laws and the rules for word building, there is in the letters themselves a power which seems to follow the same lines as in chemistry, music, mathematics'' [*SS,* XII, 14].

An examination of all these works reveals Strindberg's ardent and industrious study of dictionaries, grammars, and other publications about language; his true interest in etymology, sound laws, word structure, and shifts in meanings; his fascination with languages as revelations of human beings as well as means of communication; and real pleasure in using his active imagination while speculating about scholarly problems.

While some laymen may have found his "scientific" and "scholarly" writings convincing, scholars have not. Perhaps as typical a comment as any is the judgment made by The Svedberg, winner of the Nobel Prize in chemistry in 1926, in commenting on *The Blue Books* while considering Strindberg as a chemist: the articles in the *Blue Books* "are often little masterpieces of plausible idiocy, genuine gems of absurdity."

Professor Hjalmar Öhrvall, who quotes Dr. Svedberg, wrote: "on the whole his scientific works as such are totally worthless. ... From a scientific point of view *The Blue Books* are the most sweeping pecoral in existence, which does not keep them from having been written with stylistic mastership and can be read advantageously as light reading."[6] But his wide knowledge of both humanities and the sciences is obvious in his literary masterpieces.

CHAPTER 5

The Poet

So one wasn't born a verse writer; one didn't learn it either, for in school
one did learn all the kinds of verse, but it came — or did not come [*SS*,
XVIII, 341].

ACCORDING to his own account Strindberg was unable to
write verse until he was twenty. As a youngster he says "Johan
could not stand verse. It was artificial, false, he thought. People
didn't talk like that and seldom had such beautiful thoughts" [*SS*,
XVIII, 175-76]. He says a little later, "When Johan saw that the
poem [Byron's *Manfred*] was written in unrhymed verse, he began
to translate it, but he hadn't got far, before he discovered again
that he couldn't write verse. He was not called" [*SS*, XVIII, 286].
Then suddenly in his twentieth year when he turned to a friend for
help in writing namesday verse, he was told to do it himself, and he
did a couple of months later.

The results of that discovery were many, including *Hermione, In
Rome,* and *The Outlaw,* plays he calls "études" written in varying
degrees in verse; a partially poetic version of *Master Olof,* a great
many occasional poems; verse passages in some post-Inferno plays;
and three substantial volumes of verse: *Poems in Verse and Prose**
(*Dikter på vers och prosa,* 1883), *A Sleepwalker's Nights on
Waking Days** (*Sömngångarnätter på vaknadagar,* 1884), and
*Word Play and Miniature Art** (*Ordalek och småkonst,* 1905).
There are, moreover, poems in the volume *Gleanings* (*Efterslåtter,*
volume 54 of the collected works).

I Poems in Verse and Prose

It is not surprising that Strindberg did not put *Poems* on his list
of his most significant works included in his 1909 foreword to *The
Author. Poems* does not begin to compare favorably in substance

87

or form to the poems in the other two collections and certainly not in quality with the verse passages in post-Inferno plays.

On June 19, 1883, Strindberg wrote to Albert Bonnier that the work would consist of "unpublished verse from my youth, reflections about love, mood poems and dedications ... rather interesting things about biography ... the greater part like 'Loki's Blasphemies.' ... The mix will be pleasant and possibly interesting enough" [*Brev*, III, 255].

It is a fairly accurate listing of the content which was divided into four sections: *Wound Fever** (*Sårfeber,* twenty-one poems), *High Summer** (*Högsommar,* seven poems), *Storms** (*Stormar,* five poems), and *Youth and Ideals** (*Ungdom och ideal,* six poems).

In his foreword Strindberg admitted that he had not always met the requirements for standard versification, insisted that content is more important than pedantic perfection of form, and justified including "the strange section *Youth and Ideals* not as a source of poetic pleasure but as keys to his inner biography."

The contents of *Youth and Ideals,* 1869-1872, which echoes the versification of his Swedish predecessors and contemporaries, are interesting only because they are his accounts of personal puppy love, young women looked at romantically, a romantic description of a pond on a summer night, his serving as a model for a statue of the great eighteenth-century poet Carl Michael Bellman of whom he did not approve, of a group of actors' and other theater people's dinner, personal difficulties as tutor in residence to three rather nice boys. The poems are readable but in no way remarkable.

Storms contains "Exile" ("Landsflykt"), a poem about a bachelor's nostalgic Sunday afternoon in Stockholm; a "royal" visit to the Norwegian capital; a commentary on the Swedish-Norwegian union ; a sea voyage; a weighing of perfidious Albion against the England that produced Dickens, Darwin, Spencer, and Mill; an account of first arriving in France[2] and his response to Paris; "On St. Nicholas' Ruins" ("På Nikolai ruin, Visby 1870")[3], a consideration of the Catholicism that was and the pietism that is; and three pleasant little nature lyrics — "Sunset at Sea" ("Solnedgång på havet"), "Indian Summer" ("Indian-sommar"), and "Moonlight" ("Månsken").

High Summer has a facetious little poem on Perseus and Andromeda; a mixture of prose and verse called "Sun Smoke" ("Solrök") in appreciation apparently of the Stockholm skerries; a little lyric simply called "Sailing" ("Segling") which is a tribute to Siri ten years after meeting her for the first time; "High Summer in Winter" ("Högsommar i vinter"), a tribute to marital bliss; an interesting retelling of a "French" ballad; and two lyrics devoted to young family life — "Saturday Evening" ("Lördagskväll") and "Morning" ("Morgon").

The remaining section is the one that signifies most: The poems are revelations of high points in Strindberg's early life as he saw them: a treatment of the generation gap that affected him, a plea for writers to become thoroughly involved in current problems, attacks on class distinctions, a protest against the mechanical nature of society, an attack on pretenders to taste, an appreciation of Nobel's invention of dynamite[4], and commentaries on the joylessness and other flaws of the time. Of all the poems, two are particularly noteworthy — "Loki's Blasphemies" ("Lokis smädelser")[5], an iconoclastic attack on the "gods of the time" and an early Strindbergian venture into debunking both past and present and "The Esplanade System" ("Esplanadsystemet"), a highly appreciative look at letting in air and light by replacing rundown shacks, by creating broad avenues. Stockholmers in our day should find his concluding stanza still controversial as this rough translation indicates: "Ha! The way of the times: to tear down houses!/But build? — It's terrible!"/ — "We're tearing down to get air and light:/Isn't that perhaps enough?"

II A Sleepwalker's Nights on Waking Days (*1884*)

The second collection of poetry has an intriguing title: It reflects one of his dominant ideas in both his plays and his prose fiction. The collection is, moreover, as he knew, far better than the first.

As printed in the Landquist edition, *A Sleepwalker's Nights on Waking Days* consists of a brief introductory poem and five "nights." The first one had appeared in a preliminary version of "Farewell" ("Avsked") in *Poems;* the fifth one was not written until 1889, according to Landquist [*SS,* XIII, 310], after Strindberg had returned to Sweden from his self-imposed exile.

The little introductory poem suggests the dominant mood of the whole collection — nostalgia for Sweden and Stockholm. While passing a butcher shop in Paris, Strindberg observed smoking, freshly butchered meat, a seemingly throbbing animal heart hanging on the door, all of which made his thoughts go quickly to a bazaar in Stockholm where "a little book in thin cover hangs in a bookstall window — a heart removed from its owner and dangling on its hook."

The first "night" emphasizes Strindberg's love-hate relationship with Sweden and the Swedes. Paris had proved noisy and disturbing: Sanitary facilities were far from adequate, the French substituted perfume for baths, and the food was unbelievably bad. (Writing to Albert Bonnier on October 19, 1883, he asserted "My wife goes out shopping and prepares the food. ... We can't eat French food which is fit for dogs and makes us sick" [*Brev,* III, 33]. The first major poem deals with his departure from Sweden; while his body is brought farther and farther away, his spirit is returning to Stockholm across the fertile plains of Skåne, the stone-strewn landscape of Småland, the bountiful stretches of Östergötland, the dark Kolmården forest, and the approaches to Stockholm, "the place to which he steals in the night like the wandering Jew." The place in Stockholm to which he returns is here particularly Adolf Fredrik's Church, the church his family had attended and in which he had been confirmed, the church that represented both pleasant and unpleasant memories, unpleasant largely because in its larger context it had failed to give him "a single solution to the puzzle of life." The poem is a highly effective revelation of Strindberg's longing for home and an interesting revelation of his conviction in the 1880s that religion does not provide answers to man's fundamental questions.

While the second "night" also emphasizes the poet's nostalgic mood, it primarily concerns the sleepwalker's rejection of art as providing the solution to his search for answers. The carefree, happy life in the artists' colony at Grez[6] provided welcome relief from the noise of Paris by its simple social pleasures, to be sure, but his "return" to the museums and galleries in Stockholm makes him reject art for nature itself: "Farewell, beauty, delightful for some, now usefulness comes, useful for all!"

The third "night" is probably Strindberg's frankest commentary on the shortcomings of Paris, a city he considered in many ways the center of the world of culture but confusing and disturbing as well. The poem becomes a questioning and then a rejection of the idea of usefulness or practicality and a turning to knowledge, to books, to science, only to conclude with Omar that books do not have the answers.

The sight of a Scandinavian spruce in the midst of an out-of-the-way corner of an artificial, restricted Paris park continues the emphasis on nostalgia in the fourth "night" with its commentaries on the limitations of the natural sciences ("say, you [science] can surely answer where the dead have gone, where we shall all go, where we came from! You do have answers, but not to those questions, answers to many things that do not concern us, but you don't admit your inability but bring us ever into greater darkness.") Readers who have doubts about the perfection of advanced education, who worry about such matters as the mutilation of our environment and human indulgence in over-population, will find Strindberg was very much aware of problems like those: What must startle many a Swede who has had the notion that Strindberg hated Sweden are his lyrical tribute to "my Sweden" and his appeal to Swedes to live in freedom true to themselves and not afraid of democratic progress.

The "night" written after his return from exile is probably one of the most poignant statements that one can never really go home again. Having been exiled and burdened with ever-recurring thoughts of and longing for home, the poet returns to the home city of which he is so proud to find old friends dispersed or dead, no acquaintances at the old meeting place, he himself thought probably dead, and unavoidable loneliness in the midst of crowds — no answer for the sensitive poet to feel at home even though his country really shows signs of progress.

III   *Word Play and Minor Art*

Strindberg did have an eye for street scenes — he saw them often enough on his solitary walks — and speculated on how they affect eyes and ears; results include a series of those brief vignettes called "Street Scenes" ("Gatubilder"); a lyric called "At the End of Day" ("Vid dagens slut"), nostalgic recollections of youth stemming from seeing the harbor in his loneliness; "Thunder Storm" ("Åskregn"), a recalling of marital love; "A Singer's Reward" ("Sångarlön"), a dream of achieving happiness again; "May on the Heath" ("Maj på heden"), a description of a Mayday demonstration for universal suffrage; and "Figures in the Clouds" ("Molnbilder"), an imaginative interpretation of cloud formations suggestive of happy days on Kymmendö years before.

"The Trip to Town" ("Stadsresan") is far more ambitious than the pleasant little poems already noted. In the first part ("Första sången") of a poem in hexameters reminiscent of Esaias Tegnér, a Romantic, Strindberg describes the rural environment of Lake Mälare and relates how the organist at Årby prepares to take the steamer for Stockholm on a very special Midsummer Day — the twentieth anniversary of his wedding by, among other things, enjoying the very good breakfast his wife has prepared after telling her they have to watch every penny now that their numerous children make greater demands and they themselves are aging. The second part is a descriptive account of the round trip by steamer through a beautiful area; it tells about the organist's careful protection of a large box on his return, and the third part narrates how the organist steals out of church during the sermon to open the box and bring the new piano in it into his home as a delight and a joy for his wife and himself on their anniversary. "The Trip to Town" is delightful as a genuine revelation of thoroughly Swedish landscape and a very special Swedish holiday, Midsummer.[7]

Any foreigner who has observed the Swedes' delight over the coming of spring, their rituals in welcoming spring on Walpurgis Night (April 30), and their flight to the country as soon as possible after spring has come should find the slightly dramatized part of "The Evening Before Trinity" ("Trefaldighetsnatten") evocative of memories of a people who know how to celebrate special occasions and times with joy and exuberance and with more than a touch of impressive pomp and ceremony. For those who know Swedish and *A Dream Play,* this poem in a collection attached to *Fairhaven and Foulstrand (Fagervik och Skamsund,* 1905) will throw light on the sharp contrasts at a resort (the real Furusund in Strindberg's day) and a quarantine station in the Stockholm skerries. The section concludes with a rapid survey of a Swedish summer in the country, details recalled with nostalgic pleasure from earlier and happier days.

Inserted in the cycle are, strangely enough, two lyrics that have fascinated and challenged readers — "Chrysaëtos" and "I Dreamt" ("Jag drömde") as well as the more easily interpreted "Haze Above the Rye" ("Rågen ryker"), "The Meadow Barn" ("Ängsladan"), the onomatopoeic "The Vane Is Singing" ("Flöjeln sjunger"), and "The Song of the Nightingale"

("Näktergalens sång").

"Chrysáëtos" is the very sort of lyric that would appeal to the devotees of one of Strindberg's disciples, Ingmar Bergman. The poem is a beautifully conceived and executed account of a man's desperate sorrow over the death of a woman he has loved. Whether it is based on Strindberg's difficulties in adjusting to the ups and downs of his relationship to his third wife with its alternating moods of fulfillment and loss or a challenging recreation of vaguely suggested but highly suggestive moods of a human being isolated in loss is a question that could cause a Bergman fan to speculate creatively. It is most likely Strindberg's lyrical summary of his last profound love for a woman.

For those who are repelled by Strindberg's accounts of marital hells in prose, "I Dreamt" must be a verse parallel to these. It treats in a relatively few lines the perennially observable effects of what human beings do for and to each other: a cripple is transformed physically and spiritually into youth and health by a woman's love but shortly afterwards he transforms her from "a perfect [woman] in ways and manners and not least in dress" into a nagging, bickering harridan because in demanding perfection in her he calls her attention to an offending bit of red ribbon on her right shoulder. The result: a dance of death as evocative as the marital hell in the plays by that name and the contrast between the wedding evening and the morning after in *To Damascus* III.

"Haze Above the Rye" and "The Barn on the Meadow" are nature lyrics which reveal Strindberg's sensitivity to sights and sounds and fragrances — in short, the nuances of beauty in rural Sweden. The other two poems are experiments in trying to produce "bird" songs in combinations of human sounds.

Readers of Pär Lagerkvist (1891-1973), another of Strindberg's prominent disciples, may well wonder if "Laokoon" and "Ahasuerus" were not two of the many impulses in Strindberg that led to the composition of Lagerkvist masterpieces.[8] The former is a provocative protest and appeal ending: "Forget that it wasn't enough for me/ to be the priest of Apollo, the voice of the oracle/ but even the divine animal man. Forget! — — — —." The poem about the wandering Jew may well be considered as closely related to "The Flying Dutchman" in terms, among others, of Lagerkvistian interest in exiles and pilgrims.

"The Flying Dutchman" should, on the one hand, comfort

women's liberation advocates for its apostrophe at some length of
the perfection of the feminine form and its promises to man and,
on the other, the cynics who find perfection in neither form nor
spirit. Those who know their Strindberg will find the three songs
that comprise "The Flying Dutchman" an effective statement in
verse form of Strindberg's concept of love-hate, a restatement of
his personal dream of fulfillment and completion through union
with woman and his personal assessment of the Lauras of this
world as Omphales.[9] "Ahasuerus" had definite Strindbergian
emphasis in its presentation of the popular old tale — loss of family
and home, loss of friends and relatives, utter isolation.

"At the Last Headland" ("Vid sista udden") is an expressive
account of the effects an unseen pianist's playing an unseen piano
has on an unseen man in a sailboat, on unseen people on a steamer,
on birds, insects, and animals — playing in a gray, deteriorating
villa on the headland. As perceptive as Strindberg was to *all*
nuances in the skerries he was equally alert to those of Stockholm;
"The Wolves Are Howling" ("Vargarne tjuta"), not only in-
terprets the cries of the animals at Skansen, Stockholm's outdoor
museum[10], as cries of protest against inhumane imprisonment but
also presents breathtaking views of Stockholm at night (partly
lighted by a raging fire) and in early morning.

Divided into five short lyrics, "Long, Heavy Evenings"
("Långa, tunga kvällar") is perhaps Strindberg's most poignant
expression of loneliness and isolation: empty rooms, silence,
walking back and forth, listening, thinking, remembering, trying to
forget, watching the one light across the heath, wondering, waiting.
"Night on the Heath" ("Natt på heden") is Strindberg's lyrical
interpretation of what he saw one winter night as he looked out
over the heath to the east of his apartment on Karlaplan.

Two poems, "Rosa mystica" and "The Laws of Creation"
("Skapelsens tal och lagar"), are didactic poems in the manner of
Lucretius' *De rerum natura,* the former a textbook-like description
of the briar rose (*rosa canina*) and a suggestion of its occult values,
the latter an account of creation as a series of steps and an interesting revelation of Strindberg's continued interest in the occult.

"Visor," the concluding title, covers four little ballads: "My
Troll Castle" ("Mitt trollslott"), "Seven Roses and Seven Fires"
("Sju rosor och sju eldar"), "Semele," and "Villemo." The
"ballads" are little songs written for Anne-Marie, his youngest

daughter, and contain a great many characteristics of ballad style — repetitions, parallels, refrains. Their contents are suggestions of moods evoked during his last marriage. They have been set to music by two of Sweden's greatest composers, Ture Rangström and Wilhelm Peterson-Berger.

V *Strindberg and Verse*

Strindberg's best verse is probably to be found among the many verse passages in his post-Inferno nonhistorical plays, particularly in plays such as *A Dream Play* and *The Great Highway*. In the former, for example, the happy harmony between intensely felt and expressed emotions and ideas and Strindbergian free verse can, in translation, give the reader who has no Swedish at least some notion of Strindberg's control over verse and lyric.

For those who know the riches of Swedish poetry in the original, Strindberg's achievements as a poet in the sense of a creative artist expressing himself in verse can never rank with those of such predecessors as, say, Carl Michael Bellman (1740 - 1795), Esaias Tegnér (1782 - 1846), Erik Johan Stagnelius (1793 - 1823), Per Daniel Amadeus Atterbom (1790 - 1855), C. J. L. Almqvist (1793 - 1866), and such contemporaries as Johan Ludvig Runeberg (1804 - 1877), Viktor Rydberg (1828 - 1895), Gustaf Fröding (1860 - 1911), Verner von Heidenstam (1859 - 1940), Erik Axel Karlfeldt (1864 - 1930), and even Oscar Levertin (1862 - 1906) as masters of poetic form. The explanation lies in his early suspicions about the honesty of poetic expression, in his admitted difficulty in versifying, in his preference for prose as the vehicle for expressing his personal feelings and emotions as well as his ideas.

In a national culture that has for many generations placed poetry very high on the scale of artistic performance, Strindberg did, however, feel the need of showing that he, too, could do very well at writing verse. He experimented with almost every form of verse — he insists he knew the principles and theories of versification — and succeeded best, I think, in his use of the traditional hexameter and, above all, in his free verse. His poems range from biting satire of artificial and idealized diction such as his imitation of a resented and even despised contemporary in *The Journey of Lucky Peter* to charming little lyrics (reflective, nature, and narrative) to moving expressions of universal truths in the post-Inferno dream plays.

His importance as an artist working in the medium of verse lies in his rejection of idealized diction in poetry, in his striking and rich use of realistic imagery and realistic detail, in his use of free verse, in his revolutionary expansion of the Swedish vocabulary, and in his provocative material and ideas. His poetry was and is read: The best evidence for that can be found in the testimony of his contemporaries, enemies as well as admirers, and in the poetry of the host of Swedish poets in our century.

CHAPTER 6

The Story Teller

So the author was just as right when he insisted to a friend that he could show photographs of the characters as he was when he explained he had not taken photographs. It was fiction and it was reality. ... he still had the ability to produce characters and scenes with his imagination [*SS*, XIX, 165].

F OURTEEN of Strindberg's works are by general agreement classified as novels: *The Red Room* (1879), *The Son of a Servant* (1886), *Time of Ferment* (1886), *In the Red Room* (1886), *The Author* (1886), *The People of Hemsö* (1887), *A Madman's Defence* (1887), *At the Edge of the Sea* (1890), *Inferno* (1897), *Legends* (1898), *The Gothic Rooms* (1904), *Black Banners* (1904), *The Roofing Celebration* (1905), and *The Scapegoat* (1906).

A great many others are fairly long narratives, too long to be called short stories, too short to be called novels, but probably justifiably to be classified as novellas. Most of these narratives appeared in the collections, *Town and Gown* (1877), *Swedish Destinies and Adventures* (1882-92), *Actual Utopias* (1885), *Life in the Skerries* (1888), *Fairhaven and Foulstrand* (1902), and *Historical Miniatures* (1905).

Then there are short narratives that can justifiably be called short stories, particularly some of those in *Married* (1884, 1886)[1] and *Tales* (*Sagor,* 1903). For all practical reasons including the fact that Strindberg himself did not insist on distinctions between his short narratives and his very, very short ones, all of the narratives except those listed above as novels will here be considered short narratives.

I *From* Town and Gown

His first volume *Town and Gown*[2] should delight angry young people who have taken a more or less close look at university life

97

anywhere and found it wanting. The twelve tales — "The Boarders" ("Inackorderingarna"), "The Loner" ("Ensittaren"), "The Vole" ("Sorken"), "Between the Struggles" ("Mellan drabbningarna"), "A Snob" ("En snobb"), "A Public Entertainment" ("Ett folknöje"), "A Promising Youngster" ("En lovande yngling"), "The Skald and the Poet" ("Skalden och poeten"), "The Sacrifice" ("Offret"), "Irresponsibility" ("Lättsinnet"), "The First and the Last" ("Primus och Ultimus"), and "The Old and the New" ("Det gamla och det nya") — were all based on Strindberg's recollections of university life and on observations he had made on visits in Uppsala after his student days were over. None of them is the kind of story loyal friends of a university establishment would want to gain wide circulation.

"The Boarders" is an account of a naively idealistic student who without guidance or goal wastes several terms at the university, substituting social activities for self-directed study toward a degree and thereby disappointing an indulgent father. The "loner" makes no attempt to become "one of the fellows" but protects his privacy and pursues his studies until he achieves his realistic but not idealistic goal. The vole, however, spends some twelve terms at the university without ever fitting in but making do with things as they were:

That's how his life passed — quietly and calmly: he never did any harm, was never criticized, was a good human being, had all the pleasant qualities, went to church, wrote to his parents, never got into arguments, attended lectures, but never came up for any degree.

He left Uppsala when he was twenty-six, without any bitterness toward instructors or comrades, just as appreciated and liked as when he came [*SS*, III, 25].

Then there are the stories of the little hunchbacked medical student whose extreme poverty is interrupted occasionally by little or big breaks ("Between the Struggles"); of the handsome young student whose good manners, good clothes, and fine cane, made him the object of envy, and got him labelled a snob, but who, after four unpleasant years, took a law degree with honors; of four hundred students less rather than more seriously engaged in taking the Latin examination required until 1873; of the burial of the golden boy among medical students, a victim of meningitis and the object of the ritualistic pomp and ceremony of that thoroughly Swedish institution, the provincial house (*nationshus*); [3] of the two young student poets, the romantic idealist who ultimately catches on to what is in the current taste and becomes a happy lumber inspector up north and the opportunistic young poet who plays the game, gets his degree with honors and succeeds in getting into the histories of literature; of the young pastor, a sacrifice to his father's stinginess and ambition and the product of poverty and humiliation; of the irresponsible Big Man at the University who led his fellows not only in standard student extracurricular activities but in vandalizing the community, only to end up in debt and beginning to prepare for the ministry; of the handsome young humanist (*primus*) and the poverty-stricken and not so handsome chemist (*ultimus*) at another impressive Swedish ritual (*promotionen*), the ceremonies when various doctoral degrees are awarded and the laurel wreath is placed on each new doctor's head, and the unexpectedly different lots life dealt them; and of the two sharply contrasting points of view on life, [4] the university, and a professor-philosopher who has an older student as his admiring disciple and who faces rejection by a new generation of realistic students represented by a bright fifteen-and-a-half year old.

While Strindberg tells the stories of a series of atypical students, the major thrust of the whole collection is directed at the university system and what it does to its students. The lack of guidance, definite requirements, and supervision overwhelms the youngsters who are suddenly plunged into a kind of freedom for which the strict discipline of the lower schools and the watchful care of parents at home have not prepared them and which leads to a meaningless pursuit of distractions ("wine, women, and song") plus vandalism and waste. The collection was Strindberg's first major contribution to a lifelong examination of the educational system, a system that he believed should be revamped so as to prepare boys and girls both for making a living and living.

Strindberg later insisted that he wrote these stories without any intention of exposing flaws and weaknesses or to attack the system, but he added: "The experiences of the past few years had trained him in a genuine humanity, which extends its sympathy to all social classes, even the highest, to wherever he found an unfortunate person who is waging his bitter struggle for position whether it is high or low. He had seen that it was a harder fate to step down from a position where birth and training had placed him without any of his own doing than to remain on a low place where he was

born. He had seen how difficult it was to realize the dream of
equality. If anyone stepped or fell down to a lower class, he was
trampled still farther down by this class, instead of being welcomed
as an equal. Trample or be trampled, seemed to be the rule; below
me or above me, not beside me!'' [SS, XIX, 155]

But in stories that reflected his memories and his later observations, he could, by his very nature, not refrain from exposure
of flaws and hypocrisy any more than he could avoid recording his
keen observations of changes that had taken place. The romantic
idealists of his own day, for example, had given way to practical,
even cynical realists.

University people of any period will recognize the validity of his
presentation of gifted youngsters with great expectations frustrated
by the facts of university life or forced to compromise their ideals
or his presentation of open-eyed youngsters ready to make use of
whatever advantages are available for their personal gain. Told
with humor and light irony, these narratives reveal a sharp eye for
both the comedy and the tragedy in student life. Non-Swedes can
with profit speculate a bit about models such as Charles Dickens
and Hans Christian Andersen[5], two of Strindberg's foreign
favorites, but they will not find them slavish imitations but original
masterpieces.

II   The Red Room

While it was neither the first important nor the first great
Swedish novel, *The Red Room* (1879) was the first novel to
examine the Swedish community from almost every conceivable
point of view and the work which made the Swedish reading public
acutely aware of Strindberg. Both in form and content, it probably
has been more influential than any other on the development of the
Swedish novel from the late nineteenth century through the
twentieth.

One passage explains Strindberg's intention: ''. . . he had had the
opportunity to observe people as social animals in all possible
ways. He had attended parliamentary meetings, church councils,
shareholders' meetings, philanthropic meetings, festivals, funerals,
police investigations, meetings of the public; everywhere big words,
and many words, words that are never used in daily talk, some
special kind of words, which do not express any thought, at least

not the one that should be expressed. That had given him a one-sided conception of human beings and he never could look at them except as deceitful social animals, bound to be that since civilization forbids open war'' [*SS*, V, 212].

While Swedish critics tried to find foreign models in Zola and others for *The Red Room* upon its startling immediate success with the reading public, Strindberg was undoubtedly correct in saying that the inspiration came from Charles Dickens [*SS*, XIX, 160]. A comparison of the Circumlocution Office in Dickens' *Little Dorrit* (1856) and Strindberg's government departments supplies merely one striking proof.

The novel presents the Stockholm and the Sweden of the 1870s through the eyes and ears and mind of the idealist Arvid Falk — Swedes consider him a slightly disguised August Strindberg — an idealist who has been brought up to have great and romantic expectations of himself, his fellow human beings, and his society. When he is set loose after inadequate preparation as a participant in and an observer of his community his perceptiveness forces him quickly to note the vast discrepancy between what human beings and their activities and institutions are said to be and what they actually are. An idealist addicted to self-scrutiny and self-judgment and a reporter dedicated to scrutiny and judgment of his world, Arvid Falk examines both with care and in detail.

Strindberg got much of his material from sessions and discussions with fellow artists and fellow observers in the habit of gathering in the so-called Red Room in Bern's Restaurant in Stockholm, from visits to artists' hang-outs, from his own thorough knowledge of Stockholm, and, perhaps, most of all, from his own observations as a journalist.

With relatively good-natured humor and a good measure of Dickens-inspired exaggeration, Strindberg presents Arvid Falk's exposure to the family, the church, and the school, to the whole gamut of the political system (parliament, bureaucracy, limited political participation) to attention to public welfare (sanitary conditions, charity, social welfare, housing), to the business world (business standards and practices, labor relations), to sharply defined class distinctions, to the place of artists including writers and actors, to critics and reviewers, to emigration — in other words, to wellnigh every conceivable aspect of Stockholm and Sweden in the 1870s. Strindberg, moreover, presents Arvid Falk's development through confrontation and conflict and attempts toward adjustment with his fellows, his community, and himself.

The result of his efforts is a novel that has continued to delight one generation after another of Swedes ever since its appearance in 1879 — a fairly recent proof of that fact was the nationwide popularity of the TV series based on the novel in 1970. Not only has the plot, the bird's-eye view of Stockholm, and the telling exposé of the Sweden of that day fascinated readers, but a great many of the characters — Arvid Falk; his Philistine brother Charles Nicholas Falk; the deplorable do-gooders Eugenia Falk and Evelyn Homan; the artists Ygberg, Olle Montanus, Lundell, and Sellén; the opportunistic journalist Struve; Smith the publisher; Pastor Nathaneal Skore; Falander the actor-manager; Dr. Borg the rationalist cynic; and the honest member of parliament Sven Svensson at least — have become part of Swedes' common body of knowledge. Swedish scholars agree that the novel has had great influence on Swedish prose fiction both in form and in substance, not least through Strindberg's use of contemporary matters expressed in colloquial language.

III   Swedish Destinies and Adventures

Strindberg's interest in history found expression in every one of his areas of creative activity. Born at a time when both historical prose fiction and historical drama were highly popular in Sweden and when "popular" histories of the Swedish people appearing as "stories" from the Swedish past were what we would call best sellers, Strindberg from his early boyhood on read widely both in Swedish and foreign historical prose fiction, historical drama, and histories. Walter Scott and Victor Hugo were, for example, at times among his favorite foreign novelists. Closely related to such matters was his interest in folk literature, in medieval and Renaissance literature in general, and in Rousseau's assessments of nature and society.

His reading in folk literature, Romantic and post-Romantic Swedish literature, Boccaccio, E.T.A. Hoffmann, J.P. Jacobsen, H.C. Andersen, and others served him well in his composition of a series of historical prose narratives that he called *Swedish Destinies and Adventures: Tales from All Periods* (1882-1892).

The eighteen stories or novellas all are set in the past, do deal with far more than the atmosphere and the setting of a time long since part of history, but are decidedly pertinent to Strindberg's time and amazingly to ours. They may be read as treatments of modern social problems in historical settings as some scholars insist, but the fact that the historical dead faced problems very similar basically to those faced by human beings during any other age probably is most accurate in identifying Strindberg's intention and procedure: "The author's intention is to give in short prose narratives depictions out of our country's social and cultural history, each of which can stand by itself but through chronological arrangement can make a coherent whole when the work has been completed. To make reading it more pleasant the four volumes, comprising the four periods the Middle Ages, the 1500s, the 1600s, the 1700s, will be published parallel to each other with their different titles and own pagination" [*Brev,* III, 499]. These novellas would then complement what he had done in his social and cultural histories (*Old Stockholm,* 1880; *The Swedish People,* 1882), and in his satire *The New Nation* (1882).

The human dilemmas and problems treated are timeless and universal: the inability of an inadequately trained upperclass man to cope with the world once artificial supports (wealth, for example) have been taken away in "Cultivated Fruit" ("Odlad frukt"); the unhappy consequences of celibacy and the church's hypocritical solution to the demands of sexuality in "Higher Goals" ("Högre ändamål"); the need for accepting new superior techniques and methods in spite of tradition and regulation in "Patrons" ("Beskyddare"); the need for exposing corruption even at the risk of the ultimate in punishment in "For Good and Evil" ("På gott och ont"); the meaning of life (joy in living or forsaking) in ecclesiastical art in "Evolution" ("Utveckling"); conflict between city and country in "Paul and Peter" ("Pål och Per"); and the duty to defend one's own against injustice in "New Weapons" ("Nya vapen").

The novellas do contain anachronisms and illustrate Strindberg's habit of compressing historic time, but they do give in turn a clear insight into and interpretation of the life and times of a medieval nobleman, the struggle for survival in the Stockholm skerries in a distant past, the contrast between the reason celibacy was required and the reason the church gave for its requirement back in the middle ages, the medieval guilds and the role of the Germans in

Stockholm, the dangers of putting into print the truth about the establishment back in Gutenberg's day, the contrast between Renaissance and Reformation, social customs and government regulations back in the old days, and attempts at reducing free farmers to serfs in the 1500s.

The details concerning Scanian students' behavior in the lecture halls of the University of Lund and the general antagonism of the Scanians to Swedish authorities' firmly proceeding to Swedify them in the late seventeenth century do give a nice touch of historical local color in the novella *Tschandala,* but the story itself is glaringly modern and the setting very much that of the late nineteenth century in Denmark in spite of Strindberg's assertions: "but I thought you and your public would enjoy more a narrative out of Charles XI's time when absolutism caused strong opposition and the annexation of Skåne led to conflicts. ... To get information about the time and its costumes I'm asking for books and am using them, but I'm taking the warp out of my own life as always and as I have done *the whole time* in *Swedish Destinies*" [*Brev,* VII, 1674]. The last assertion is valid.

While Strindberg rented rooms for his family from May through September, 1888, at Skovlyst, a rundown manor house near Holte, Denmark, he had some of his most disturbing and probably embarrassing experiences: exposure to filth and decay, a contest of wills with the gypsy manager of the estate, adultery with the manager's unwashed young sister, scandal in Danish newspapers, charges and countercharges, and a conviction that he was the object of persecution.

Strindberg was frightened and fascinated by the whole situation: the setting, the people (the gypsy, the gypsy's sister, the strange "noblewoman" who supposedly owned the estate, her employees and her neighbors), and, perhaps most of all, by his own role as a superior human being harassed and persecuted by barbaric inferiors. Very much impressed by Nietzsche's concept of the superman[6], just then, Strindberg considered himself a superior human being, cultured, civilized, learned: "So he has to perish, because he was civilized, the human being developed for a higher life in the community, the one who had to see himself struck by the same fate, which had struck the civilized peoples of ancient times, the ones who had gone under before the barbarian, because they could not murder like the barbarians, could not steal like the barbarian, not deceive like the barbarian. So this was the fruit of enlightenment, of morality, of consciousness of justice, that the enlightened, moral and learned human being necessarily would fall at the moment of self-defence, because he did not have the required coarseness" [*SS,* XII, 362-363].

In *Tschandala* he transformed his personal experiences to a superficial degree: Andreas Törner, a teacher at the University of Lund in the late seventeenth century, spends several months with his family at a rundown Danish manor house, finds himself in conflict with the gypsy manager, and uses his power of suggestion to destroy his enemy. The cultured, learned Törner unlike the cultured, learned Captain Adolf in *The Father* (1887) stoops to primitive self-defence against a primitive human being, to morally questionable murder of a member of the lowest caste in society.

Tschandala is impressive as a psychological study: Strindberg scrutinizes in detail what happened as seen by a superior human being convinced an inferior is trying to destroy him psychically. Surely Strindberg's (or Törner's) failure to leave such an environment and such a situation can be explained primarily by his reluctance to forego a rewarding source of material for his pen even though the experience was, as he says, hell for him and cannot have been more pleasant for his family. As effective as anything in this impressive novella is the presentation of the setting and its inhabitants: It is a study in the horrible and the grotesque, a study of a nineteenth-century Danish Tobacco Road.

Three novellas — "Lord Bengt's Wife ("Herr Bengts hustru"), "At the Wake in Tistedalen" ("Vid likvakan i Tistedalen"), and "A Royal Revolution" ("En kunglig revolution") — are counterparts of much in three of his historical plays, *Lord Bengt's Wife* (1882), *Charles XII* (1901), and *Gustav III* (1902). These novellas demonstrate not only Strindberg's imaginative insight into historical events and characters but also can be used as controls to his stated intentions in the three plays. One — "The Strawman" ("Stråmannen") — is such an effective and persuasive reappraisal of King Fredrik I (1720-51) that one can wish Strindberg had put that king's story into dramatic form; it could have made a fascinating piece for both stage and screen.

"A Triumph" ("En triumf") is a stinging attack on war set in Erik XIV's day (1560-68) when Swedes and Danes were engaged in war for questionable reasons. "The Last Shot" ("Sista skottet"), set at the end of the Thirty Years' War in 1648, is still another depiction of the horrors of war and an implicit plea for peace. "A Funeral" ("En begravning") is more an examination of perennial family obligations and self-sacrifice than a study of a human destiny set pretty vaguely in a remote past.

"A Witch" ("En häxa") is an impressive study of Tekla Degener, a seventeenth-century woman shaped by environment and heredity to addiction to pretense of illness and amoral selection of means for getting attention including ultimately the desire to be executed as a witch. The novella is one of Strindberg's finest portrayals of women characters deserving to be ranked with Laura, Lady Julie, Tekla of *Creditors,* Alice, and Queen Christina.

"The Isle of the Blessed" ("De lycksaliges ö") is, on the surface, an account of the fortunes and misfortunes of a group of Swedes who are shipwrecked on a luxuriant island while on their way to New Sweden (founded in 1638 in the Delaware Valley). This long novella is far more than an imaginative account of human beings turning to a Rousseauistic world of primitive nobility and their corruption into typical members of a complex and sick modern society. It is, aside from its merits as a decidedly entertaining story, a devastating attack on accepted standard historians' accounts of Swedish history and a placing of royalty and commons in what Strindberg justly considered proper perspective.

IV   Married

Married (1884, 1886) is the title given to the two volumes of novellas or fairly long short stories about what happens to men and women in marriage. The first contains twelve stories and a preface, the second eighteen and a preface. While these thirty stories contain Strindberg's most concentrated contribution to the debate then raging about three closely related human problems — the woman question, the double standard of morality, and marriage — there is a world of difference between the two collections in substance and in mood.

The debate about these matters was not new in Sweden: It had become acute since Carl Jonas Love Almqvist's novel *Sara Videbeck (Det går an,* 1839) and Fredrika Bremer's novels, among others, had appeared in a fairly steady flow; Ibsen, Björnson, and several others had later contributed to the discussion; and Swedish women had become insistent in their demands for equality.

The 1884 volume was, Strindberg says, primarily directed at the relatively small percentage of people at the top of the social scale, say ten per cent of the adult population, at *kulturkvinnan* and *kulturmannen*, the people privileged socially and economically. Marriage for the vast majority of people, he insisted, was a natural, cooperative venture. For the people at the top, marriage, he believed, was a highly artificial arrangement. Still under the influence of Rousseau, Buckle, and Darwin, Strindberg assumed that certain basic matters are natural to human beings and that, if these are artificially curbed, trouble, even tragedy results for the individual, the couple, the family, and the community. Strindberg's approach is both Rousseauistic and deterministic; he looks closely at the biological, social, economic, and moral aspects of being married.

The program for the improvement of marriage as stated in his foreword sounds like what is theoretically true in much of the Western world today: free association of boys and girls, the simplification and rationalization of education for both boys and girls, general release from excessive attention to the past, the elimination of gallantry, the introduction of civil marriage, the easing of divorce proceedings, the elimination of male guardianship, legalizing marital agreements, granting women the right to work at any job (except the military!), giving them the right to keep their own names, providing for individual privacy even within marriage, sharing expenses if the wife has a job, insuring the husband if she does not, and providing a definite income for the housewife, the homemaker.

The very titles of the twelve stories — "The Reward of Virtue," "Love and the Price of Grain," "Just to Be Married," "Had to," "Compensation," "Bad Luck," "Conflicts," "Unnatural Selection," "Attempts at Reform," "Natural Obstacles," "A Doll House," and "The Phoenix" — suggest Strindberg's extensive and searching examination of the marital relationship at its most intimate.

Take "The Price of Grain," for example. It tells the story of a young couple, very much in love, without substantial means or common sense, at the mercy of their drives and addicted to living beyond their means. They enjoy marriage, they do not worry about grocery and other bills until it is too late, the wife becomes pregnant, and her father literally keeps his daughter and his son-in-law apart. A moving, even humorous tale, it is an application of the facts of economic life and an application of Buckle's theory of economic determinism.

"A Doll House" is a narrative gem, not only because it is a delightfully detailed examination and criticism of what may well be a popular misreading of Ibsen's *A Doll House*, but it is also a superb account of a happy marriage that almost founders because of the influence of an unawakened, appreciably pedantic advocate of woman's liberation.

"The Reward of Virtue" was singled out by the establishment as the basis for bringing Strindberg to trial for blasphemy in 1884. In telling the story of Theodore Wennerström, Strindberg had frankly blamed Theodore's misfortunes and death on social pressures (his mother's, the schools', and the church's) which prevented Theodore from securing healthy expressions for his sexual drive, gave him guilt feelings about masturbating and having wet dreams, destroyed his health, involved him in a scandal, and led to his death shortly after his marriage to a radiantly healthy woman. Even if the frank treatment of sex had not offered the authorities an excuse for prosecuting Strindberg, one passage concerning communion after confirmation did:

He was confirmed that spring. ... The shameless deception committed with Högstedt's Piccardon [wine] at sixty-five öre a can and Lettström's wafers at one crown a pound the minister offered as the blood and the flesh of Jesus of Nazareth, the agitator executed more than eighteen hundred years ago, did not trouble him for he did not think things through then but got "moods" [*SS*, XIV, 63-64].

What happened as a result was to change Strindberg's life, his view of himself and his fellow human beings, and his contributions to literature.

Strindberg may have been right in suspecting that Queen Sophia[7] inspired his being charged with blasphemy and brought to trial in the fall of 1884. On October 4, Strindberg learned that unsold copies of the volume had been confiscated by the police and that, if he did not appear in court on October 21, his publisher Albert Bonnier would have to. Bonnier urged the unwilling author to return from Geneva, apparently got Björnson and others to try to persuade Strindberg into returning, and finally sent his son Karl Otto to Geneva to bring him home. Extremely tired, highly upset and nervous, Strindberg arrived at the railroad station in Stockholm, was the object of an ovation there, stayed at the Grand Hotel, was forced to keep a hectic pace because of reporters and admirers, was acquitted on November 17, and was lionized at a banquet in the Grand Hotel, in certain theaters, and by his supporters. His enemies were to establish a fairly widespread notion that Strindberg was anything but "nice." Personne's famous pamphlet is only one representation of this strangely irrational reaction, traces of which exist to this day.

When Strindberg returned to Switzerland on November 18, he was on the verge of nervous collapse; he was not only emotionally torn but physically ill. Perhaps the two factors that affected him most were the well-intentioned interference on the part of friends such as Björnson and, even more, Siri's inability to rise to the occasion: Beautiful, socially gifted, sexually attractive, and well enough intentioned, she was apparently unable to think the situation *through* for herself or to talk *with* him about it. The crisis for Strindberg helped lead to his loss of faith in Rousseau, socialism, and religion, and affected his views on woman and woman's liberation. In his bitterness toward his persecutors, real and imagined, he struck out at what he considered evil, not least in the institution of marriage.

V   Married *II*

The most immediate literary result was *Married* II (1886), published after some difficulty in finding a publisher. The eighteen narratives were written in bitterness, partly because of his own increasing marital troubles for which he was substantially to blame and partly because he believed the upperclass leaders of the women's emancipation movement were among his worst enemies.

In the eighteen narratives — "Autumn," "Bread," "The Child," "Nature the Criminal," "For Compensation," "With or Without the Marriage Ceremony," "Duel," "Misfits," "It's Not Enough!," "The Stronger," "Like Doves," "The Ideal Demands," "His Poem," "Cheated," "A Business Deal," "Blind Faith," "His Servant or Debit and Credit," and "The Bread Winner" — Strindberg considers the roles of man and woman in courtship, marriage, and parenthood and at work, play, and studies.

Strindberg prepared a bitter preface for the second volume, a preface that is preceded by pertinent quotations about women and their flaws from Schopenhauer, Rousseau, Aristotle, Max Nordau, Godin, Georg Brandes, J. S. Mill, Herbert Spenser, and a misquotation from Anne Besant, and that is concluded by a quotation from Paul Lafargue and the warning, "watch out, men!" The preface itself is a series of looks at the whole matter of woman's emancipation from the point of view of a furious, irritated male; his exaggerations are no greater than those of some extremists in the liberation movement.

If one story were to be singled out for special consideration it should surely be "For Compensation" ("Mot betalning"), the story of Hélène, a general's daughter without meaningful training, who marries an Uppsala lecturer in ethics to secure status and power and sells her sexual favors to him as a means of increasing her power. This story, which like the other seventeen deserves close scrutiny as provocative revelations of marital purgatories and marital hells, is also important because of its striking similarities to *Hedda Gabler* which Ibsen was to publish four years later (1890)[8].

Married is ultimately no more or no less than an appeal for human liberation from ignorance about the nature of human beings, sexuality, and the man-woman relationship, and for freedom from irrational, artificial codes of conduct. It is a highly effective series of appeals for the elimination of the conspiracy of silence about basic matters.

VI   The People of Hemsö

From 1871 to 1883 Strindberg had spent several happy summers on Kymmendö, his favorite island in the archipelago. On October 31, 1887, when he was in one of his most difficult and unhappy periods, he wrote to Axel Lundegård:

Unhappy and weary, tortured to death, hunted like a wild animal I sat down at my desk in August to amuse myself. Wrote: the story of a hired hand, my summer memories of unforgettable days in the Stockholm Archipelago (for I have even had a lot of fun in my days).

[I] cut out the woman question, cast out socialism, politics, all nonsense, and decided to write a Swedish and an entertaining and an earthy priceless story, showing how a hired hand with sound nerves and healthy blood, without spite, makes his way through life, taking whatever is available, letting go without shedding tears what he couldn't hold.

[I] chose Dutch genre painting as my model, since that has always seemed to me to resemble the life of simple rural people in Sweden [*Brev,* VI, 1457].

Strindberg insisted that *The People of Hemsö* was never intended to be a major serious work but rather an escape from his personal troubles and from the very serious literature he was then creating in autobiography and in drama.

The result of his interlude of relaxed creative writing is one of the most delightful of novels and surely his most pleasant and least irritating prose fiction. It is personal in the sense that his recollections in tranquillity of life on "his" island and his imaginative reconstruction of what happened and might have happened to its natives are the bases of a story delightfully, humorously, and brilliantly told. The very chapter titles reflecting as they do an old device of, say, eighteenth-century novelists suggest as much:

1. Carlsson takes on his job and turns out to be a "loudmouth." 2. Sunday rest and Sunday chores; the good shepherd and the wicked sheep; the woodcocks who got what they had coming, and the hired man who got *the* room [for himself]. 3. The hired man plays his trump card, becomes master of the place and puts the young roosters in their place. 4. There is loud talk of a wedding and the old woman is taken for her gold. 5. There's violent quarreling on the third Sunday of announcing the bans, [Carlsson and Madam Flod] go to communion and get married, but don't get into their marital bed anyway. 6. Changed conditions and changed opinions; farming is neglected and mining flourishes. 7. Carlsson's dreams come true; the bureau is watched, but the Administrator comes and crosses out everything.

It is proof of what Strindberg could do by way of telling entertaining stories which could offend at most only the islanders who were his models.

Strindberg had studied the islanders with delight and sympathy both as fellow human beings and as country people in speech and customs different from Stockholmers. He has exploited these differences in producing not only an excellent novel about the archipelago from many points of view from appearance to climate but also a whole gallery of unforgettable characters such as Carlsson, the "picaresque hero" and "superior" outsider from the mainland; Madam Flod, the aging widow anxious for a bedmate;

her son Gusten, a fisherman and hunter but not a farmer; maids and hired hands; Pastor Nordström, who has become a victim of his environment; and summer paying guests from Stockholm and their servants. It is no wonder that *The People of Hemsö* has become a favorite not only with Swedish readers but with Swedes and other Scandinavians who have seen it in its stage, film, and TV versions.

What has helped make it popular beyond anything else Strindberg wrote is Strindberg's wide use of humor ranging from deliberately crude slapstick to the subtlest kind. Admirers of Strindberg may be inclined to overlook the humor to be found in almost all of his works because of his primary emphasis on extremely serious matters, but even in, say, *The Dance of Death,* there is a great deal of humor, dark and even grotesque though it may be. In *The People of Hemsö* no one can possibly overlook the humor in the haying, the proposal, and the wedding scenes, and closer scrutiny will reveal less earthy and far subtler humor elsewhere.

VII   Life on the Skerries*

When Strindberg had completed *Life on the Skerries* (1888), a work that he had originally thought of as a sequel to *The People of Hemsö,* he prepared an introduction which depicts the rich variety of nature in the archipelago and presents a summary of his views of the natives and their ways:

[here] live a people, who according to their means can be divided into three classes: those who farm, living mainly on the larger islands; those who farm and fish, or the middle class; and finally the genuine men of the skerries who make their living mostly by fishing and hunting but who keep a cow, a sheep and some chickens besides ...

The bright, smiling aspects of the skerry dweller's life when it turns out bright I have pictured in the preceding part, *The People of Hemsö;* in this part I have presented the half shadows. ... [*SS,* XXI, 186, 191].

This second part is not a novel, however, but ten novellas.

While none of these admirable narratives is without humor, they have relatively little of the slapstick or the earthy. If one may justifiably think of *The People of Hemsö* as primarily comic, one will have to consider the ten novellas as ranging from tragicomic to tragic. In presenting the halfshadows of life on the skerries, Strindberg has paid far greater attention to the ideational implications of his stories than he did in "the preceding part."

"My Summer Minister" ("Min sommarpräst") tells the story of an island pastor kept from achieving his potential because of limiting factors in an unfavorable environment. His taking on coloring from exposure to islanders and cultivated outsiders is both tragic and comic, while Pastor Norström's loss of a moose badly needed for the family larder because of his willingness to court the favor of royalty and count on rewards in "The Pastor's Moose" ("Pastorns älg") is primarily comic — the pastor and his wife can survive the winter on a diet of salt herring and smelts. "The Promise Made While in Distress at Sea" ("Sjönödslöftet") is a tall tale about an islander whose improvised harpoon leads to a wild flight of his imagination. "The Tailor Just Had to Give a Dance" ("Skräddarn skulle ha dans") is the tale of a badly crippled tailor who is a small-scale combination of Luther Burbank and Carl von Linné and who pays a big price for a little attention. In all of these stories, however, handicaps stemming from heredity or environment or both run like red threads and keep the stories from being hilarious.

Much the same can be said about "Feminine Love" ("Flickornas kärlek"), "Höjer Takes Over the Farm" ("Höjer tar gården själv"), and "The Customs Inspector" ("Uppsyningsmannen"), which Strindberg had thought of calling "The Flying Dutchman." The first is a look at the island servant girls' use of premarital sex, the second the story of a man "who was not created to be a master," and the third the story of a man engaged in essentially meaningless activity.

Two of the novellas — "A Criminal" ("En brottsling") and "Superstition" ("Vidskepelse") — are fascinating revelations of Strindberg's current interest in criminal psychology. The young twenty-two-year-old in "Superstition" who terrorizes a whole neighborhood into helplessness through his effrontery and brazen behavior verging on vandalism should appeal to anyone in a time when people no longer dare to intervene. "A Criminal" examines the idea that the victim rather than the murderer may be the real criminal or at any rate the cause of the crime.

"The Romantic Organist on Rån Island"* ("Den romantiske klockaren på Rånö") is, however, the novella in *Life on The*

Skerries that Strindberg valued most and that has received most attention from scholars and readers. Strindberg's most interesting comment is his recollection of a conversation in Copenhagen with Georg Brandes: "I was writing 'The Organist on Rånö' then and had published *The People of Hemsö,* my break with pure realism, before the 1890s' supposed Swedish renaissance" [*SS,* LIII, 557].

That statement together with his first manuscript classification of it as "Idyll by August Strindberg," his insertion of the word "romantic" into the title, and various references to the tale or, as he called it, novel, suggest that Strindberg may very well have played with the idea of creating a pastiche:

Gifted Alrik Lundstedt a native of Rån Island who escapes into a dream world because of a crime he does not want to recollect is trained at the Academy of Music in Stockholm, shows great promise, but has to give up his dream of great achievements in music to return to his island as organist and teacher because of impulsive foolish behavior toward his father who he had apparently seen murder his mother years before. Addicted to living in his imagination rather than in reality, Alrik becomes a fantast whose only means of genuine expression is music until he marries a lighthouse keeper's daughter and with her and their children "plays the most precious games with real toys" [*SS,* XXI, 257].

The power of dreams to sustain the fantast until he is forced to face reality — his father's exhaustion of meager resources and the reality of the schoolroom on Rån Island, for example — was a recurring motif for the neo-Romantics of the 1890s, and Strindberg was justified in pointing out that in his novella he had been well in advance of Heidenstam and Levertin in turning away from "shoemaker realism." "The Romantic Organist on Rån Island" can indeed be read as a pastiche of the romantic tale.

VIII   At the Edge of the Sea

On May 1, 1889, Strindberg wrote to Albert Bonnier: "I'm sending ... the two first chapters of my novel *At the Edge of the Sea* which will be my *Workers of the Sea* in grand style" [*Brev,* VII, 1832]. On July 6, he wrote to Ola Hansson: "I'm living in spiritual dog days reading an unbelievable amount of natural science, which I'm collecting for my coming *Antibarbarus.* Writing at the same time a modern novel on the model of Nietzsche's and Poe's" [*Brev,* VII, 1867]. When he sent the last installment to Bonnier on June 7,

1890, he wrote: "So here is the promised major work in new grand renaissance style! The last chapter is grandiose and I build on Homunculus, the Dolls and Hercules — Jesus ... This is the new direction that began with the novella *The Little People* [p. 64] ..., was continued in "The Battle of the Brains" [p. 64], *Tschandala* [p. 105], *Lady Julie* [p. 143] etc." [*Brev*, VIII, 1976].

The novel, probably his one major work about which there has never been even an approach to consensus of critical opinion, may be summarized as follows:

Brought up by his father to analyze every aspect of himself and life and frustrated in his efforts to advance in professional life, Axel Borg accepts a position as fishing commissioner in the outermost skerries. He finds himself unable to help the islanders effectively because of their ignorance, stupidity, gullibility, addiction to old ways, and suspicion and resentment of him. A preacher brought to the island at Borg's suggestion turns out to be a former classmate who hates and works against him. He analyzes the woman [a summer resident] he "loves" and thereby destroys their relationship. In analyzing himself into isolation, he breaks all ties with life and commits suicide.

The strangely moving novel has not bored its readers; instead, it has stirred them up either to enthusiastic approval or to hesitant disapproval.

Axel Borg is not merely a geologist and a metallurgist, not merely an expert on fishing but an intellectual who has taken all fields of knowledge as his province. His father has trained this intellectual superman to look at every aspect of life scientifically, to analyze it scientifically, to come to conclusions about it scientifically. Borg himself becomes his primary object of study: He observes, experiments with, and analyzes himself as a superior being, classifying his intellectual powers as higher and his emotional and physical ones as lower. But Axel Borg is no physical giant: "His [the little man's] face, as much of it as one could see, was thin and pale as a dead man's, and a pair of small black, thin moustaches, trained upwards at their ends, emphasized the paleness and added something exotic to its expression" [*SS*, XXIV, 6].

The exotic effect was set off by his dandified clothes, his haircut, his rings, his bracelet, and a generally decadent air. While Borg is a small and even delicate man, Strindberg makes it clear that even physically Borg is a refined specimen of humanity.

To tell Borg's story, Strindberg read scientific and popular material on every aspect of the archipelago from its geologic formations to its inhabitants, summer vacationers as well as natives. For the natural scientists, his reporting is not flawless, but for the lay reader, the reporting is detailed and impressive. In one area — the psychology of an Axel Borg — he has succeeded superbly.

Dr. Borg is a gregarious human being as well as an intellectual titan. Unfortunately for him, his addiction to analyzing everything and everyone and to classifying even his own powers and instincts as higher or lower has led to suspicion of others and to inability to find satisfactory expression for his "lower" emotions. In his exposure to his peers, to his professional "superiors," to ordinary people, to inferiors, and to a woman who attracts him sexually, his refinement of taste, his extreme sensitivity, and his constant analysis prevent him from establishing meaningful communication with anyone and condemn him to isolation.

Suspicious of others and paranoiac, Dr. Borg himself plots, tries to arrange other people's lives, and apparently assumes they are doing much the same to him albeit in an inferior, cruder fashion. Having analyzed every one of his fellows and rejected them all, he turns more and more inward. Having cut himself off from his fellow human beings and from life itself, he deteriorates and disintegrates. His sailing beyond the edge of the sea to inevitable death is one of Strindberg's finest conclusions to his numerous accounts of psychic suicide.

IX Tales

As influential as Strindberg's realistic-naturalistic prose fiction has been on recent and contemporary Swedish novels, novellas, and other narrative forms, the influence of his *Inferno*, *Legends*, and *Alone* has been equally great. The remarkable leaps forward in both form and content that Swedish prose fiction has taken in the last eight decades or so are appreciably attributable to the impact of Strindberg's two-fold influence. Not least has been the tremendous growth in insight into man and his world, both externally and inwardly.

Hans Christian Andersen (1805-1875) was one of Strindberg's favorite authors; evidence of his impact on Strindberg's prose fiction can be discerned particularly in his shorter narratives and most of all in the collection of thirteen stories *Tales* (1903). While there are affinities and parallels that can easily be detected between all of them and various Andersen tales, the thirteen stories are thoroughly Strindbergian in both substance and structure. The parallels and affinities are mainly matters of seeming naïveté, attention to virtues and vices, suggestion of morals (didactic points), imagery, and appeal to both children and adults. Much of the similarities can, of course, be traced to both authors' knowledge of and debt to folk literature and folklore.

"At Midsummer" ("I midsommartider") presents the tribulations of a young wife and her child while the unhappy husband and father is abroad — Strindberg was extremely conscious of what separation could mean for parents and children. In "The Deep Sleeper" ("Sjusovaren"), a lonely musician remains faithful to the memory of his beloved wife. In "Half a Sheet of Paper," Strindberg created a short story about a happy marriage:

There it was recorded: all of this beautiful story, which had taken place in the short time of two years; everything he wanted to forget was recorded there; a part of human living on half a sheet of paper ...

He was not bowed when he went out; on the contrary, he carried his head high, a fortunate and proud human being, for he had had the most beautiful [part of life]. How many poor souls never have! [*SS*, XXXVIII, 51-53]

"Half a Sheet of Paper" is in its concentrated, tight structure a stylistic narrative masterpiece that compares with any short story in world literature; in substance, it is surely Strindberg's most moving persuasive presentation of positive possibilities in the man-woman relationship.

Strindberg's primary interest in human relations and human problems plays an important part in most of the stories. In "Blåvinge" ("Blåvinge finner Guldpudran"), it is the problem of finding a source of drinking water on an island in the archipelago; in "When the Tree Swallow Was in the Buckthorn" ("När träsvalan kom i getapeln"), the need for human friendliness in reconciling unfortunates with life; in "Photography and Philosophy" ("Fotografi och filosofi"), the need for understanding and cooperation with one's fellow human beings; in "Sankt Gotthard's Saga," the need for eliminating ethnic antagonisms; in "Jubal Without an Ego" ("Jubal utan jag"), the need for being oneself and avoiding falling into phony roles; in

"The Secrets of the Tobacco Shed," the evils of pride and arrogance; in "The Victor and the Fool" ("Triumfatorn och narren"), an illustration of "Pride goeth before a fall"; in "The Large Gravel Screen," the human tendency to read meaning into what is not understood; in "The Pilot's Tribulations" ("Lotsens vedermödor"), actuality transformed into dream; and, finally, in "The Golden Helmets of Ålleberg," Swedish history in capsule form.

With the exception of "Half a Sheet of Paper," all of the stories can be read as if they were told to children; they do have the elements of fable, allegory, parable, and didacticism that children's tales usually do, but all of them are essentially tales told as much for grownups as for their offspring.

X   The Gothic Rooms

Even if *The Gothic Rooms* (*Götiska rummen?*, 1904) is not one of Strindberg's greatest novels, it is important as a revelation of his thinking about his world and its problems and not least of results of his exploration and exploitation of his generally dormant streak of cruelty. Undoubtedly thought of as a sort of continuation of *The Red Room* (1879), some of the action does take place in Bern's Restaurant in Stockholm — the Red Room had given way to renovation and redecoration. Some of the characters in the earlier novel do reappear in *The Gothic Rooms*. But the latter does not begin to compare with the former as fiction likely to hold the reader through suspense. Its appeal lies in other matters.

The plots deal primarily with the marital, social, and political fates of Dr. Henry Borg and a number of his relatives, in-laws, and acquaintances. The brilliant doctor with his three marriages, his brother Gustav's marriage to a woman who accepts the programs of the emancipated women's movement without understanding them, two nephews with unhappy marriages, plus a niece's "unblessed" union with her friend are used primarily as a means of discussing such perennially pertinent subjects as the family, the man-woman relationship, sex, life styles, the parent-child relationship, divorce, and woman's revolt against what nature has made her.

Argumentation and exposition take precedence over narration and description in this novel, so the most interesting fact about its content is that Strindberg foreshadowed the whole contemporary women's liberation movement of our day. Strindberg believed both men and women were paying a high price for what he considered excesses.

There are, to be sure, discussions of almost all other aspects of Swedish life from child rearing to, say, journalism. No other matter in the novel has made it as memorable as this brutal and cruel passage, however:

Yes, you women have good days now; consider our women writers! Drinking ale; Tuesday soup; little variations on other writers' themes and they're labelled geniuses by Little Sakris! Look, there he goes. Born with a bay window, eyeglasses, a shorn crown, and pension; the protector of literature, the friend of the ladies; the sponge; the shadow. He hatches silk worms after he has bought the eggs; he looks like a scarecrow detective, a *faux bonhomme*, who is terrible; a swindler against whom one never gets proof, but from whom one senses one must flee; inexplicable and therefore terrifying; flatters in order to get to claw; uses everything for his own ends, even the bodies of the dead; forgiving when something can be gained and vengeful when nothing can be lost. He talks in woman's name as if he were a woman; slanders his own sex like a masturbator and toadies to the ladies like all pederasts [*SS*, XI., 88-89].

That Little Sakris was Gustaf af Geijerstam, Strindberg's "friend" and benefactor, colleague and, for some time, editor, was clear to many Swedes. That af Geijerstam was an opportunist may have salved Strindberg's conscience a little, but it was not to prevent him from exploiting his generally dormant cruelty in his next novel, a novel in which af Geijerstam was to be only one of several colleagues to be assassinated in print.

The Red Room which had been the gathering place of young artists and other intellectual rebels in the 1870s had given way to Gothic Rooms — in varied but less flamboyant colors — and they were to be succeeded by the black banners of evil.

XI   Black Banners

Strindberg was hesitant about the publication of *Black Banners: Morals and Manners about the Turn of the Century* (*Svarta fanor: Sedeskildringar från sekelskiftet,*[10] written, 1904; published, 1907): "The novel is a continuation of *The Gothic Rooms* and consists of depictions of morals and manners about the turn of the century. They are horrible but based on actuality. I have not had any pleasure in writing it. But the work pursued me so it had to be written. Even if I would suffer while doing it ..." [*SS*, XLI, 292]. And later: "I'm reading proof for *Black Banners*. As you know, I break with the Blackguards [literally, the black ones] in this work. People are sure to cast stones at me. But that I'll take as my lot. As far as that goes, I'm already used to it" [*SS*, XLI, 292].

He had good reason to expect repercussions: Only *A Madman's Defence* compares with *Black Banners* as a cruel exposé of living human beings as he saw them. He had, he believed, stripped himself bare in works such as *Inferno, Legends*, and *Alone* and in his Damascus trilogy. He had then set out to expose the evil in others, living and dead, in both dramatic and nondramatic works.

Black Banners has two story lines folded in or interlaced: the story of media people who are little more than vampires and the story of some of their victims who have taken refuge in a "cloister." On one hand are people who, though they are supposed to be devotees of the art of communication do not succeed in communicating as human beings, on the other are men who have withdrawn from a world of humbug, double-talk, and corruption to a refuge where they can attempt to communicate with each other about humanity and the world.

While the latter story line concerns a home for people who have achieved a measure of resignation and humaneness, the first concerns primarily the "home" of Little Zachris [stet], his wife Jenny, and their two boys, Brunte and Pirre. Zachris makes awkward, selfish moves, is repudiated by his "party," rejected by his "friends," betrayed by his wife and sons, and thereby acquires material for his writing. Zachris is a vampire and a parasite, his wife a fury, his boys monsters, and his marriage a marital hell.

Zachris represents the opportunists who manipulate people, who steal (things, ideas, people), and who, in a Strindbergian sense, are engaged in a grotesque dance of death in which life is essentially absurd and meaningless — for them. As Jenny says when she is awakened from her sleepwalking: "You are as far away and as small as dolls in a store window; you are blue in the face like dead people; but that is because you are dead; you have committed suicide..." [*SS*, XLI, 263]. The living dead in thought and deed are, in Strindbergian terms, guilty of psychic murder and psychic suicide.

Strindberg's procedure for telling the story of his colleagues and acquaintances was to exploit his capacity to hate and to be cruel: Departing from his resentments, he used many facts from his models' lives and appearance and rounded out and filled in with personal and imagined material: "Friends, ... there has always been misunderstanding between me and my readers about my writing. They have believed, you see, that I have only punished them when I have reacted against evil in myself. In order to get to write my collected [works] I have sacrificed my biography, my person. It occurred to me, rather early, you see, that my life was staged for me, so that I could be able to see it from all [points of] view. That reconciled me with my misfortunes, and taught me to grasp myself as object. When I now in my little diatribe hit at irreligious people, I include myself, myself most of all" [*SS*, XLI, 196]. The result is deliberate distortion and caricature.

The characters could easily be identified. (For examples: Lars Petter Zachrisson = Gustaf af Geijerstam; Jenny = Mrs. Nennie af Geijerstam; their two sons; Smartman = the journalist, Pehr Staaff; Professor Stenkåhl = Professor Karl Warburg; Hanna Paj = Ellen Key, the feminist author; Kilo = C. Gernandt, the publisher).

What horrified readers most — and perhaps fascinated many of them — was what Strindberg had done to Gustaf af Geijerstam, his wife, their two boys, their home, and their marriage. Gustaf af Geijerstam (1858-1909) was probably the most widely read author among the general reading public at the turn of the century. His realistic novels of the 1880s and 1890s, his criminal novels, and his two memorable, humorous, charming, and even sentimental narratives about his sons and his family — *My Boys* (*Mina pojkar*, 1896) and *The Book about Little Brother* (*Boken om lillebror*, 1900) — were read and were highly popular as were his folk comedies in the theaters; but the reviewers, critics, and scholars then and since have not reached a consensus of opinion about him as a human being and never place him among the really great writers. Instead the accounts either state or suggest that he was very much interested in establishing useful contacts and connections with publishers, editors, reporters, reviewers, critics, theater people, and writers. The accounts suggest, too, that he did indulge in namedropping, flattery, and even fawning, that he exploited his family and acquaintances in his writings, and that his motives and acts could not always bear scrutiny.

Geijerstam's greatest misfortune may very well have been his relationship with Strindberg. Geijerstam's offers of assistance in getting Strindberg's works published — especially from 1897 to 1902 when Geijerstam was a literary consultant for Gernandt's Publishing House in Stockholm, his tendency to become too curious about and familiar with Strindberg's creative activities and personal life, and his inability to deal discreetly with Strindberg made Geijerstam and his family tempting subjects for caricature and satire.

While *Black Banners* was undoubtedly cruel and merciless to the Geijerstams and to a number of other intellectuals, it is one of the greatest satires in literature and eventually — when all personal implications are no longer significant — may well be so recognized. It has interesting Platonic dialogs indulged in by the men who have withdrawn, temporarily at least, from a corrupt society of vampires — dialogs which concern finite human beings' examination of such matters as memory, imagination, inexplicable experiences, natural science, and the nature of man and the world. The novel is filled with dark, grotesque humor, usually related to the malicious delight (*skadeglädje*) others take in stripping or unmasking one of their fellows. Its primary appeal will probably always lie in its devastatingly effective exposé of professional scheming and intrigue, humbug, and manipulation of human beings.

XII   The Roofing Celebration

In *The Roofing Celebration* (1906) Strindberg created a short psychological novel that illustrates beautifully his flare for making even his prose fiction dramatic, his constant experimentation with structure, and his never-ending consideration of the possible meaning of human existence. He has told the fascinating story of an articulate and thoughtful man who on his deathbed recalls major and minor events in his personal pursuit of happiness. Injured so severely in an accident that there is no hope for recovery:

he was an educated man and a hunter, a fisherman, a sportsman, a traveler in Africa, a sailor; son of fisherfolk, born by the sea with simple habits in his profession, a spontaneous, healthy everyday person, used to command and to kill, in his emotional life tender, nice, self-sacrificing, faithful to wife and child. Not promoted because of a bit of thoughtlessness stemming from his bringing up, he had been wise enough not to be affected by the insult but made it a point of honor to take the defeat as something quite natural, and his life had gone along calmly and smoothly until the beginning of the last year when misfortunes had struck one after the other ... [*SS*, XLIV, 13].

Those Job-like tests and trials and their possible backgrounds comprise the gist of the contents.

Structurally, the novel consists of a series of dramatic monologs (monologs in the sense, say, that Robert Browning and Gustaf Fröding illustrated the term) interrupted by comments and exposition by the narrator or by actual conversations between the dying man and his nurse Sofia or between the doctor and the nurse, or by imagined dialogs between the dying man and his friend, the museum curator. The elements of the dramatic monolog are all present in every part except, of course, in the interludes of dialog or narration: one speaker, an audience. These dramatic monologs vary in intensity according to the effects of the patient's fever and of the morphine injected into his veins and of the relief brought by camphor.

Important in the far from loose flow of memories are his enemy (the professor who blocked his professional advancement and who lives within sight of his windows), the apartment house being built next door, his family, and particularly his estranged wife and their son. Important, too, is Strindberg's use of parallel marriages: the dying man's own and that of the younger couple in the apartment below. The two marriages deteriorate, each in its own way; the last possibility of seeing any reminder of the enemy disappears just as the builders celebrate the completion of the roofing of the house next door and Death releases the injured man from the agony of existence.

The wealth of symbolism can here be merely suggested: for examples, the use of specific musical compositions, the house that is far more than an actual house being constructed by a master builder and his crew, a celebration that is at once an actual event and a representation of the completion of an earthly life. In such ways *The Roofing Celebration* is closer to *A Dream Play* and the chamber plays than to novels like *Black Banners* and the pre-Inferno novels.

While the details about the two parallel marriages, his family's destruction of the dying man's marriage, the building of the house next door, the father's unfortunate choice of a gift for his son, and the nature of one human enmity are realistic enough, the major emphasis is placed on the central figure's inner review of his life, his brief interludes of happiness, and his isolation.

Perhaps as interesting as anything in this short masterpiece of psychological fiction is the assessment of life: "Life is like that ... a ... ball with masks and domino; removing the masks at twelve o'clock" [SS, XLI, 77], and "human existence is pure misery and nonsense" [SS, XLI, 77]. Terms like masks, acting, unmasking, covering up, constant adjustment to bewildering circumstances, the complexity of human individuals, the web of human interrelationships, unexplained loose ends such as three figures haunting the island home are all important in the exposé of life as a web.

XIII   The Scapegoat

Strindberg's last novel, *The Scapegoat* (1906), is probably the most moving of all his narratives that are not intentionally autobiographical. It concerns the lot of a human being who does not deserve the treatment that his fellow human beings mete out to him; it concerns a community and a world in which morality and justice may be little more than idle words.

Originally given the title *Small Town Life* (*Småstadsliv*), *The Scapegoat* can be read as an early exposé of small town life related, on the one hand, to Balzac's accounts of village life and, on the other, to such later treatments as Hjalmar Bergman's *Markurells i Wadköping* (*The Wild Orchid*, 1919), Sinclair Lewis' *Main Street* (1920), Edgar Lee Masters' *Spoon River Anthology* (1915). The idyllic setting in a beautiful valley surrounded by protective hills contrasts with the prison-like atmosphere and the ugly behavior of many of its "inmates." The small town is "a home for elderly pensioners, widows and sick people," but the small town people do not suffer from physical sicknesses alone.

Strindberg's major concern is, however, the matter of human destiny in a far from perfect world. In his narrative that explores and illustrates that world is a group of secondary people — Askanius, the restaurant owner; Tjärne, the chief of police; Karin, one of Askanius' waitresses; Sjögren, a clerk; and Libotz Senior — all of whom play a role in the drama of the central character,

Edvard Libotz, the scapegoat. In the tragicomedies of what human beings do to themselves and each other in an evil world, each of these people, unconsciously or consciously, helps make continued living in the town impossible for the gentle, sane citizen Libotz: Karin through her inability to understand and communicate with him; the corrupt father through insensitive humiliation and merciless exploitation of his son; Askanius through his ambivalent attitude toward the man who badly needs his friendship; Sjögren through his deliberate disloyalty and opportunist actions; and Tjärne through his probing for soft spots in a tender conscience and his ready use of them.

Tjärne and Askanius are particularly interesting in their own right: Tjärne, the opportunist ready to exploit anyone and anything for his personal gain, is most likely a bastard biologically and certainly, in his behavior, a "bastard" in the vulgar but popular sense; he is one of Strindberg's finest presentations of a psychic murderer. Askanius, the psychic suicide, is thoroughly human in his inability to judge his close associates, to identify and accept his limitations, and to refrain from extending his efforts beyond his grasp. But the writer who said "Human beings are to be pitied" does not damn any of these people who touch Libotz' life. Instead he raises the questions: Is the lot of man predetermined? Are people mere marionettes? Or, as Strindberg had said years before in *Creditors,* is there a margin of responsibility?

Certainly his central character believes he is destined to play a definite role:

But this fine intellect was naive about living, could even seem simple minded when he sat revealing his little weaknesses, helping his enemy procure weapons and ammunition, delivering his head on a platter to the firstcomer. But all this stemmed from his gullibility, which was not based on ignorance of the evil in human nature but principally on his efforts to believe good, to imagine he believed good [in others], and, when disappointment followed, just the same try to put up with his fellow human beings' weaknesses, and forgive [them]without end. That was his nature, quite simply, innate ideas about the world, human beings, and his own shadowy destiny, all of which he called his religion [*SS,* XLIV, 158].

A brilliant lawyer and a practitioner of a high ethical code, Edvard Libotz is a gentle human being whose unusual name, unusual appearance, unusual manner, and unusual behavior make the small town people shy away from him until they find him a useful object on which to heap their troubles, resentments, and hates. Socially inept and self-effacing, he makes no effort to use his clients' self-defensive techniques — techniques he knows very well — but goes on with what is apparently his destiny: to bear the guilt of others, to rise above hate, to serve as a sacrificial offering — up to a point. In a modest fashion a Christ figure reminiscent of the Lawyer in *A Dream Play*, Edvard Libotz is charged, though innocent, with many things such as drunkenness, failure to treat his deplorable father and his demanding brother decently, and slander, and is ultimately forced by his fellows to leave the community. Strindberg more than implies that he is destined to serve as a scapegoat wherever he goes.

Strindberg has made no effort to present Libotz as a romantic or realistic hero; instead he is a tragicomic figure of flesh and blood, usually admirable when understood, frequently comic and even ridiculous on occasions, but always very close to Strindberg's central concern with answers to the problem of coping with existence in an evil world: unawareness and apathy for most, psychic suicide through withdrawal into egotism for some, or humaneness and resignation for anyone with an extremely tender conscience.

CHAPTER 7

Apprentice Dramatist

... the herald, the prophet, the teller of truth — [SS, XVIII, 313]

I Preparation

FROM the time he saw a play on the stage for the first time at the age of eight, August Strindberg was fascinated (his own word is *hänryckt*) by drama and theater. He saw in his early years comedies of manners and other light comedies, many of them adapted or translated from French and English; folk plays such as F. A. Dahlgren's *Värmlänningarna,* still part of Swedish repertory; *Hamlet* and other historical and pseudohistorical plays, native and foreign; operas and operettas. While he does not give us a complete list of plays that he actually saw and heard, he emphasizes his taking advantage of theater fare in Stockholm, his reactions to the plays and the performers including his penchant for personal identification and his extensive reading in dramatic literature and in books and articles on acting.

He admitted frankly the very great impact of predecessors or contemporaries on him. For example:

... the melancholy Hamlet affected him more profoundly. Who is this Hamlet, who is still alive, after having seen the lights on stage during the time of John III [1537 - 92] and always remained just as young? People have interpreted him in many ways and used him for all possible purposes. Johan [Strindberg] immediately used him for his own. ...
But it was wonderful to weep over one's own fate and see it wept over. Hamlet for the time being did not become anything but the stepson, however; later on he became the doubter, and still later, the son, the victim of family tyranny. That's how interpretations grow [SS, XVIII, 182-183].

In his teens, Strindberg "gulped down" all of Shakespeare in C.A. Hagberg's excellent translation (1847 - 1851) and was to

127

return to Shakespeare time and again. He read not only the plays of Goethe, Schiller, and Lessing but also studied what they had written about theater and acting. In addition to such native Swedish playwrights as August Blanche (1811 - 1868), Johan Jolin (1818 - 1884), and Frans Hedberg (1828 - 1908), he studied the plays of the Dane Adam Oehlenschläger (1779 - 1850); became early acquainted with the plays of Henrik Ibsen (1828 - 1906) and Björnstjerne Björnson (1832 - 1910); and was aware of what Georg Brandes (1842 - 1927) was beginning to say about literature.

The nineteen-year-old Strindberg, while tutoring Dr. Axel Lamm's sons and living in the doctor's home, while taking the first steps toward becoming a medical doctor, had the good fortune of being treated as one of the family, of being allowed to mingle with the writers, actors, and other artists who were the Lamms' guests, or frequently having the chance to see plays at the nearby Royal Dramatic Theater, and of being included as an equal in discussions of artistic and intellectual matters.

But he gave up medicine to become an actor: "He had probably got the desire by seeing others act, and the theater was, of course, an unreal, better world, which lured one out of boring reality, which probably wouldn't have seemed boring if his bringing up had been more harmonious, realistic and not so romantic as it was. ... In these fantasies about the theater something of what he had felt when he preached [he had as a youngster preached in a Church of Sweden pulpit!] showed up, and when he spoke up in opposition during Christianity class in school — the herald, the prophet, the teller of truth" [SS, XVIII, 312-313]. In his enthusiasm, he prepared for a career in acting by reading what Schiller, Goethe, Lessing, and others had written about the profession; accepted Schiller's assertions about the great significance of theater; tried desperately to practice what Goethe had to say about walking, standing, having stage presence, sitting down, making an entrance and making an exit, and read with appreciation what Lessing had written about drama critics and reviewing.

Instead of creating the desired major role of Karl Moor in Schiller's *Die Räuber,* he was given — as his first assignment — a one-speech part in Björnson's *Maria Stuart*; he was expected to serve as an extra time and again and was advised to enter the training school for actors; unwilling to take the first preliminary steps, his eyes were opened, he says, to the disillusioning facts of theater life. His failure to establish himself as an actor in Stockholm was repeated later in Göteborg. His experiences on stage were not unfruitful, however: Never again was he to confuse the roles of actor and playwright. The latter, he had learned, is the herald, the prophet, and the teller of truth.

II *The Experimental Plays*

Disappointed by his unhappy experiences as an actor and disturbed by difficulties with his father, Strindberg tells us he was reading in Topelius' *Fältskärns berättelser* (*The Fieldsurgeon's Tales*) about a stepmother and a stepson who came to terms:

A woman worshipper as he was, and with guidance from tales about the barber-surgeon, he spins together the idea that only a woman can bring about a reconciliation between himself and his father. And this beautiful role he gives his stepmother.

While lying there, he feels an unusual fever in his body, and while that rages, his head works away, at arranging memories of the past, eliminating some and adding some. New minor characters appear, he sees them involved in the action, hears them talk. It is as if he saw them on stage. After a couple of hours, he has a comedy in two acts ready in his head. It was a both painful and delightful work, if it could be called work, for it went of itself for itself, without his will or interference. But then it had to be written. In four days the play was done [*SS,* XVIII, 340-41].

He called his play *A Namesday Gift* (*En namnsdagsgåva*); it has disappeared, but his account shows that he had discovered at nineteen that he had the gift of writing for the stage. He dealt, significantly, with family difficulties and with the role of woman in settling them.

The second play was *The Free Thinker* (1869), an apprentice piece in three scenes. It tells in largely summary form the story of Karl, a University of Uppsala student, who under the influence of Theodore Parker, becomes a deist and breaks with the establishment; blurts out some bitter truths about the doctrines and practices of the Church of Sweden, his father's hypocritical behavior, and social hypocrisy and pressure; and pays the penalty by losing the woman he loves, his parents' support, and a place in the community and by having to contemplate emigrating to America. The little play expresses rather awkwardly what any undergraduate rebel would recognize as typical for a young man with ambitions to become the herald, the prophet, and the teller of truth: the elderly as enemies of the young, the corruption of the people in power, the need for confrontations, the needs of the underprivileged, unfairness within the family, efforts at weaning the very young from corrupting influences, and idealization of the man-woman relationship.

Always fascinated by history and aware of the great interest historical and pseudohistorical plays had for theatergoers, Strindberg's next three extant plays — *Hermione* (1869), *In Rome* (1870), and *The Outlaw* (1871) — demonstrate that he could write a historical tragedy, a historical proverb in one scene, and a one-act historical tragedy on a theme from early Scandinavian history, all types then in vogue in Sweden.

Hermione is a rhetorical tragedy, divided into five acts, sprinkled with monologs and soliloquies as "numbers" or "scenes" for star actors. It is written largely in blank verse and ends with a couplet; it is oratorical in manner and vocabulary. A highly artificial drama, it tells the story of the daughter of a priest of Ares, Hermione, who is sent to murder Philip of Macedonia when he threatens to destroy Athens' freedom but who, falling in love with Philip instead of murdering him, is killed by her father.

Since it is a highly derivative play, Swedish scholars have had an easy time in identifying Strindberg's sources in, among others, Viktor Rydberg's *The Last of the Athenians* (1859), Shakespeare, Ibsen, Oehlenschläger, Schiller, Lessing, and native dramatists and writers of prose fiction. The play does demonstrate, however, Strindberg's ability from very early in his career to deal effectively with exposition, preparation, presentation of issues, and plot structure.

In Rome is a one-act comedy in rhymed pentameters or a proverb based on an episode in the life of Bertel Thorvaldsen (1770-1844), the Icelandic-Danish sculptor. In dealing with Thorvaldsen's struggle for achievement and recognition as an artist, Strindberg was, very much in a way, dramatizing his own inner conflicts about his duty to be faithful to his call to be an artist as opposed to his needs for making a living at some other occupation. The play presents Thorvaldsen at the time of creating his first masterpiece, penniless and about to be forced to return to Denmark to take a job in a shipyard. Fortunately, a wealthy Englishman buys the statue and thereby saves Thorvaldsen for art.

In Rome was performed eleven times at the Royal Theater, was not treated too unkindly by the critics, and probably did give Strindberg a lift, not least royalty to the amount of 209 *riksdaler* and 66 *öre.*

Oehlenschläger, Ibsen, Björnson, and various Swedish dramatists had tried their hands at writing historical tragedies with themes from pre-Christian Scandinavia and had achieved a measure of popularity as a result. In *The Outlaw* Strindberg did the same, largely as a result of studying Danish and Old Icelandic literature and noting with care what his fellow Scandinavians had done. The play deals with the conflict between Scandinavian paganism and Christianity and concerns itself primarily with the tragedy of the Swedish viking Thorfinn, the outlaw, his "last of the vikings," who is brought to his knees by forces beyond his control: the loss of most of his fleet in a storm at sea, his daughter's conversion to Christianity, and his being declared an outlaw by the Allting. He is killed by his enemies.

In *The Outlaw* Strindberg demonstrated that he knew the traditional concept of tragedy (the fall of a superior human being through his own arrogance and other inner flaws), could write a prose tailored to his characters (here conciseness in the saga manner), and already could give his characters an appreciable measure of life by exploiting what he sensed within himself.

From October 16 on in the 1871-1872 season the Royal Theater presented *The Outlaw* eleven times along with other one-act plays. The most striking result was King Charles XV's summoning Strindberg to the Royal Palace, praising him for his achievement, and awarding him financial support for his studies at the University of Uppsala. Unfortunately, the award turned out to be only a one-time thing.

III   *The Breakthrough:* Master Olof

If any figure in Swedish history suited Strindberg in 1872, emotionally and intellectually, it was Olaus Petri (born Olof Pedersson in 1493 or 1497; died 1552), the man who had had the conviction and the courage, the desire and the dedication to accept Martin Luther's religious ideas and to force through their acceptance in his native Sweden. Interestingly enough, the great Swedish reformer had been not only a heroic idealist who dared to break with authority but also a very human being who had succumbed to the temptation of compromising with authority when confronted with the danger of losing his life.

As a result of justified confidence in his own ability to create dramas, his wide reading in historical and popular accounts, his acquaintance with Shakespeare's and others' stageworthy historical plays, his already great understanding of human beings, and his enthusiasm, he wrote *Master Olof,* a play that certainly proved he was far more than an apprentice dramatist and that should have been accepted as superior to every other Swedish play written before 1872.

Many years later when he wrote his memoranda to August Falck and the actors at his own Intimate Theater, he asserted accurately: "In my first version of *Master Olof,* I . . . substituted prose for verse, and instead of the opera-like blank verse drama with solo and special numbers, I composed polyphonically a symphony, in which all the voices were interwoven (major and minor characters were treated equally), and in which no one accompanied the soloist" [*Open Letters,* 10][1]. For the most part the conversational prose is adapted subtly to every character: Most of it is free of declamatory and oratorical artificialities. The reader or the audience is unobtrusively but carefully prepared for what is going to happen, supplied with adequate information about the background of what is happening, and gradually permitted to sense or grasp the significance of each bit of action. *Master Olof* was the first strikingly realistic Swedish play.

The central character or hero is not a simple character who believes the Bible should be substituted for the Church of Rome as the basis for Christianity in Sweden, who fights without fail for the achievement of that goal, and who dies for his cause. He is instead a complex human being hard to catch hold of at any moment and capable of change at any time. He does believe in Lutheran reform, he does fight for its realization, he does reject priestly celibacy, he does take delight in challenging authority, he can resist compromise when it does not involve much personal danger, but he can compromise when it is a matter of his life and justify doing so, dimly perhaps, on the basis of needing to serve others. Master Olof and the other important characters with one exception (Gert) are, moreover, intimately characterized in their littleness as well as in their strengths: King Gustav I, Bishop Brask, Archbishop

Laurentius Petri, Brother Mårten, Master Olof's mother, and his wife Kristina.

Strindberg avoided simplifying the basic struggles for goals and power (religious and ecclesiastical, intellectual, political, social, economic) except in presenting Gert, the idealist who remains static and who advocates complete freedom. Very appropriately the Roman Catholic bishop Hans Brask would retain his church's control over beings not ready for anarchy; King Gustav wants religious, political, and economic independence for Sweden for selfish as well as practical reasons. All these approaches to the problems involved in the double struggle for reform and independence are in counterpoint to each other and in the course of the action it becomes clear that the playwright had good reasons for toying with "What Is Truth?" as its title.

But the play did not please Frans Hedberg, the director of the Royal Theater:

[He said] Gustav Vasa and Olaus Petri were misrepresented and reduced in stature. Johan [Strindberg] insisted that on the contrary they were restored to the [human] condition in which they had once most likely existed but which through patriotic and idealistic errors had gradually been distorted. ... the blow was crushing, although it was given as gently as possible and the author was encouraged to rewrite the play [*SS*, XIX, 37].

In the years that followed Strindberg did rewrite it in various versions, two of which have been staged: the middle version (*Mellanspelet*, 1875) and the so-called verse *Master Olof* (1876). In 1877 he wrote *The Epilogue* (*Efterspelet*), which he called a mystery play and which tells briefly the story of a fat and prosperous, middle-aged Master Olof, who had reaped the "rewards" of compromise. The only one of these plays about Master Olof that has claims to greatness is the prose version of 1872. Strindberg's ordeal of waiting for its recognition lasted until 1881 when it was first produced; the effects of the ordeal lasted until his death in 1912.[2]

In the midst of striving to write a version of *Master Olof* acceptable to the theater people, Strindberg dashed off *The Year 1848*(*Anno fyrtioåtta*, ca. 1875), a minor four-act comedy whose major interest lies in its foreshadowing the content of his first great novel, *The Red Room,* and not in its merits as a comedy. In the year of revolutions 1848, there were a few indications of unrest even in Stockholm, hence the title, but the emphasis is placed on the exposure of the wealthy brewer and Philistine Larsson and a fairly sympathetic treatment of the bohemian artists who serve as his "court."

IV   *Plays Tailored for Siri Strindberg*

An unfortunate result of the rejection of the various versions of *Master Olof* in the 1870s was that Strindberg turned away from the drama and devoted himself to prose fiction, social history, social satire, and miscellaneous writing. To be sure, his efforts in those areas led ultimately to such works of art as *The Red Room* (1879), *The Swedish People* (1882), *The New Nation* (1882), but from 1877 to 1886 he wrote only three plays, only one of which (*The Journey of Lucky Peter,* 1882) is particularly noteworthy. The other two — *The Secret of the Guild* (1880) and *Lord Bengt's Wife* (1882) — are pieces, apparently written without much enthusiasm, to provide roles for his wife. Both of these plays reflect his awareness of the prejudices of the men who controlled the Swedish theaters, the need for tailoring both form and content to suit them and yet do well by Siri, and the value of appeal to current interests.

Strindberg had written the chapters on guilds in *Old Stockholm* [3] and was considering them for *The Swedish People;* he was very much interested in the ongoing controversy about the restoration and renovation of the cathedral in Uppsala, seat of the Archbishop of Sweden. He used his knowledge of guilds and of the building of the cathedral back in the Middle Ages to give *The Secret of the Guild* a historical setting and atmosphere.

But the major thrust in the so-called comedy is not history but rather the idea that it is the grasping and unscrupulous opportunist and not the sensitive and genuinely endowed and dedicated idealist who reaps both opportunities and rewards. Sten who had the faith and the skill to be the master builder initially has to give way to Jacques, the unscrupulous opportunist, who is elected. But since the play had to have a happy ending in order to take, Jacques is exposed and reforms and Sten reveals the secret and is made the master builder.

Strindberg demonstrated very nicely he could meet every qualification necessary to have a play accepted in those days: one setting per act; a beginning, a middle, and an end per act; places for applause; "numbers," rousing speeches, emotional outbursts, revelations; avoidance of irritating the audience; and rewarding roles.

While the play represents no advance in dramatic composition, it has the very real merit of involvement in characterization of figures that do come alive as flesh and blood human beings. The major characters — Sten and Jacques — are not types but vital products of heredity and environment, time and chance — complex and dynamic people. The others, too, are an interesting group of people, each of them revealed to the extent necessary for grasping both theme and plot.

Strindberg probably was right in assuming Ibsen borrowed a great deal from *The Secret of the Guild* (1880) in writing *The Master Builder* (1892).

Lord Bengt's Wife is both in substance and structure transitional:

> ... *Lord Bengt's Wife*! Well, first of all, it's an attack on the romantic bringing-up of women. The cloister — the pension! He is the knight; all men are knights to young girls. Then they face the realities of life, and she learns he is a farmer. He thinks she is a fool, but reality develops her into a woman, which the *pension* could not do. In the second place, it's a defence of love as the natural force which survives all nonsensical notions and conquers free will. In the third place, it's a defence of woman's love as higher in quality (with the added factor, maternal love) than man's. In the fourth place, it's a defence of a woman's right to be her own. Fifth, it's a play for the theater, and that's too bad [*SS*, XIV, 34-35].

He met the demands of the theater sufficiently to have the play produced; but he made a very personal contribution to the debate about woman's rights and the man-woman relationship that had been raging in Sweden at least since 1839 when Carl Jonas Love Almqvist's novel *Sara Videbeck* (*Det går an*) appeared.[4]

The dramatic composition is traditional in such matters as division into five acts; noticeable attention to the old idea that each act should have a beginning, a middle, and an end; unbelievably artifical intrigues and devices; the use of soliloquies; expressions of love and hate that can serve as "numbers"; and, overlapping most of these, occasional declamatory lapses. But most of the dialog is intense and conversational, reminiscent of the kind of dialog dominant in *Master Olof* and foreshadowing the superb, typically Strindbergian dialog of *The Father* (1887).

The historical elements do give some coloring to the story of a convent-trained girl who marries a young nobleman in the early sixteenth century only to find that her notion that they were to live happily ever after was not realistic. There are evocative hints about cloister and castle life, to be sure, but the story, the people, and their problems are as modern as they can be — in essentials.

The treatment of the theme — the relationship of husband and wife before and after the vows were taken — is a decided advance over what Strindberg had to say in, for example, *Master Olof.* In *Lord Bengt's Wife,* it is obviously a married man who presents two young people's romantic love for each other, their difficulties in making the transition to reality, the perennial problems of the precedence work and practicality take over love, the necessity of overcoming false training if the marriage is to work.

Strindberg's fascination with human beings resulted in impressive characterizations, not least that of Lady Margit, whose role was designed for Siri Strindberg and which served her well in the initial production in the 1882 - 1883 season. In 1971, Alf Sjöberg produced *Lord Bengt's Wife* with the conviction that it is extremely pertinent to our day with its far-from-settled problems of conflict between the sexes, woman's right to equality, the burden of guilt each partner must try to bear, and based on Sjöberg's belief that it is an early contribution to the theater of cruelty.

V   The Journey of Lucky Peter

Of all the plays written before 1887, *Master Olof* and *The Journey of Lucky Peter* (1882) alone have become important parts of the Swedish repertory. Swedish audiences, young and old, have appreciated the latter more than any other Strindberg play over the years even though it is not one of his greatest plays. He himself wrote to Ludvig Josephson on January 17, 1882:

Peter has gone out into the world; has tried the best things in life; riches, friendship, honors, power and found all of them empty and meaningless; now he stands in the Caliph's palace, curses humanity and wishes he were out in nature which would heal all his wounds: He curses society. ...

As far as Peter's unmotivated sharpsightedness goes, I think you'll find when you read it again that it's precisely his uncorrupted sound common sense that has seen through the perversity of things and his naïveté which (as in Voltaire's *Candide*) tempers the satire. ... Now his usual youthful common sense leads him to make too hasty, narrow conclusions about matters which later have to be corrected! [*Brev,* II, 398]

Strindberg classified the play as a *sagospel,* which may be translated a *fairytale play.*

It can be read as a simple child's play about life, but like the medieval morality plays, it is allegorical in its appeal to the inner man. It is Strindberg's *Everyman* and, as such, deals with the vanity of seeking happiness in nature, wealth, fame and good deeds, power and position. In its treatment of love, Strindberg insists the only source of human happiness even approaching the ideal — a man's and a woman's love for each other — comes only as a gift from a chastening Deity. The play is one of the most direct statements of Strindberg's core values as a perfectionist: *love, work,* and *truth.*

The Journey of Lucky Peter is a forerunner of his dreamplays and plays of pilgrimage with medieval and Catholic overtones. Peter makes the pilgrimage from the innocence of sheltered childhood to the resignation of adulthood, resignation and acceptance of life as the mysterious, imperfect thing it is. It deals with the universally human: Peter could be any man or everyman, Lisa a typification of woman, a visible counterpart of Victoria in *A Dream Play.* It deals with the dual capacity of the nature of man, his capacity for both good and evil. It gets at "truth" as much through flashes of insight as through observations and analyses.

But *The Journey of Lucky Peter* is not restricted to wonders and miracles, free play of the imagination, flashes of insight, and dreamlike implications. It contains a great deal of satire and good humor that adults "in the know" would recognize as directed at specific individuals or institutions. Take, for example, the ceremonies at Schultze's monument: They would have given any well-informed Stockholmer in the 1880s a good laugh at Strindberg's enemy-number-one, Carl David af Wirsén, poet and member of the Swedish Academy.[5] *The Journey of Lucky Peter* should be fun for anyone to see: the child who delights in allegory and is not handicapped by addiction to analysis and the adult who delights in shocks of recognition.

CHAPTER 8

Master Dramatist

I find the joy of life in the strong, cruel struggles of life, and my pleasure in getting to know something, in learning something. — Preface to *Lady Julie* (1888).

FROM the early 1880s until, roughly, 1894, Strindberg's approach in his search for knowledge about man, the universe, and Deity was analytic and questioning. He deliberately acquired as much knowledge as possible about the psychological, biological, and sociological factors in human development. Scholars have emphasized the influence of Darwin and other scientists on him, his increasing devotion to the natural sciences, and his efforts to become and remain a nonbeliever, and his deliberate exploitation of himself as a source of knowledge and material. During the years after 1882 until the Inferno period was over, he did not write a single historical play nor a single play in which religion is given favorable treatment.

Yet in those years he wrote fifteen plays, five of which are great — *The Father* (1887), *Lady Julie* (1888), *Creditors* (1888), *The Stronger* (1889), and *The Bond* (1892) — and the rest with perhaps one exception at least competent and stageworthy — *Comrades* (1886, 1888), *Pariah* (1889), *Samum* (1889), *The First Warning* (1891), *Debit and Credit* (1892), *Facing Death* (1892), *Mother Love* (1892), and *Playing with Fire* (1892). The exception is *The Keys to Heaven* (1891), which, while it is not much of a piece for the theater, has its own claims to attention as we shall see.

Two essays about dramatic theory and criticism are exceptionally important — the preface to *Lady Julie* and "On Modern Drama and Modern Theater" (1890). The latter concerns the rise and success of naturalistic drama:[1]

... naturalism, which had been declared impossible on the stage by theorists and others, had already made a brilliant entrance on stage. One can already see the signs of a search for a form, which seems to lead the new drama in a direction somewhat different from the first attempts in [Zola's] *Thérèse Raquin* [1873], and which breaks completely with Zola's adaptation of both *L'Assommoir* and *Germinal* with their mass effect and elaborate apparatus.

Hardly a full-evening play shows up, and Zola himself makes his debut with a one-act play; and where three-act plays do appear, a strong inclination toward the unities of time and place is noticeable. All attempts at intrigue seem to have been given up as well, and the major interest placed on the psychological course of events [*SS,* XVII, 297-298].

"On Modern Drama and Modern Theater" is, moreover, Strindberg's reflection on what he himself had done from *Marauders-Comrades* on and was to do through his whole so-called naturalistic period: simplify and tighten the form more and more and place the major emphasis on the psychological course of events: "In the new naturalistic drama an effort to search out the meaningful motif was immediately apparent. For that reason it concerned itself preferably with the two opposites in life, life and death, birth and death, the struggle for one's mate, the means of existence, honor, all these conflicts, with their fields of battle, cries of misery, wounded and dead, during which one heard the new world view about life as a struggle blowing its stimulating southerly wind.

Those were tragedies such as one had not seen before" [*SS,* XVII, 298-299].

The preface to *Lady Julie* emphasizes his objectives: departure from a play divided into acts to the achievement of a one-act play presenting a segment of life without intermissions (hence his use of monolog or soliloquy, mime and ballet in *Lady Julie*); a meaningful, universal and timeless theme; a plot illustrating that theme without the use of artificial intrigue; dialog like that of conversational speech; utterly realistic staging, setting, lighting, and scenery; and complex, dynamic characters (i.e., characterless characters, individuals not types).

He had been very much influenced by naturalism and determinism. He knew, for example, what Auguste Comte had written about getting at natural laws and their relationships as *the* object of study; John Stuart Mill's insistence that egotism is the central fact of the individual's life and that human behavior should be ethical, i.e., calculated enlightened self-interest; Charles Darwin's emphasis on such matters as man as animal, the struggle for existence, and natural selection; Thomas Huxley's statements about agnosticism; Arthur Schopenhauer's pessimistic views of man as mere marionette with a built-in will to live; Friedrich Nietzsche's glorification of the superman, the man who has the will to power without regard for others except insofar as they can be used. He knew also Herbert Spencer's rather optimistic faith in progressive evolution; and, of course, Hippolyte Taine, who applied naturalism to the development of literature, and Émile Zola who supplied the formula for naturalistic literature: *faire grand, faire vrai, faire simple* — and applied it. Strindberg read, considered, and digested what all these men and others had written and practiced.

II   Marauders-Comrades

Late in 1886 Strindberg completed a five-act play that he labelled a comedy, called *Marodörer* (*Marauders*), and sent to Albert Bonnier in November. On December 3, he wrote to Edvard Brandes: "But the thing is I've just finished a comedy in five acts called *Marauders* (dealing with the ladies naturally): I think the play is highly effective, balanced nicely, and to the point. The fourth act is excellent, and the fifth has two dynamite sticks (figuratively speaking). I have a certain hope for this play, my first contemporary comedy" [*Brev,* VI, 1344].

In another letter to Edvard Brandes (January 3, 1887), Strindberg said that *Marauders* was the second part of a trilogy, that the first[2] would deal with Bertha (the major female character) and her father during her childhood and that the third part would deal with Bertha's later life as mother and the wife of a butcher.

The play, as finally revised and called *Kamraterna* (*Comrades*), tells the story of the marriage of a would-be painter, Bertha, who initially refuses to sacrifice her art for marriage (i.e., becoming, as she says, a man's slave) but does marry the gifted painter Axel to make ends meet and to improve her health. When she believes her painting has been accepted for exhibition and his rejected, she becomes puffed up and humiliates her husband. Driven beyond endurance, he reveals that he has put his name on her painting, that hers has been rejected, that he no longer wants her in his home, and that he is installing a mistress instead.

Such a brief summary should suggest that Strindberg was dealing with the relationship between husband and wife and with men and women as competitors professionally. It should suggest, too, that Strindberg had not freed himself from artificial devices of intrigue. What the summary cannot suggest are some of the very real merits of the play: generally brilliant dialog, intensely challenging substance, and rewarding roles: Axel, a gentle and gifted artist who believes in sex equality but who does not allow himself to be murdered psychically; Bertha, a vampire and a painter not because of endowment but because of determination to prove her superiority over men; Abel, a realistic bisexual; Willmer, a little feminized author; Dr. Östermark, who sees into what is happening; his former wife and her two daughters (of questionable repute); and Carl, a highly masculine military man.

Marauders was not accepted for publication or performance, and Strindberg faced an old problem: revising the play. He did so, with some help from his friend and fellow writer, Axel Lundegård, and in 1888 its final version appeared as *Comrades*. It is a serious drama even though Strindberg insisted on labelling it "A comedy in four acts." While it does not have compactness of form and is not free of artificial intrigue, it does deal with meaningful motifs, approaches placing major interest on the psychological course of events, and observes the unities of time and place. It requires no elaborate apparatus and does not try for effects beyond those in life itself. Its implications are hardly comic.

Its major attractions, aside from superb lines and memorable characters, are the treatment of various aspects of the woman's liberation movement such as competition between men and women in the labor market and the light it throws on Strindberg's thinking about the characters in *The Father*, which he completed before the revision of *Comrades* was ready and to which *Comrades* was a sort of sequel.

III   The Father (*1887*)

In writing *The Father*[3] Strindberg concentrated on the creation of an extremely realistic play about the father in one modern marriage. After his trial for blasphemy, he had speculated about his own deteriorating marital situation, extended his speculations by imagining possibilities about his wife's behavior in the present and reinterpreting episodes in the past, and contemplated others' marriages. His response to Ibsen's *Ghosts* (1881), which centers about one mother without, as Strindberg thought, adequate attention to the father, probably was a major factor in his choice of subject and the manner of its presentation.

The Father represents a very significant advance toward the ideal structure of a naturalistic play — as he was to explain in "On Modern Drama and Modern Theater" and in his preface to *Lady Julie*. While it is divided into three acts it does observe the unities of time, place, and action; it is free of artificially contrived intrigue, and the major emphasis is on the psychological course of events. The motif could hardly be more meaningful; the conflict could not be closer to the very core of family life.

The psychic destruction of Captain Adolf, the father — as much a matter of suicide as of murder — is tragic in the true meaning of tragedy as the destruction of a superior human being. The plot illustrates the destruction of the captain by his wife Laura just below the level of consciousness ("an unconscious little crime"), consciously or unconsciously by the other characters, and by the limitations the captain places on himself in the struggle for survival. The action is limited to the catastrophe, the final clinching hours of a struggle that has been going on in a marriage that has lasted for over twenty years. Functioning in a culture emphasizing individual freedom and responsibility, Captain Adolf has been brought up as a moral human being with strong convictions about his role as a man, husband, and father; with a strong sense of consideration for others and their well being; with a capacity to observe, choose, and act; with acceptance of responsibility; and with the limiting acceptance of such traditional views as the husband's duty to head the family, to look after his wife and child, and not to question these duties.

It is an unforgettable characterization of a superior, civilized human being brought low primarily by a fascinating human being not handicapped by the blinders of traditional curbs on behavior. The Captain is a strong man or a Hercules, he has the handicaps of accepting blindly the traditional concepts of man as superior to look after and woman as inferior to be looked after. Laura very much wants to be an Omphale who controls everything and everyone in her environment, including her Hercules whom she does not consider a Hercules nor herself "a little woman." Essentially untrained morally and undisciplined intellectually,

Laura has become an extremely effective manipulator of people during a twenty-year marital hell, the climax of which is brought on by the question of the daughter Bertha's education. The ghastly technique she employs in destroying her husband's will (his desire to do, his making up his mind to do, and his doing) becomes "an unconscious little crime," during the course of which Laura never quite permits herself to take a good, close look at what she is up to (note the significance of the ugly, hastily suppressed laugh, her never using a mirror, her instinctive use of "rails" laid down by Adolf, making her "home" a cage full of "tigers" for him, and her weaving of webs). Laura is not merely a feminine beast of prey, an animal with a thin veneer of socially desirable behavior: Strindberg indicates that lack of training and discipline have made her the stronger in a relationship that Strindberg believed should be cooperative rather than competitive.

While Captain Adolf and Laura are characterized as dynamic, complex people, the rest of the cast are dealt with only as they affect the two principals: Margaret, the lovable old nurse who does not quite understand what is happening; Pastor Jonas, who is a Christian in name and position only; Nöjd, who is merely a young private bent on sexual expression; Dr. Östermark, who from personal experience and alert faculties senses what is happening but does not make serious efforts to prevent it; and Bertha, a seventeen-year-old who has learned to take on protective coloring.

The Father is one of the great plays in world literature, and it is a play that arouses strong reader and audience reaction. It has superb structure; flawless use of dramatic techniques such as exposition, preparation, and presentation; thorough control of dialog; wealth of telling but fully understandable imagery; and searing impact on both reader and audience. But for many people, *The Father* has been and is a disturbing play. Back in Strindberg's day, it shocked many of his fellow Swedes because they thought it was a distasteful exploitation of his own marital difficulties. For all those that think the detailed consideration of the basic facts of human relationships is not "nice," *The Father* is both a play that causes an uncomfortable shock of recognition and a play that violates their conspiracy of silence.

IV   Lady Julie (*1888*)

Because of *Lady Julie* itself, Alf Sjöberg's film version, Elsa von

Rosen's ballet, and the preface, the play is probably the most widely known of Strindberg's dramas. Whether one translates *Fröken Julie* by *Lady Julie* or *Miss Julie,* Strindberg dealt with the "fall" of an unmarried Swedish noblewoman through her sexual involvement with Jean, her father's servant of lowly origin but patently an individual with the potential of rising socially and economically.

To illustrate the universal and timeless theme of social rising and falling Strindberg presents a plot that can be summarized as *before, during,* and *after* the mutual seduction. Based to some slight degree on a contemporary Swedish scandal involving a noblewoman and a servant, Strindberg filled out the bare outlines of that scandal through speculation and imagination. The procedure illustrates nicely his method of dramatizing "segments of actual life": On the basis of stimulating facts and situation, he selected, eked out, and arranged the material for his plays of this period. His first wife was, of course, a noblewoman from Swedish Finland.

The form of *Lady Julie* goes beyond that of *The Father* in achieving the goals of naturalistic drama that he was to outline in the preface and in the essay about modern drama and modern theater. The one-act form eliminated all intermissions. The fact that it is Midsummer Eve, a time for appreciable relaxation of social distinctions and of formal and even moral behavior as well, made it possible for his countrymen to accept Lady Julie's stooping to seek out Jean as a partner in Midsummer dancing. According to naturalistic thinking, even noblewomen are basically animals and therefore are in heat at intervals and not above mating with the most attractive male available. The actual act of sexual intercourse could not take place on stage in 1888, hence Strindberg's use of the ballet. All the techniques — monologs or soliloquies, mime, ballet, exposition, preparation, and presentation — are in strict keeping with the naturalistic notion that drama was to present a slice of life: Note Strindberg's extremely careful and detailed use of the manor-house setting, lighting, and staging.

In the course of the dialog — conversational and adapted to the course of action and the moods of the characters — this naturalistic tragedy, as Strindberg called it, reveals that the determinative factors in the fall of Lady Julie and the probable rise of Jean are heredity, environment, time, and chance. There is constant awareness of the basic animal nature of human beings, problems arising from instincts and desires, the individual's urge to live, the struggle for existence, and natural selection. The universe in which these characters live is mechanistic and, theoretically, they do not have much, if any, freedom of choice.

Both Julie and Jean are excellent samples of what Strindberg called "characterless characters," dynamic and complex human beings, individuals not types. Lady Julie may represent aristocracy in decline and Jean richly endowed plebeians, potentially aristocrats of nerve and brain, but they are much more than that.

Julie is the product of her own nature: She is at the mercy of her own drives and her conditioning by her mother and her father. On the one hand, she has been urged and "trained" to become a manhater and an emancipated woman by a mother with a confused and confusing past and, on the other, she has been encouraged to become an aristocrat by her nobleman father with his sense and code of honor. The result is a twisted, confused human being who is only to a relatively slight degree a sheltered artificial product and who goes to her death out of fear of being dishonored.

Jean has the endowment to become a superior being in an amoral world of rugged individualism. While his origins are lowly, his brain and his nerve will stand him in good stead when he grasps a chance to rise. From the point of view of naturalism, Jean is a far healthier and more promising animal than Julie. Far from incidentally, he has sensitivity of a kind (wine rather than beer, for example). He has, moreover, no scruples except about what may hurt him; he fears the count, for example, because he is still under his control.

Strindberg prided himself on his use of parallel actions, and those in *Lady Julie* can hardly be disregarded. Diana is a thoroughbred aristocratic dog usually on a leash, a "civilized" creature supposedly finer and more sheltered because of her heredity and environment but, all the same, a bitch in heat and at the mercy of her drives. The mate that chance provides is the gatekeeper's cur or mutt, a healthy animal without any hesitation about self-expression or determination to get all he wants and can get when the opportunity comes. These are curiously striking parallels to the two central characters. Even Serena, the finch, is a parallel: That caged creature is a product of careful breeding, a domesticated singer, a protected pet of "society" and an object of sentimental but not realistic regard. Even the axe and the razor are, in a way, parts of the parallel action: The axe is the heavy and crude instrument of death wielded by an unhesitant brute, the razor is the finely honed instrument that a person of honor and refinement can wield only in a hypnotic state induced by a temporarily fear-ridden brute.

Fortunately, after completing this naturalistic tragedy, Strindberg wrote the preface for it, a preface that throws light on all the plays written during the late 1880s and early 1890s. Since then it has been accepted as one of the most important contributions to the literature about drama and theater. The play itself has gone from triumph to triumph.

V   Creditors (*1888*)

Structurally, *Creditors* is a tightly packed act without intermissions, observes the three unities (time, place, and action), and has reduced properties to bare necessities. The remarkably conversational dialog of confrontation, nicely adjusted to each speaker's mood and purpose, reveals Strindberg's awareness and gift for expressing such matters as the battle of the brains, the power of suggestion that approaches hypnotic effects, and startling differences in people's ability to cope with each other.

Since the play concerns the universal and timeless theme of credit and debit within marriage, the framework is appropriately that of accounts or bookkeeping. At all points terms such as creditors, bills, payment, first mortgage, settling up, tearing up bills, presenting bills, and everyday financial transactions are there as shocking reminders of the principals' egotistic concern with the give and take within matrimony.

The plot is a simple succession of overlapping confrontations: Husband 1 vs. Husband 2, Husband 2 vs. Wife; Wife vs. Husband 1 (with Husband 2 listening in next door). It is the story of one woman's two marriages extending over about a decade with what happens on stage limited to the catastrophe, the completion of the psychic murder of the sensitive and most highly civilized — and therefore the most handicapped — principal. It is, moreover, another effective Strindbergian illustration of "innocent little crimes," on the one hand, and, on the other, a ghastly presentation of what he called the dissection of a soul.

The three characters are unforgettable: Gustav, the richly endowed intellectual; Adolf, the intensely sensitive artist; and Tekla, the decidedly attractive woman neither of the men can disregard or discard.

Gustav is Strindberg's greatest characterization of a professional educator. Proud of his own superiority as an intellectual, he has learned, he thinks, how to deal with people through analyzing, probing, dissecting, and counselling. He can and does force Adolf to analyze his art, his ideals, his wife, and his marriage, and to act about Tekla. He nicely adjusts his approach to both his successor and his former wife. He does all this because of hurt pride, seven years of humiliation before his teenage pupils, loss of honor, addiction to probing and analyzing, and his very human desire for revenge. But as Strindberg makes clear, everyone is vulnerable, even the conscious manipulators of other human beings.

Adolf is decidedly different from Captain Adolf in *The Father*. The Adolf in *Creditors* is no scientist who can make important contributions through research in the library or laboratory; he is primarily an artist who feels and senses rather than analyzes and speculates. He is a moral idealist about himself, his wife, and his marriage as well as an idealist about art and life. Strindberg demonstrates how these facts make him vulnerable emotionally, mentally, physically, and professionally.

Tekla is neither a Laura nor a Lady Julie. Unlike Laura, she has no ambition to control her child's future as a credit to her or dispose of a husband who would stand in the way of achieving her quest for power. Unlike Lady Julie, to cite just one matter, Tekla is no noblewoman who is likely to commit suicide because of the code of honor. Tekla is a physically attractive woman with some pretence to success as an author, who enjoys sex without feeling guilty, and who has the gift of not being very much aware of the real effects of what she does. Tekla is a woman whose two marriages have not worked out the way her two husbands had hoped: Gustav had planned to make her "the little woman" who would be just right for him as bedmate, hostess, and homemaker; Adolf had hoped for the idealistic mating of two people who love each other.

Tekla is no mere vampire, that is, a person who steals things, ideas, and people, although she takes advantage of opportunities whenever they are offered to her. She has been a fairly apt pupil of Gustav's: She has, for example, learned to analyze a little — when driven to it. But her role in the murder is essentially unintentional and unconscious, even though Gustav with substantial justification calls her a cannibal, a serpent, a phonograph, a thief, a little devil, and a monster.

It is in this play with its thorough application of his theory of characterization, compactness of structure, economy of staging, naturalness of dialog, and telling detail, that Strindberg has stressed "the margin of responsibility" that qualifies the deterministic, naturalistic assumption that human beings do not really have any freedom of will. But Strindberg classified *Creditors* as a naturalistic tragicomedy.

There can be no denial of its tragic implications or even of its gruesome humor or of its commentary on the tragicomic nature of life. It is a great play, which deserves Herbert Grevenius' succinct appraisal, "It is a pretty terrible play, but it is terribly good." [4]

VI   *The "Cynical" Plays*

Between the completion of *Creditors* and the beginning of the Inferno period Strindberg wrote *The People of Hemsö,* a folk comedy; *The Keys to Heaven or St. Peter Wanders on Earth,* a fairytale play; and a series of short one-scene or one-act plays: *The Stronger, Pariah, Samum, Debit and Credit, Mother Love, The Bond, Facing Death, The First Warning,* and *Playing with Fire.*

The Stronger (1889), a "fifteen-minute," one-scene play of the kind then receiving encouragement at the Théâtre Libre in Paris, is the most widely popular of the short plays. Without intermissions and with simplicity of staging, small number of characters, and representations of one-wall-away Strindbergian naturalism, *The Stronger* has been produced so often in so many places that it would be impossible to get even a fairly reliable estimate of the number of productions.

It has been called a monodrama, a dramatic monolog, a battle of the brains in one scene, and a tour-de-force. However one wishes to pigeonhole it, the facts remain that it is good theater, that it does have something important to say, and that it has presented people who do not accept the deterministic point of view with an interesting gambit for argument and discussion.

Strindberg answered the question of which woman is the stronger when he wrote to his wife about her creation of the role of Mrs. Y:

"Play it 1. as if she were an actress — that is, not an ordinary housewife, 2. as the stronger, that is, the pliable person who bends and rises again, 3. dressed in the best of taste. ... 5. Study the role extremely carefully, but play it simply. That's to say, not "simply." Put 50% charlatan into it ... and hint at depths that do not exist" [*Brev,* VII, 1784].

The wife's final solving of a puzzle by putting the two heaps of pieces together is an illustration of Strindberg's diabolic insight into the struggles the individual must engage in if she (or he) is to survive and win.

A brilliant result of Strindberg's extensive study of psychology and criminology is the short one-act *Pariah: A Free Dramatization of a Story by Ola Hansson* (1889). Strindberg had from time to time considered dramatizing various works of prose fiction, but it was not until he read his fellow writer's story, that he did so — in typically Strindbergian fashion: Borrowing some details and suggestions, he transformed the material into a study of crime and punishment. The confrontation of Mr. X who had unintentionally killed an old man years ago and Mr. Y who had committed forgery out of extreme need becomes a fascinating illustration of a Strindbergian battle of brains. Mr. X, a superior intellectual with moral standards, has developed his gift for analysis to the point where he can in the manner of Edgar Allan Poe not only determine the truth about Mr. Y's guilt, punishment, and nature but also protect himself from punishment by society for a crime he never intended to commit. *Pariah* offers actors superb opportunity and challenge: material that should have universal interest (if Strindberg's assertion that "everyone has a corpse in his cargo" is true), excellent lines, suspense, and a provoking conclusion.

On March 10, 1889, Strindberg wrote to Ola Hansson: "...I have written a brilliant Edgar-Poe play — called *Samum* (in one act, of course) in which I have used the desert wind's ability to evoke terrifying visions which drive French soldiers [in Algeria] to suicide" [*Brev,* VII, 1793].

The depiction of a psychic murder by an Arabian girl disguised as a young man is, as Strindberg said, a brilliant one-act play, which exploits the general interest in an exotic and terrifying setting and serves as a striking means of demonstrating how suggestion, hypnosis, and ventriloquism can be used in destroying a weakened human being.

When Strindberg in October, 1909, wrote a brief preface to *The Author,* he listed his works, labelling the one-act plays of 1892 "one-acters out of cynical life." The covering title is appropriate for all six and could justifiably be extended to the plays of the late 1880s as well. Egotism, selfishness, self-interest dominate all of them.

Perhaps the most delightfully amusing of all his short plays is *The First Warning* (1892), a presentation of jealousy as a unifying factor in a marriage that has not been satisfactory to either mate. The wife has irritated her husband in many ways and aroused his jealousy through getting the attentions of other men, but the infatuation of a fifteen-year-old girl and her middle-aged mother for the husband together with the loss of one of her front teeth makes her not only jealous but also aware of aging. The result is reconciliation "for at least eight days," as the husband puts it. Aside from the presentation of jealousy as a reconciling factor, the play has such merits as excellent lines, amusing situations, and an interesting set of characters (particularly Rosa, the fifteen-year-old, a lively, precocious adolescent decidedly different from his *seemingly* retarded girls of the late nineteenth century such as Bertha in *The Father*).

Debit and Credit (1892) is a telling presentation of the price that has to be paid for success not only by the individual who achieves it but also by the people who have, financially or otherwise, helped him on the way. The situation and the problems raised are timeless and universal, but the solution — flight from obligations — is startlingly reminiscent of Strindberg's own behavior on occasion.

Still another set of causes of family unhappiness — daughters' mistreatment of a father whose dead wife had made their marriage miserable and guaranteed that the misery would continue after her death — is the material in *Facing Death* (1892), a fifteen-minute tragedy. It involves a marital hell, ugly possibilities in the parent-child relationship, psychic murder, psychic suicide, arson, and actual suicide. *Facing Death* is the least satisfactory of all these short plays: The lines are surprisingly awkward, the characterizations thin, and the exposition far from adequate.

For those who may wonder how a seventeen-year-old Bertha in *The Father* can take on the protective behavior of a seven-year-old on occasion, *Mother Love* (1892) should be a revealing study of one method of discipline and training and its effects on a sensitive youngster. Strindberg presents the results of a middle-aged ex-prostitute's rearing of her illegitimate daughter Hélène (with assistance from a morally questionable dresser) in isolation, selfishness, vulgarity, and bitterness. One does wonder, however, how such an environment and such exposure can produce an Hélène, a lovely, sensitive, and refined young actress. Lisen, her halfsister (the still younger legitimate offspring of Hélène's fine father), is rare among Strindberg characters in her unbelievably precocious knowledge of life and people (in spite of her protective, refined upbringing) and in her ability to analyze and communicate the analysis to others. *Mother Love* is a curiously contrived but nevertheless stageworthy little play.

Strindberg never wrote a lighter play than *Playing with Fire: A Comedy in One Act* (1892), in which he examines the emotional lives of five idle rich people, who might have been ironically called beautiful people at a later date — a father (60), a mother (58), their son (27), their daughter-in-law (24), a niece (20), and a male friend (26) who has just been divorced. Without work and with no need for concern about food, shelter, or clothing, at least four of them play with the fire of sexual attraction in trying to make time pass in a beautiful setting and an atmosphere of whimsical abandonment of serious concern about much of anything. The roles are very good indeed, the lines excellent, and the solution amusing.

VII   The Bond

Strindberg's first divorce (1891) and the legal system to which that divorce exposed him were the point of departure for an appreciably imaginative treatment of what in his less emotionally involved moments was at the very core of the tragedy of divorce: What happens to the children?

While the title *The Bond* suggests that the child as victim of parental incompatability is the major theme, Emile (the child) does not appear and he is not uppermost in the minds and thinking of the baron and the baroness as they confront each other in court. Strindberg suggests that one should not expect too much of the baron and his wife even though the former is capable of a measure of self-restraint and the latter, while undisciplined, does want custody of her child.

The two principals are complex and dynamic products of

unhappy homes themselves. Baron Axel resembles Captain Adolf in *The Father* and Gustaf in *Creditors:* The baron has been trained and disciplined so that he can analyze himself and his wife, their relationship, their two agreements (premarital for the protection of the emancipated woman and predivorce agreement for the protection of the child), and the plight of their child as victim (disgrace; humiliation; loss of social standing, advantages of a real home; a twisted upbringing). But the baron shares with his far less trained wife the human frailty of not being able to rise above the need to indulge in self-defence. For anyone who has witnessed a divorce trial, *The Bond* should be particularly pertinent in the "washing of the dirty linen in public" (the charges and the countercharges) and in its presentation of marital love-hate.

Three of Strindberg's major conclusions about people and their community are stated memorably in *The Bond:*

JUDGE: In any event, it's ghastly to see two human beings who have loved each other try to destroy each other like this! It's like watching animals butchered!
PASTOR: That is love, Judge!
JUDGE: What is hate, then?
PASTOR: The lining of the garment!

and

PASTOR: One becomes that [a terrible skeptic] when one's sixty and has cared for human souls for forty years. Lying persists like original sin, and I think all people lie; we lie out of fear as children; out of self-interest, necessity, for self-preservation when we get older. I know people who lie out of pure human kindness. In this case, so far as these two are concerned, I think you'll have a hard time figuring out who comes closest to speaking the truth.

These two matters — love-hate and the basic flaw in human nature (lying to protect one's ego and one's interests or to be kind) — are linked, of course, to Strindberg's striking presentation of the imperfections of the laws set up and applied by human beings.

The Bond is one of the great plays about divorce. It is probably as wise a statement as has ever been made about marital discord, separation and divorce, and the price not only the child but the parents, too, pay.

VIII   Two Potboilers

The People of Hemsö: A Folk Comedy in Four Acts (1889) is a dramatization of episodes in the great novel. On February 17, 1889, Strindberg wrote to Gustaf af Geijerstam, just then advising the powers at *Södra Teatern* in Stockholm: "The piece is like this: Four good, superior acts. One setting; the fishing room in various lightings and furniture that varies as the luxury increases. 12 roles. The tone of a folkcharacter play, coarsely comic, but strictly unified and extremely effective. Ends with the wedding which is a Bambocciad [a depiction of scenes from low folklife] without going beyond the limits [of decorum]" [*Brev,* VII, 1769].

On February 19, 1889, he wrote more frankly to Ola Hansson: "I have stooped to dramatizing *The People of Hemsö* for *Södra Teatern*!!! so that I can write more tragedies" [*Brev,* VII, 1771]. Although the folk comedy was a potboiler designed to bring him enough income so that he could get on with his work — the creation of serious literature — the play has enough merits to have served as popular entertainment quite often in Swedish folk parks.

One of the strangest plays ever written is *The Keys to Heaven or St. Peter Wanders on Earth: A Fairytale Play in Five Acts* (1892). The story of the Smith's pilgrimage with St. Peter to find the lost keys of heaven is unbelievably cluttered with matters involving Don Quixote, Sancho Panza, Tom Thumb, the Wandering Jew, the Old Man of Ho Cliff [5], Cinderella, Romeo and Juliet getting ready for their silver wedding, the Pope, a woman leper (who supplies the love interest), Doctor Allknowing, dwarfs, and others. Apparently concocted as a potboiler when he missed his children (whose custody had been awarded to Siri) and he needed money for child support and other expenses, the play does have a moving first scene depicting a father's distress over the loss of his children, does have some pre-Inferno foreshadowings of his dreamplays, and may very well have served as a source of ideas for later writers.

CHAPTER 9

Dramatist of Penetration
and Representation

Twelve years ago I committed hara-kiri; I executed my old self. ...

    Yes, I remember you were stupid enough ... to confess publicly ... all your faults and weaknesses ...

    ... after ten years of suffering when I had set things right, it occurred to me that I ought to confess your sins, too!

— The Great Highway

I   *The Resumption of Creative Writing*

STRINDBERG was delighted he could write plays again when his Inferno crisis was over.[1] He believed he had an assigned mission as a medium or instrument of Providence. In terms that Strindberg had known since early childhood, that had been reinforced throughout his lifetime, and emphatically driven home to him during the Inferno years, he was to confess his sins publicly, testify first about himself and then about others, and, in the process, interpret human beings, their world, and their finite knowledge of and shadowy relationship with Providence and the powers. All his post-Inferno works are part of that program: his autobiographical volumes, novels, novellas, short stories, poetry, essays, memoranda for the theater, *Blue Books*, contributions to public debate, and certainly his thirty-six plays.

Of the extremely personal plays, four (*To Damascus*, I, II, III, and *The Great Highway*) are devoted primarily to the author himself, the first three concentrated on his flaws and weaknesses, his self-conviction of sin, his public confessions of sin, and his post-confession situation. His last play took a close look at the author's whole life as his journey on the great highway of living.

One play — *A Dream Play* — extends such matters to all humanity; several — *Advent, Easter, There Are Crimes and Crimes,* the dance-of-death plays, and the chamber plays — are dramas of testimony, primarily about other human beings he knew personally, and the fifteen historical dramas dramas of testimony about people of the past. *The Crown Bride* and *Swanwhite* deal with the folk, the first with folk in the mid-nineteenth century, the second with folklore, presumably medieval. Even the two plays primarily designed for children — *Casper's Shrove Tuesday* and *Abu Casem's Slippers* — fit into his newly reacquired pattern of faith in a moral world with its finite human beings, still subject to the factors of heredity and environment, time and chance, with watchful forces in control of all four and with the individual human being burdened with the responsibility of choice and accountable for his actions.

Religion and morality always played major roles for Strindberg. As a child and as a youngster, he had been exposed to and influenced by pietism and Lutheranism: Terms such as sin, faith, doubt, guilt, conviction of sin, backsliding, free-thinking, damnation, salvation, hell, heaven, eternal punishment, and reward were terms that were very real to him always, even if exposure to the liberal theism of Theodore Parker's Unitarianism gave him some respite from gnawing torturous concern about his spiritual and moral condition as a young man; and free-thinking (atheism, agnosticism) may have given him some relief in the 1880s and early 1890s.

Then during his period of genuine suffering came his exposure to such matters as occultism, theosophy, hypnotism, telepathic suggestion, alchemy, spiritualism, sorcery and witchcraft, and, far from least, Emanuel Swedenborg's visions of heaven and hell and of earth. All of these matters related very directly to himself and to the universal and timeless questions about Man, the universe, and the supernatural, questions about the origin and the nature of human beings, their relationship with higher powers that might exist and be in control, man's freedom of will, his possible responsibility, the meaning of this life, and the possibility of a hereafter.

In the pre-Inferno autobiographical volumes, the emphasis is on his perception of actual outward experiences that his senses could take in. But even in these pre-Inferno volumes, he did not neglect the distortions of actuality his limitations imposed on his reporting of how heredity, time, and chance had shaped his environment, and he succeeded to a remarkable degree in revealing his inner life, his feelings, his thoughts. His Inferno experiences led to still greater concern about his own nature and spiritual condition, the meaning of whatever happened to him and what he did, and the nature of his relationship with divinity and its powers.

II   *The Damascus Trilogy*

In his most influential post-Inferno plays, he examined the inner life against the backdrop of outer actuality and represented his findings on the stage to be seen and heard by others. The substance was a combination of dreamstate inner perceptions and outer reality as perceived by the limited senses, and the form was what some scholars have labelled Expressionistic but that he called dreamplay:

In this dream play as in his earlier dreamplays *To Damascus*, the author has tried to imitate the disconnected but apparently logical form of a dream. Everything can happen; everything is possible and likely. Time and space do not exist; on an insignificant basis of reality the imagination spins and weaves new patterns: a blending of memories, experiences, free inventions, absurdities, and improvisations. — Prefatory note to *A Dream Play*.

If one takes the dream in its broadest meanings and does not limit it to the obvious dream proper, all his post-Inferno nonhistorical dramas are essentially dreamplays, and even some of the historical dramas have dreamplay elements.

Certain characteristics of the Strindbergian dreamplays, most of which Carl E. W. L. Dahlström[2] noted years ago, are crucial to understanding them: their deliberate subjectivity ("emanation of the ego"); their expression of the inner man (his dream world, his Unconscious); his search for the spiritual, the elemental, the ecstatic; his use of lyricism and musical counterpoint; his search for the divine; and their assertion of the dignity of the human individual. Inevitable distortion, reliance on synthesis rather than analysis, characters that are types rather than complex and dynamic Strindbergian characterless characters, and close ties to periods of faith rather than to periods of doubt are also involved in Strindberg's projection of inner reality into visible outer representation.

In the Damascus trilogy Strindberg put into dramatic form his Inferno experiences which led to his conversion to his own brand of Christianity and earlier experiences as well, particularly matters of commission and omission that had made him feel guilty. Applying St. Paul's journey [3] to Damascus to himself, Strindberg presented in the trilogy detailed testimony about his own life and personality, his own record as a rebel, and his own conversion and reluctant submission.

The simplified diagram on the next page indicates the broad outline of its structure and suggests its substance.

The pilgrimage or wandering concerns Strindberg's journey through his private hell of rebellion and guilt to his coming to some sort of terms with himself, with others, and with divinity and its powers. The dream experiences stem from his setting his imagination free to play with actual experiences, his deliberate speculating about anything that came to mind or that the Unconscious had to offer or that memory served up — in distorted form. These plays deal far less with the appearance of outer actuality than they do with inner reality.

The Damascus trilogy is an attempt to let the theatergoer or the reader witness a sensitive human being's attempt to penetrate below the surface, to plumb the depths of the self, the ego, the persona, and to find reconciliation. These three plays, along with the post-Inferno autobiographical volumes, were Strindberg's public confession of faults and weaknesses. In both substance and structure the plays have affected the development of modern drama.

III   Advent (*1898*)

In *Advent*   Strindberg presented the advent season's message of the good news of salvation as he understood it in an astonishing combination of childlike and adult experiences. Labelling the play a fairytale tragedy with mysticism, he made it an examination of self-righteousness on the part of a judge and his wife. The two share abundantly in the human ability to rationalize, to lie to oneself as well as to others, and to distort truth to make life comfortable for oneself. The play examines human evil and its effects, but it also examines human goodness and its effects — as

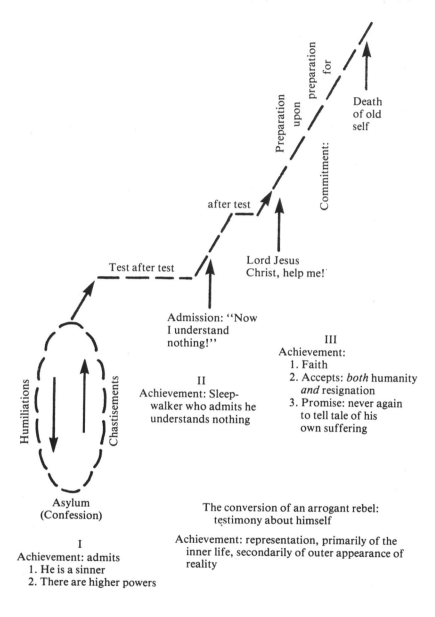

Preparation upon preparation for

Death of old self

Commitment:

after test

Lord Jesus Christ, help me!

Test after test

Admission: "Now I understand nothing!"

III
Achievement:
1. Faith
2. Accepts: *both* humanity *and* resignation
3. Promise: never again to tell tale of his own suffering

II
Achievement: Sleep-walker who admits he understands nothing

Humiliations

Chastisements

Asylum
(Confession)

The conversion of an arrogant rebel: testimony about himself

Achievement: representation, primarily of the inner life, secondarily of outer appearance of reality

I
Achievement: admits
1. He is a sinner
2. There are higher powers

observed and interpreted by children and by adults.

The contrasts between appearance and reality are applied directly to the apparently fortunate aging couple who in moments of control count themselves a model couple and the dreamlike self-scrutiny when the control that permits rationalization and self-deception is not functioning. *Advent* is a modern morality play, many of the elements of which reflect Strindberg's very great interest in the Middle Ages: for example, the procession of shadows led by Death, allegory, the Other One (Satan on his way to salvation), the ball (a dance of death in reverse in which the Other One is master of ceremonies and the seven deadly sins are in attendance about the throne of royal sinners, an orchestra that plays but produces no sounds), a trial scene which takes place in the minds of the sinners, and childlike, naïve scenes involving children and the Christ-child.

IV   There Are Crimes and Crimes (*1899*)

Strindberg considered his next play, *There Are Crimes and Crimes*, *Advent*'s companion and had the two plays published together under the covering title *Before a Higher Court* (*Vid högre rätt).* Just as *Advent* deals with the breaking of human and moral laws whether detected or not, the other play examines the commission of crimes and sins that are a matter of wish and thought, whether intended or not. As Strindberg said, "I've now wanted to deal with the problem of the Evil Will and the responsibility for evil thoughts and the individual's court of self-punishment" [*Brev,* XIII, 4019].

But Strindberg knew that good and evil may very well be interwoven in a web that is hard or impossible to disentangle, so in a four-act play that has a fairly happy ending for the attractive and decent Maurice Gérard, he presents an important aspect of his testimony about crime and punishment. Maurice commits such "crimes" as rejoicing over the success of his play on a Paris stage, celebrating that triumph with a demonic woman who has helped a friend get rid of an unwanted pregnancy, neglecting the faithful woman he loves, and indulging in loose and careless remarks about matters that have popped into his mind.

There Are Crimes and Crimes has always appealed to actors, directors, audiences, and readers: It is decidedly actable, has touches of both humor and irony, a vital group of characters, and, perhaps as important, universally and timelessly applicable ideational content: the problems of the individual's responsibility for his thoughts and wishes and for carelessly putting both into words.

V   Midsummer (*1900*)

Swedes deserve the reputation of arranging celebrations impressively and effectively, whether it be the formal and solemnly controlled awarding of Nobel Prizes or making Midsummer a decidedly special and unrestrained occasion for Swede and foreigner alike. Back in 1888, Strindberg had used a Swedish Midsummer celebration as a key factor in *Lady Julie*. In 1900, when he wrote *Midsummer: A Serious Comedy in Six Tableaus*, he confused his intention of writing a comedy about a Midsummer celebration in Stockholm and its skerries with his ongoing intention of presenting testimony about human behavior. As a result, *Midsummer* is an amazing drama that is interesting as a revelation of his attitudes toward Stockholm, the islands, and Midsummer — when read — and could conceivably serve well as a scenario for a film on Swedish folk life at the turn of the century. But it is not a play fit for the stage although, if cut and otherwise adapted, it might serve very well in an outdoor summer theater.

The story line is a web of overlapping plots none of which is developed with care and logic. Even if one takes the story of the student Ivar Larsson, the nasty, arrogant, and far from brilliant student who passed the entrance examinations by cheating, as the apparently central plot, its development must be judged as slight, fragmentary, and, in terms of its principal's "conversion," unconvincing. The gist of the ideational content is clear enough: "Everything repeats itself, even the good," "human beings are to be pitied," and it is a good thing to be resigned to the human condition and to be decent to oneself and others.

VI   Casper's Shrove Tuesday (*1900*)

One of the thoroughly interesting elements in *Midsummer* is the puppet play, *Kasperspelet*, that Strindberg inserted as one part of Stockholm Midsummer entertainment. An expanded version, *Casper's Shrove Tuesday: A Play for Lent*, is apparently proof of

Strindberg's appreciation of one type of theatrical entertainment he was exposed to very early and — without emphasizing the point — an illustration of the human tendency to be amused by conflicts, misunderstanding, and physical abuse — of others. Seen in production, the little morality play is primarily a rather delightful reminder of a once-popular type of public entertainment.

VII   Easter (*1900*)

The three-act passion play, *Easter*, is a curiously happy combination of elements of the church's celebration of Holy Week or the Week of Suffering and the welcome return of spring to the North. The form, as Strindberg said, comprises the three acts of the passion play: the day of purification culminating in partaking of the flesh and blood at communion services; the long, long Good Friday (*Långfredag*) of suffering and death, a suffering that can ennoble; and the evening before the resurrection with the promise and the bringing of hope. Parallel to all this is the human joy as the harsh northern winter gives way to sunlight and warmth, to renewal of life in nature.

Strindberg applied the Easter message of hope to a human family suffering misfortune upon misfortune appreciably due to egotistic concern with self rather than to external blows over which they have no control. The nicely presented characters include a stubborn and arrogant adult son, a mother and wife who pretends she believes her husband imprisoned for forgery is innocent but really knows better, a sensitive young boy capable of rising above egotistic concern with self, a prospective daughter-in-law who is no longer a sleepwalker, an elderly man who knows the ways of the world but who has achieved both acceptance of humanity and resignation, and Eleonora, a teenager who is "a poetic figure of light in a world heavy with bitterness."

Impressionistic and dreamplay elements are subtly interwoven in *Easter*: The music from Haydn's *The Seven Last Words of Christ* underscores the dominant mood and atmosphere — among them, fear, anxiety, and anguish giving way to hope; distortion of both tangible people (Lindkvist, for example) and intangibles (other people's attitudes) as well as essentially realistic details; the interpretation of Eleonora as a Christ figure; and poetic overtones. The contrasting roles of Eleonora, an "innocent" on the way to

Christlike self-sacrifice and self-negation, and of Elis, a resentful and arrogant egotist who is forced to his knees in acknowledgment of his own inadequacy and of the existence of good make Strindberg's interpretation of the Easter message believably human and comfortingly warm.

VIII   The Dance of Death, *I and II* (*1900*)

Strindberg's fascination with human beings and their behavior, his conversion, and his great interest in the Middle Ages were factors that account for the superb quality of the companion plays, *The Dance of Death* I and II. Turning his attention from his own failures in marriage to that of two people close to him, he observed, distorted what he observed as finite beings will, and concluded the two principals were engaged in a nightmarish marital hell, a pattern of human misery as real as Christians have imagined Hell will be.

The story in *Dance of Death* I is the story of a marital hell created by a frustrated army officer and a frustrated would-be actress living at the end of twenty-five years on an island called Little Hell. *Dance of Death* II tells the story of the same wife and husband, the latter now retired and so free to go to work as a vampire who steals things, ideas, and people. In keeping with the medieval dance of death, these modern ones emphasize the grotesque and the horrible in the marriage by making every line and every nuance of action thoroughly believable as parts of unreasoning torture of each other and pointless self-deception. The first play ends in a grimly humorous scene: two aging combatants about to plan the celebration of their silver wedding.

The second play is only in points of emphasis a reversal of the first: The setting is not the gray cold prison of the first but the beautifully arranged home of the one person who has befriended the couple in their isolation; the theme of the retired officer as a vampire is dominant, the theme of the possible repetition of the pattern has become very important, but the theme of the marital hell is secondary. The second play is devoted to the retired officer's active manipulation of his genuinely alive daughter, his friend, and his friend's son in order to gain sustenance for himself: things, ideas, and people.

In these "nightmare" plays which are startlingly effective blends of realistic-naturalistic and dreamplay techniques, Strindberg has created unforgettable characters: Edgar, the frustrated officer who becomes one of the living dead and a practicing vampire; Alice, the frustrated coquettish army wife who has almost sunk to the level of troll; Kurt, the friend, who has achieved acceptance of humanity as well as resignation to other imperfections in living; Judith, a young woman who could become her father's image but who also has the capacity to love; and Allan, a sensitive young man who shows no signs yet of becoming a troll.

IX The Crown Bride (*1901*)

The Crown Bride was not only an expression of Strindberg's interest in the past and the folk but a play designed to rival contemporary neo-Romantic artists' exploitation of Swedish folk culture, past and present. For example, Carl Larsson's and Anders Zorn's paintings, Erik Axel Karlfeldt's poetry, Karl-Erik Forsslund's poetic prose, not to mention nameless folk artists from Dalarna, the western mountain province famous for its retention of traditional speech, folkways, beliefs, practices, and arts. Strindberg had, as we have seen, become interested in folk culture even before doing research for his *The Swedish People* (1882), so *The Crown Bride* represents a return to a scrutiny of a way of life strikingly different from that of his native Stockholm.

The six-scene folk tragedy examines in depth the crime of adultery committed by a girl brought up in a community where wearing a bridal crown was the reward for retaining her virginity. Against the cultural background of genuine folk tradition, genuine faith, and genuine folk ways, Kersti commits her sins (adultery and child murder), tries to wear the bridal crown, receives her punishment, and is saved through penitence and death.

The Crown Bride is no idyllic folk drama about love but a very effective combination of folk drama, psychological revelation of character, a rich tapestry from the folk life of the Dales, a serious treatment of crime and punishment, and an extension of the imagination in the manner of the dreamplays. The play presents much about the introverted members of a patriarchal society who say little, mean much, and are understood by each other; it uses the Dalesmen's love of music and song, capitalizing on lures (*lur*) and fiddles. Kersti's development from a beautiful but hardened young girl through murder, pretence to the right to wear the crown, the awakening of her conscience, confession, imprisonment, and refusal of reprieve from punishment, and a multitude of visual illusions and cultural phenomena are subtly woven into a thoroughly convincing interpretation of one woman's crime and punishment.

X   Swanwhite (*1901*)

Aside from the fact that Strindberg admitted the play resulted directly from his falling in love with Harriet Bosse, in *Swanwhite* it is clearly his intention to dramatize a hymn to love which is pure or spiritual and dominates over physical love. The plot is simple enough: The daughter of a medieval duke is persecuted by her wicked stepmother, falls in love with and is loved by a young prince, is courted by a sensual young king, loses her prince who drowns, but through her love, purity, and mercy, she succeeds in bringing him back to life.

The stylized stage set suggests the setting in the Middle Ages, an age of childlike faith, myth, imagination, and antitheses. The stylized dialog — laconic, elliptic, epigrammatic — is in keeping with dialog in folktales and folksongs just as the characters are as impressionistically presented as those in folktales.

But Strindberg made the play far more explicit. Folk wisdom is pretty well hidden though always present in the folktales. Strindberg makes it clear that he is presenting an unfortunate family situation, a close scrutiny of evil and the means of coping with it, and a decidedly pertinent commentary on the difficulties of passing from childhood to adulthood and of learning the facts of the human condition and adjusting to them.

It is a charming play which can evoke a childlike response or, with some suspension of disbelief, even a sophisticated adult's appreciation.

XI   A Dream Play (*1901*)

The two finest statements Strindberg ever made about *A Dream Play* [5] are the prefatory note and his explanation in a letter to Emil Schering: "To understand *The Dream Play*? Indra's daughter has descended to Earth to find out how human beings have it: And there she learns how difficult life is. And the worst is: Injuring or doing evil to others if one wants to live. The form is motivated in a preface: The conglomeration out of a dream in which, however, there is a definite logic. Everything *nonsensical* becomes believable. Human beings appear at several points and are sketched, the sketches flow together, the same person splits into several persons only to flow into one again" [*Brev,* XIV, 4715].

His purpose was then to interpret and judge human life primarily through what dream or dreamlike states have to testify about it when they are not controlled by consciousness or censors and only secondarily through what the senses and reasoning power offer. The material was to be that which is served up by dreamstates, by memory, by imagination, and by the Unconscious.

The form of *A Dream Play* is an imitation of the dream proper, the loose flow to the mind of ideationally related elements, particularly from the Unconscious and the memory, supplemented by elements from the poet's imagination or, if you will, flights of the poet's fantasy.

A basis of outer reality consists of echoes from the dreamer's waking past as adapted, recorded, and stored. To present all this material visibly Strindberg used symbols, some of the most important of which are the Growing Castle (the physical prison of the soul), the chrysanthemum (the soul struggling for expression and ultimate freedom), the shawl (the accumulation of human misery), the secret door (the riddle of life, the meaning of life), Victoria (the ideal woman, always longed for, never attained), the green fishing box (but not *that* green!), Agnes (an incarnated Victoria = womanhood = the dreamer's hope for adjustment to life through woman).

The refrain, "Human beings are to be pitied," states the theme that life on earth is rarely interrupted suffering, that the cause for that suffering is human egotistic, selfish desire for love (Agnes and the lawyer, Ugly Edith, Alice, the naval officer), for power and place (the wealthy shipowner), for possessions (the guests at Fairhaven, the doorkeeper), for recognition and fame, knowledge. And human nature? "All these are my children!" says Agnes; "Each one by himself is good, but all you have to do to turn them into demons is to bring them together." The play illustrates in one area of life after the other the conflicts that result from human beings' desire for perfection right now and of the imperfect nature of finite life itself. Human beings, says Strindberg, are extremely limited creatures, whose key problem is the control of the ego in the imperative adjustment to others and to life itself. And, since the possibilities for improving, not to say perfecting, human beings and life itself are slight but worth making, the individual's greatest need is to accept human beings (himself included) for what they are and resign himself to the imperfections of life about which one can do nothing.

Since *A Dream Play* has been and is a highly seminal play, Strindberg's out-and-out subjectivity, expression of the inner man, his emphasis on the ecstatic, his use of lyricism and musical counterpoint, his search for the divine (an outside point of reference), his assertion of the dignity of human beings (not merely naked apes), his use of antitheses (Fairhaven and Foulstrand), his synthetic rather than analyzed characters ("types" rather than "characterless" characters), his use of distortion (that of the senses as well as that of the Conscious and the Unconscious) are elements which make this play one of the greatest in world literature.

XII   The Chamber Plays

Always interested in and amazingly well informed about music, a bit of a composer, and an amateur performer on the flute, the guitar, and the piano, Strindberg used music in various plays and applied such musical techniques as counterpoint in his dramatic composition. In 1907 he did even more by composing four chamber plays for his Intimate Theater (1907 - 1910), the little theater in Stockholm in which for the first time all the offerings were to be his plays directed by his good friend August Falck, watched over with great care by himself, and performed by enthusiastic young actors:

Last year Reinhardt went the whole way by opening the Kammer-Spiel-Haus [in 1906], which by its very name indicates the real program: the concept of chamber music transferred to drama. The intimate action, the highly significant motif, the sophisticated treatment. ...

If anyone asks what it is an intimate theater wants to achieve and what is meant by chamber plays, I can answer like this: we seek the strong, highly significant motif, but with limitations. We try to avoid in the treatment all frivolity, places for applause, star roles, solo numbers. No predetermined form is to limit the author, because the motif determines the form. Consequently: freedom in treatment, which is limited only by the unity of the concept and the feeling for style. — *Open Letters to the Intimate Theater*, 19.

So he was composing chamber plays that demanded ensemble playing, a new cooperative and dedicated style of acting, and simplified staging: He wrote *Stormy Weather, The House That Burned, The Ghost Sonata, The Pelican* in 1907, and added *The Black Glove* in 1909.

A Dream Play is, among other things, a presentation of the earth as the world in which human beings must try to make their home. The chamber plays deal essentially with individual homes — *Stormy Weather* is set in an apartment house whose inhabitants for good reason call it "the silent house"; *The House That Burned* takes a close look at a family house that had not been the home it seemed to be; *The Ghost Sonata* is anything but the home of beauty and refinement it seems to be; and *The Pelican* is a presentation of a dwelling in which the dance of death did not end with the death of the husband. *The Black Glove* deals with an apartment house in which various people indulge in selfishness and cruelty.

Stormy Weather (Opus 1) deals with loneliness as exemplified in the lives of a number of people trying to eke out a bearable existence by withdrawal into solitude. The quiet and the isolation are broken for the aging gentleman rather comfortably by brief but welcome contacts with a few others and most uncomfortably by the reappearance of his younger ex-wife and her second husband. It is her reappearance that provides the stormy weather, which gives way to the silence and peace implicit in a line such as "I'm settling my accounts with life and people, and I've already started packing for the journey. Living alone is so-so, of course, but when no one else has any claims on one, one does have freedom. Freedom to go and come, think and act, eat and sleep as one wants to."

The play is a thorough application of Strindberg's definition of a chamber play: The plot is slight; characterization is more a matter of suggestion than analysis; every character has an important role to play in the presentation of human loneliness; the atmosphere and the mood are highly important. The silent house has little of the warm comfort of human comradeship that Strindberg believed a home should have; yet it does have the cold comfort of a place into which to retreat from the struggles of life.

The House That Burned (Opus 2) is a strangely moving presentation of the impossibility of going home again in any comforting sense: Arvid Valström, a stranger to others and to himself, returns to his childhood neighborhood only to find that his "home" has literally been destroyed by fire and that the neighbors and his brother are quite willing to destroy it figuratively by blurting out the truth about his parents, his family, and their neighbors. The block is appropriately named the Morass or the Swamp (Swedes have the practice of naming city blocks): "We all know each other, for there's something special about this street. The people who once move in here never get away from it; that's to say, the ones who move away always come back, sooner or later, until they're taken to the cemetery up at the end of the street. ... And all of us hate each other, slander each other, torture each other. ..."

In *The House That Burned*, Strindberg dealt superbly with the differences between appearance and reality in the "home," with the human desire to belong, to have friends and neighbors in meaningful, enrichening ways, and with, as Strindberg saw it, the essentially unbreakable isolation and loneliness of the human individual.

The Ghost Sonata (Opus 3) deserves the extensive attention and general approval accorded it by readers, audiences, and theater people: Its structure and its substance are such that it has rivalled *A Dream Play* both as literature and as theater. These two plays have apparently become the outstanding representatives of Strindberg's greatest impact on modern drama and modern theater abroad; most Swedes and many other Scandinavians have been fortunate enough, however, to have chances to see in performance other post-Inferno plays rivaling them in importance.

As the title suggests, Strindberg has adapted such techniques as the division into three parts or movements and the statement, development, and recapitulation of two contrasting themes from the sonata form, specifically from that of Beethoven's Piano Sonata in D Minor (Opus 31, No. 2). The play is indeed in three parts: the vision of the home and the people in it as they seem to be, their unmasking and stripping (of all artificial props, including lies), and the presentation of a doctrine that can make life on earth bearable. The two contrasting themes — transferred from the idiom of one art form into that of another — are *perfectionism* as represented by Arkenholz, the student, and *vampirism* as represented by Hummel. When applied as they inevitably will be, both destroy, says Strindberg.

While *The Ghost Sonata* is not based structurally on the form of the dream proper, it belongs, as Strindberg believed, with the dreamplays: In its cruel revelation of truth about a "home" by stripping it of all pretence and revealing the truth with its distortions, the play is a nightmare evoked by a creative observer. As he said in his prefatory note to *A Dream Play*, absurdities do show up when controls are not functioning: Note, for example, the vampire cook and her role.

In *The Ghost Sonata* the inhabitants of one apartment and two outsiders, the manipulator and exploiter of others and the idealistic young student, provide one of Strindberg's most vital statements about the human condition, another and even more striking demonstration of his conviction that human beings are to be pitied. The aging inhabitants of the aristocratic apartment house may in Strindbergian terms have become the living dead who, ghostlike, go through the motions of living, but the lengths to which even an idealist may go in his demands for getting at the truth is a matter of some importance. Strindberg's doctrine is acceptance of human beings as imperfect creatures and resignation to the facts of earthly existence.

The Pelican (Opus 4) is a sort of sequel to *The Dance of Death* I and II: It is, as Swedish scholars insist, a reexamination of the relative guilt of husband and wife in making their marriage a marital hell and in preventing their children from developing into healthy human adults. The plot is slight enough: The husband is dead, a psychic suicide as well as the victim of psychic murder; the son and the daughter are distressingly incomplete; the mother is still a sleepwalker who refuses to examine the truth about herself as a person, a wife, a mother, and a mother-in-law. When awakened, she cannot bear the implications of reality (the pose of the self-sacrificing mother versus the actuality of being an egotistic vampire who has destroyed her husband and crippled her children).

It is a strange "house" that has never been a "home" except in name. The chamber play, again with all the voices — mother, children, son-in-law, servant, and even the dead father — contributing to the ensemble is decidedly stageworthy.

According to Strindberg's stage directions, *The Ghost Sonata* ends with the death of Adéle; then:

(*The room disappears; Böcklin's Island of the Dead [the painting]*[6]*becomes the backdrop; soft, quiet, pleasantly sad music can be heard from outside.*)

Shortly afterwards when he was writing *The Pelican,* he started a chamber play that was to be called *The Island of the Dead* or *Hades* (*Toten-Insel*) and was to depict awakening after death and life in the hereafter. Unfortunately, he never finished the play, and, equally unfortunately, he had burned a play which he considered so brutally true to life he did not dare to leave it intact.

The fragment is intensely interesting: A teacher has died, is awakened on the island of the dead, is still harassed by all the pressing duties of his profession and by all the problems at home and in the community. Almost any of the longer speeches can suggest the rich possibilities. Take, for example, one colleague's evaluation of the dead man:

As a colleague and competitor he was like a wild beast; in company a lamb; as a superior thoroughly humane; as a teacher a model; as an underling a monster; as a husband faithful for he loved only her the bride of his youth; as a father, he gave his children more than himself; as a master indulgent; as a citizen law abiding ...; as a son sacrificing for an inferior father, respectful of his mother beyond what she deserved; variable toward his brothers and sisters as they, false toward the false, faithless toward the faithless; a faithful friend but not always.

His wife testifies that he was the worst tyrant that ever lived.

The Black Glove: A Lyric Fantasy for the Stage in Five Acts (Opus 5) is quite different from the first four chamber plays. While it does have elements of that sort of play, it has, unfortunately, a great many other elements that distract one from one "strong, highly significant motif but with limitations" by including several, every one of which deserves primary attention. Written partly at least as a Christmas play, it reminds one more of *The Journey of Lucky Peter* (1882) than of the first four chamber plays: its plot, its use of allegory, the appearance of make-believe creatures (the *tomte* or elf, the Christmas angel), the insertion of a great deal of verse, and deliberately didactic emphasis.

But the play is interesting as another study of a house, this time a large apartment house with a gallery of vulnerable human beings: a beautiful little wife who is kind to her little child but nasty to every one else; an old scholar, the unloved father of the young wife and a lifelong searcher for the meaning of life; Ellen, a faithful servant accused of stealing the young wife's ring but which the young wife has carelessly left in her now lost black glove; Kristin, another remarkably good servant; the caretaker (apartment-house manager) who looks after heating and lighting and serves as a sort of house counselor; a young husband who does not appear. As the young wife says, "This strange house, in which human destinies are piled high on the double floors, the one on top of the other, alongside each other." *The Black Glove* has the makings of several plays.

XIII   Abu Casem's Slippers (*1908*)

In *Abu Casem's Slippers: A Fairytale Play for Old and Young Children in Uncounted Iambs in Five Acts*, Strindberg used motifs developed in a French fairy tale and in *The Arabian Nights*. It tells the story of a penny-pinching father who is a far better man than appearance suggests, the story of a prince and the young woman he loves (a dream has made her suspicious of men, except for older men such as the miser), and the story of a ruler studying his subjects in disguise and ultimately rewarding those who have integrity. Somewhat reminiscent of *The Journey of Lucky Peter*, *Abu Casem's Slippers* has never achieved popularity in spite of rather effective appeal to the naïve and childlike and its Strindbergian blunt presentation of human frailties.

XIV   *The Last Play*

The last play, *The Great Highway: A Drama of Wandering with Seven Stations* (1908), is not easy to stage but is one of the richest in substance: 1) On the Alps: The Hunter's search for his identity and protection of his soul or self; 2) By the windmills: Exposure to other human beings (the impossibility of being left alone, to be uninvolved); 3) In Eseldorf (the village of Jackasses): The struggle to retain personal independence; 4) An arcade in the city: Temptations from within himself and from others; 5) In the park outside the crematory: Consideration of the truth versus the appearance of truth; 6) At the last gate: The price of happiness (fleeting at best); 7) The dark forest: The wanderer and his epitaph. The stations are like the halts or places at which scenes in medieval mystery plays were performed, not the halts for performance of devotions in the church.

Strindberg's *apologia pro vita sua*, it presents his justification for a great many of his acts and certainly contributes to knowledge of his personal history. Many of his contemporaries had berated him for many frailties, not least for ambivalence and inconsistency, for example. His most striking previous justification for changing his mind about people, ideas, and life itself had appeared in the third Damascus play: the monastery gallery with its portraits of great men each of whom is depicted with two or more heads. In *The Great Highway* comes further justification.

A challenging blend of very fine free verse and potent prose, the play is allegorical and symbolic, a series of inner dialogs about the author (the Hermit who has tried to withdraw from involvement in other people's affairs, the Hunter who is still in search of his soul or self, and the Wanderer who has never achieved a lasting home on earth), about the beautiful Earth on which he has his being, and about the Great Teacher, who controls everything while giving his human creatures at least some freedom of choice. The various Strindbergs are still unknown strangers among strangers:

> One travels best Incognito, and believe me
> one should always become acquainted
> but never get to know,
> one doesn't, of course,
> one just thinks one does. ...

Presenting himself as a soldier who has waged war, Strindberg demonstrates subtly that all human beings need correction and that he personally felt called upon to correct many (including such contemporary Swedish writers as Gustaf af Geijerstam, Verner von Heidenstam, and Axel Klinckowström,[7] that happiness is slight and fleeting, and that, in view of everything, human beings are to be pitied. In his post-Inferno years, Strindberg had confessed and testified about himself and about others, and, when life was over, his epitaph would read:

> Here rests Ishmael, son of Hagar,
> who once was called Israel,
> because he had had to fight with God,
> and did not give up until brought low,
> overcome by the goodness of His might!
> O eternal God! I will not let go Your hand,
> Your hard hand, before You bless me!
> Bless me, bless Your humanity,

which suffers, suffers from the gift of Life!
Me first, who has suffered most —
who has suffered most from the agony
of being unable to be what I wanted to be.

CHAPTER 10

Dramatist and Historian

Even in the historical drama the purely human is of major interest, and history the background; souls' inner struggles awaken more sympathy than the combat of soldiers or the storming of walls; love and hate, torn family ties more than treaties and speeches from the throne. — *Open Letters to the Intimate Theater*, 266.

I *The Concept of the Historical Drama and the Cycle*

STRINDBERG'S historical dramas were composed during two periods: a handful of plays in the years before 1883, including one masterpiece, two fairly respectable plays, a few apprenticeship pieces, and, after his Inferno period, eleven masterpieces about figures from the Swedish past and four less happy ones about non-Swedish figures. He did not write historical plays during the years in the 1880s and 1890s when he considered himself a free-thinker and an atheist. Interested though he was in puppets and marionettes as such, he could never quite equate them with human beings. "The Great Synthesist" had provided for freedom of the human will to a certain degree.[1]

The Swedes have good reason to be grateful to Strindberg for creating a cycle of plays about their history from the Middle Ages to the late eighteenth century: With the exception of England, no other nation has such a cycle, either quantitatively or qualitatively.[2]

The cycle[3] includes *Master Olof* (1872) and eleven post-Inferno plays, here listed by time periods rather than by date of writing:

Earl Birger of Bjälbo, the late 1200s
  Earl Birger, regent, 1250 - 66; Valdemar I, king, 1250 - 75; Magnus Barnlock, king, 1275 - 90; Birger Magnusson, king, 1290 - 1318; (Torgils Knutsson, regent, 1290 - 98)
The Saga of the Folkungs, middle 1300s
  Magnus Eriksson, king, 1319 - 64; Erik XII, co-king, 1357 - 59;

Håkon, king, 1362 - 71; Albrekt of Mecklenburg, king, 1364 - 89
Engelbrekt, the 1430s
    Margaret, regent, 1389 - 1412; Erik XIII of Pomerania, king, 1396 - 1439; Engelbrekt, folk leader, 1435 - 36
The Last of the Knights, 1512 - 20
    Karl Knutsson Bonde, regent, 1436 - 40; king, 1448 - 57, 1464 - 65, 1467 - 70; Christopher, king, 1440 - 48; Christian I, king, 1457 - 64; Sten Sture the Elder, regent, 1470 - 97; 1501 - 03; Hans, king, 1497 - 1501; Svante Sture, regent, 1504 - 12; Sten Sture the Younger, regent, 1512 - 20; Christian II, king, 1520 - 21
The Regent, early 1520s
    Gustav Vasa, regent, 1521 - 23; king, 1523 - 60
Master Olof, 1520s - 40s
    The Lutheran Reformation
Gustav Vasa, 1540s
Erik XIV, 1560s
    Erik, king, 1560 - 68; John III, king, 1568 - 92; Sigismund, king, 1592 - 99; Charles IX, regent, 1599 - 1604; king, 1604 - 11
Gustav Adolf, 1630 - 32
    Gustav II Adolf, king, 1611 - 32
Queen Christina, 1654
    Christina, queen, 1632 - 54; Charles X Gustav, king, 1654 - 60; Charles XI, king, 1660 - 97
Charles XII, 1715 - 18
    Charles XII, king, 1697 - 1718; Ulrika Eleonora, reigning queen, 1718 - 20; Fredrik I, king, 1720 - 51
Gustav III, 1789
    Adolf Fredrik, king, 1751 - 71; Gustav III, king, 1771 - 92; Gustav IV Adolf, king, 1792 - 1809; Charles XIII, king, 1809 - 18

Easily and economically each play ties up with its predecessor and its successor: Strindberg knew well that the roots of the present lie in the past.

The never-ending struggle for power and the never-ending search for internal law and order give unity to the cycle; their treatment varies in depth and meaningfulness according to the perceptiveness of the central characters. Strindberg subtly wove into the fabric of each play the economic, political, social, artistic, religious, ethical, and intellectual elements of the evolving cultural patterns, both at home and abroad.

Such matters rarely detract from the primary core of the rich literary quality — the dynamic, complex characters, varied and individualized with as much attention to their inner beings as to their appearance and external behavior. Medieval Earl Birger of Bjälbo is not merely a cynical opportunist willing to do anything necessary to gain power; King Magnus, the last of the Folkungs, is not merely a dedicated servant of his people; Engelbrekt is far more than a folk leader determined to set his people free; Sten Sture is more than an unrealistic idealist; young Gustav Vasa is an impulsive realist working toward the attainment of an admirable goal; Master Olof is a brilliant reformer who does not see through some implications of his actions; King Gustav Vasa is an administrator who knows what his objectives are but is never satisfied that he has achieved them; Erik XIV, gifted but disturbed, can cope only in cooperation with and through his adviser Göran Persson; Gustav Adolf is not the saint some writers have pictured him; Queen Christina is far more than a sleepwalker; Charles XII has qualities that raise him above the role of Sweden's destroyer; and Gustav III is a cultural and intellectual force, not merely a facile actor on the throne. Each central character becomes a believable being of flesh and blood, a person as "characterless" (i.e., complex and dynamic) as any other human being. The secondary and minor characters are individualized to the degree their roles require. On occasion that can be very great: for example, Archbishop Gustav Trolle, "the Judas Iscariot of Sweden." In *The Last of the Knights* and *The Regent*, Trolle is as thoroughly individualized as the two men who have to cope with him. Strindberg's characters behave as people do, and they speak as people do.

Conversational language is adapted with care to the individual character, his or her mood, and the situation. The range is great: Gustav Vasa does, for example, speak as brutally and frankly as Edgar and Alice in *The Dance of Death* and as gently and tenderly as Lindquist when speaking to Eleonora. Strindberg avoids archaic language.

Strindberg explained his method of gathering historical material, absorbing it and adapting it for theatrical purposes in detail in many places, not least in his *Open Letters to the Intimate Theater*. Wide reading in both scholarly and popular history and in both primary and secondary sources was always his point of departure. He did, what even the effective historian must do — select, arrange, and interpret. He used realistic, impressionistic, and dreamplay (Expressionistic) techniques — as we shall see.

II   Earl Birger of Bjälbo

Earl Birger of Bjälbo is a presentation of a strong man of action in pursuit of power to strengthen Sweden through centralizing its government and enforcing law and order. As Strindberg understood Earl Birger — and historians agree — the earl was a richly endowed human being who dared to think clearly about himself, his fellows, and their environment, who knew that he frequently had to conceal his thinking if he were to achieve his goals, and who was destined to achieve many goals but never to receive the symbolic reward, the crown. While all these matters are clearly the core of the ideational content of the folk drama, theatergoers and readers will undoubtedly find Strindberg's presentation of the earl in his many roles and the people about him in theirs even more fascinating than the attention to ideas.

While Strindberg's final composition apparently came easily and quickly, his own admissions as well as his many notes in the Strindberg Collection in the Royal Library prove that he did a great deal of planning before he served as a sort of medium in writing creatively. He even felt occasional anachronisms were justifiable:

When I began to plan and consider the subject of Earl Birger about ten years ago, I discovered immediately that the material was unmanageable. His long life, with his crusades, disappointments, penance, two marriages, and the children who caused him trouble, was suitable for an epic and not for a drama, if I did not break off a piece that had dramatic force.

At first I thought of taking the whole story and using the chronicle style in Shakespeare's way, ... I noticed the strongest motifs came at the end of his career .... I took the liberty of moving this motif back and combining it with Valdemar's pilgrimage of penance to Rome and Magnus' regency. ... So I knew what liberties I was taking; I knew what the drama was gaining [*Open Letters to the Intimate Theater*, 264-65].

He compressed historical events, but he insisted rightly that he "never unnecessarily violated historic truth." For many of his countrymen his interpretation of great, near-great, and minor figures has become theirs without contradicting in any major fashion interpretations by twentieth-century historians.[4]

III   The Saga of the Folkungs

The Saga of the Folkungs is an even more ambitious historical drama in that it deals with the whole dynasty and a whole epoch. With King Magnus, the last of the Folkungs to occupy the Swedish throne, as the central character, Strindberg has presented an interpretation of a whole period during which crucial and civilizing changes took place in Sweden, not least because of the efforts of one Folkung after the other. King Magnus says to his daughter-in-law: "It's not an attractive family you married into, Blanche. It certainly has provided strong instruments for the hand of Providence — it has brought order out of chaos in our country, it has unified our laws, and made a Christian kingdom out of a badly split and unhappy country. But the Lord sometimes uses dirty instruments. ... Why? That we're never told."

The play has caught nicely the flavor and the atmosphere of the Middle Ages. Complementing its presentation of human beings and their dealings with each other is Strindberg's use of dreamplay elements such as the Plague Girl, the Plague Boy, the Madwoman, sleepwalking, rituals, and symbols, all of them highly appropriate in a play about an age of faith. Capitalizing on the biblical assertion that the sins of the father shall be visited on the children unto the third and fourth generations, he was able to do two things: give a realistic portrayal of the Folkungs and their environment toward the end of their generations of power and, at the same time, reveal his medieval characters' innermost feelings and thoughts through poetic techniques long used in allegory and in lyric poetry.

Strindberg knew how to provide historical atmosphere as well as salient facts about the past not only by settings and stage properties but also by folk scenes and by conversations involving analysis by deeply involved characters. The opening court-barber-shop scene in *The Saga of the Folkungs* is a superb realistic exposition of what people probably observed at the time and prepared the audience for what was likely to take place. King Magnus' analysis of the whole saga of his family's years of power in the last act is an excellent illustration of effective realistic technique.

IV   Engelbrekt

Swedes, Norwegians, and Danes have tried on occasion to unite, but the unions have never been quite satisfactory to any of them in spite of their cultural, historical, and linguistic ties. For the Swedes, the least satisfactory of Scandinavian unions was the so-called Kalmar Union (1397 - 1523), a union dominated by the Danes. In Engelbrekt Engelbrektsson (assassinated in 1436), Strindberg had a folk hero who would serve nicely as the central figure in a play about Swedish resistance to foreign oppression: Engelbrekt had protected the Swedes from the system of serfdom, he had laid the foundation of a national parliament, he had aroused their desire for liberty and strengthened their national consciousness. Strindberg chose the form of the folk drama for his play but went beyond that, as he said in a note: "*Engelbrekt.* A drama of character. A drama of ideas. Miniature scenes, intimate. Engelbrekt's private life is depicted as this is influenced by the great historic events." In *Engelbrekt*, he considers the practical results of a union of closely related but decidedly distinct nationalities including, among other matters, intermarriages, divided loyalties, and generation gaps.

V *Companion Plays*

The Last of the Knights and *The Regent* also deal directly with Swedish struggles to be free of the union. The two are companion plays not least because they deal with the archbishop, Gustav Trolle, who was historically one of the most difficult opponents of both Sten Sture the Younger and Gustav Vasa in their struggles for independence.

In *The Last of the Knights*, Strindberg dealt with a national leader who was not only a Christian in name but a practicing one as well. Like King Magnus in *The Saga of the Folkungs*, Sten Sture the Younger was exposed to the ideals of Christianity and chivalry and the ideals had "taken." The historical accounts of the attempts of an unrealistic idealist, a knight without fear and beyond reproach, to cope with the ambitious and nominally Christian archbishop furnished Strindberg with difficulties and challenges: The presentation of a thoroughly good man is, as Strindberg well knew, likely to devolve into something embarrassingly close to cloying sentimentality and is, in fact, never accurate factually. Except for an occasional slip, Strindberg has avoided that trap by presenting Sten Sture as a good man with human frailties.

Although Strindberg can hardly be called a royalist, he did

acknowledge merits in the kings and the queens, particularly in Gustav Vasa, the first of the great dynasty to sit on the Swedish throne: Gustav Vasa is the central character in *The Regent* and in *Gustav Vasa* and is an exceedingly important character in *Master Olof*. The three plays deal respectively with the young leader about to become king in 1523, the mature king who made Sweden a powerful and unified kingdom, and the young king in his earlier efforts at bringing order out of chaos in post-union and reformation days.

Capitalizing on the legendary stories about Gustav Vasa that Swedes through the generations have known as well as Americans have known the stories about George Washington and Abraham Lincoln, Strindberg in *The Regent* presents Gustav Vasa as the practical man who knows what his country needs, is sure he can supply the necessary leadership, and proceeds to put his plans into execution taking due regard for the imperfections of himself, his fellow human beings, and his environment. His opponents and his enemies, his admirers and every one else about are aware of him and of what he does and almost all would agree with Herman Israel, representative of the Swedes' opportunistic ally, that young Gustav is "... a very wise man, very wise, because in his younger years he had to learn the difficult art of living in a hard school, and Gustav Vasa knows that the ships and the goods weren't what they should have been — there weren't any others — and he knows that the money is defective; but instead of looking a gift horse in the mouth, and wasting time by complaining, he went ahead on rotten ships and with false money, straight to his objective ... in a straight line—."

The Regent is an admirable presentation of a relatively short but crucial segment of Swedish history. Strindberg has, moreover, caught Gustav Vasa at an early stage of his pursuit of power and reestablishment of law and order.

VI   *The Vasa Trilogy*

Strindberg's first great play, *Master Olof* (1872), can be considered from many points of view, not least from that of the generation gap or, if you will, never-ending conflict between conservative elders and rebellious youngsters. In Olaus Petri and Gustav Vasa, history supplied Strindberg with a young and enthusiastic rebel against the Church of Rome and a young and determined king set on a conflict course in their pursuit of freedom, the one interested primarily in release from Roman control and restrictions, the other convinced that the Swedes should have freedom from all foreign control under his guidance and direction. Each is a reformer in his way; each has to work with the other against the aging representatives of churchly and political power and, having overcome the elderly, confront each other. The fact that the play theoretically covers over two decades of Swedish history permitted Strindberg to note subtly the inevitable changes that took place in both protagonists. For pupils in the Swedish schools — *Master Olof* has long been a text — the play probably is the most memorable and enlightening presentation of the men who, perhaps above all others, laid the foundation of modern Sweden.

After his Inferno crisis was over, Strindberg wrote two sequels to *Master Olof* — *Gustav Vasa* and *Erik XIV* — and considered the three the Vasa trilogy. Among the links between the first two is an aging Master Olof reconciled to settling for much less than he had once dreamed, and among the links between the last two are the extremely important roles given Crown Prince Erik and his companion Göran Persson.

The structure of *Gustav Vasa* is set apart from that of the other historical plays by having everyone else keenly aware of the king whether he is on or off stage. "The wonder man of God" does not make his entrance until Act III opens, but, before that, he is constantly felt and is directly or indirectly, the center of attention: "Always this giant hand, which one never sees, only feels" and "When he's furious in the attic, people say they feel it all the way to the cellar just as when it thunders." The biblical story of Job with its accounts of the testing of one man of integrity and its revelations of his inner life serves as a parallel to Gustav's:

The destiny of Gustav Vasa begins like a legend or a miracle story, develops into an epic, and is impossible to survey completely. To get this gigantic saga into one drama is impossible, of course. Therefore the only answer was to find an episode. That was the one centering in the rebellion led by Dacke. The king was then in his second marriage with children by two wives, and at the height of his power. But Providence wanted to test him and temper its man, to whom the building of the kingdom was entrusted, and for that reason it [Providence] struck him with all the misfortunes of Job. That time of despair gives one the best opportunity to depict the great human being Gustav Vasa with all his human weaknesses [*Open Letters to the Intimate Theater*, 255-56].

That is precisely what Strindberg has done superbly in what many consider his greatest historical play.

But its sequel, *Erik XIV*, has received more attention in the theater than *Gustav Vasa*, partly because of Erik XIV's frequently bizarre behavior rather than because of King Erik's plans and efforts on behalf of Sweden and the Swedes. There were, moreover, the king's extremely close relationship to and dependence on his adviser and favorite Göran Persson and the king's marriage to the commoner Karin Månsdotter. *Erik XIV* is not a closely knit concentrated play like *Gustav Vasa* but a loose episodic play fitted remarkably well to the chaotic and irregular behavior of the king and not to the steady pursuit of a clearly defined objective:

Erik XIV is a Hamlet. Stepmother (= stepfather); murders Sture (= murders Polonius); Ophelia =   Karin Månsdotter; Erik XIV dies poisoned as Hamlet does; insane or simulating insanity as Hamlet; vacillating; judges and rejects his judgment; his friend Göran Persson — faithful unto death; Fortinbras = Dukes John and Charles; Hamlet was loved by the uncivilized masses. Erik, too, a hater of the lords and the people's king [*Open Letters to the Intimate Theater*, 80].

The play is an amazingly detailed and believable "case report" on "a characterless human being."

VII   Gustav Adolf

In the 1890s during the neo-Romantic period both writers and readers had an impressive interest in the past: Among the many indications were literary works based on history by major writers such as Verner von Heidenstam, Selma Lagerlöf, and Oscar Levertin; the founding of the famous outdoor museum Skansen in Stockholm; and, not least, the celebration of the tercentennial of the birth of King Gustav II Adolf (1594-1632). That king who, in Swedish opinion, had been a genius, a saint, and a martyr for the cause of Protestantism, struck Strindberg as interesting only after he had gone through his Inferno years and been converted to his own brand of Christianity.

Strindberg stated clearly what changes took place in his understanding of Gustav Adolf and his role in world history after reading extensively about him:

> Then I saw at once his whole character and the whole drama, and I called it my *Nathan the Wise*.
> The blond man with the gentle spirit, who always had a joke ready even in dark moments, very much a statesman and a little of the musketeer, the dreamer about a universal monarchy, our Henri Quatre who loves beautiful women as much as a good battle, half Swedish and half German, with a mother from Holstein and a wife from Brandenburg, related to Pfalz, Prussia, Hesse, Poland, Hungary, Bohemia, and Austria itself, sinful enough to be human, gets into such disharmonies and inner conflicts that make a drama rich and interesting [*Open Letters to the Intimate Theater*, 257-58].

Lessing's *Nathan the Wise* (1779) is, of course, a very long five-act dramatic sermon on religious tolerance and brotherly love set somewhat vaguely in the third crusade in Palestine in the 1190s.

Although tolerance and brotherly love are key ideas in *Gustav Adolf*, Strindberg's monumental play is much more than a plea for those virtues. It is an unbelievably effective presentation of the Thirty Years' War (1618 - 1648), a time when Sweden played a major role in world history. It is, moreover, a drama of character in which Strindberg made Gustav Adolf and many of the people about him live for the reader — few people have ever had a chance to see it on stage: Its length and great demands on the resources of theaters have prevented that.

The play has five acts, fifteen settings, more than fifty characters with lines to speak, many others without lines, and would take about seven hours for performance. The 1912 revision *Gustav Adolf, A Play in Five Acts Adapted for the Stage by the Author* was advertised: "The drama has been cut by half, half the characters have been eliminated, roles have been combined, and the dangerous Vasaborg [Gustav Adolf's illegitimate son] removed although the Vasaborg crypt remains at the rear of Riddarholm Church [the burial place of royalty]." Strindberg was obviously willing to make concessions to get a play produced.

The uncut form could serve beautifully as the basis of a scenario for a film. In a country with as rich traditions, achievements, actors, photographers, and directors as Sweden it strangely enough has not been used by the cinema. Until it is filmed, the uncut play will serve admirably as an interpretation of one of Sweden's periods of greatness and of some of the people who played roles in achieving that greatness.

VIII   Queen Christina

In his historical dramas, Strindberg by no means neglected women although only in one, *Queen Christina*, did he make a woman the central character. He could, of course, have written a play about Birgitta, who helped make life miserable for King Magnus, the last of the Folkungs, and who aspired to power and canonization; he did present her in *The Saga of the Folkungs* as a gifted egotist grasping for control of her environment but not totally untrue to her nature as a woman. The women in the Strindberg plays are as human and varied as the men: Take, for example, Gustav Vasa's lovely Queen Margareta Leijonhufvud, Erik XIV's commoner queen Karin Månsdotter, Gustav Adolf's neurotic wife, the sensitive child Queen Beatrice, and the adulterous, scheming Dowager Duchess Ingeborg.

Gustav Adolf's brilliant daughter, Queen Christina, struck Strindberg as strangely fascinating:

A woman reared to be a man, fighting for her self-existence, against her feminine nature and succumbing to it. The favorites — translated lovers, frankly speaking — but with forbearance for the daughter of the great Gustav Adolf. Stiernhielm includes among her lovers even Holm the tailor, but I did not want to do that. Charge that to my credit, Quiriter! Christina was so genuine a woman that she was a womanhater. In her memoirs she says frankly that women should never be permitted to rule. That she did not want to get married, I think natural and that she who had played with love was caught in her own net, is, of course, highly dramatic [*Open Letters to the Intimate Theater*, 258].

These comments indicate some of the important facts or allegations about the queen, but they do not mention that Queen Christina was very much interested in the theater, that she encouraged and supported theatrical performances and even took part in some, and that it is very easy to think of her as an actress on the throne who had made acting a dominant fact in her behavior in private as well as in public.

It is that sort of understanding that gave Strindberg both structure and substance. The four-act structure of *Queen Christina* is basically that of the well-made play, a highly artificial dramatic form remarkably well suited to the story of a crowned actress. The relevant implication is that the queen usually lived in an artificial world, a world of make-believe rather than in a world of harsh reality, that Christina was a sleepwalker. In presenting her and her story, Strindberg has combined the realism of her environment and the dreamlike quality of her sleepwalking to show not only the sleepwalking but also the awakening. Strindberg has gone far beyond a typical well-made play.

The highly appropriate interweaving of realistic and dreamplay (or Expressionistic) techniques has proved a welcome challenge to several of Sweden's greatest actresses: extensive discussion of the queen who abdicated in 1654, became a convert to Catholicism, and astonished Europeans before and after these acts because of astonishing behavior and gossip. The interpretations of the queen, the people about her, and her period have fascinated foreigners as well as Swedes.

IX *Charles XII*

Charles XII, the king who was primarily responsible for bringing Sweden's time as a major power to an end, was never an object of Strindberg's admiration even though romantic Swedish poets and Swedish historians had idealized and idolized Charles:

> Charles XII, the man who ruined Sweden, the great criminal, the champion fighter, the idol of the ruffians, and the counterfeiter, was the one I was going to present on the stage to my countrymen.
>
> Well, everyone does have motives for his actions, every criminal has the right to defend himself, so I decided to plan my drama as a classical tragedy of fate and catastrophe. The end of a life that was a big mistake [*Open Letters to the Intimate Theater*, 259].

Instead of concentrating on the sleepwalker's realistic environment and concealment of inner life as in *Queen Christina*, Strindberg deliberately placed his major emphasis on the king's innermost experiences and to represent them used the impressionistic-dreamplay techniques he had used in revealing his own inner experiences in the Damascus trilogy. Consequently, the play seemed to many early critics disjointed and loose. Later readers and theatergoers understand and appreciate the deliberate blend of reality and dream experience, the symbolism, the stress on emotions and feelings, the dark moods, and the effective use of music.

It seemed to Strindberg that the last three years in the life of the king had been years of frustration, indecision, waiting, and inner defeat. They had, he thought, been the years when the king's character in all its complexity had been frozen in a mold, or, to put it in another way, he had become one of the living dead.

The happy combination of realistic and dreamplay techniques gives us a synthesis and an analysis of an "arrogant egotist who believes he is the man of destiny and the center of the world; who conceals his inordinate desire for honor beneath extremely simple speech, attire, tastes, and manner; who despises his fellow men to whose sufferings he is insensible; who is not religious in any ordinary way but who uses religion to get power and support; who is unable to forgive anyone; and who is willful and stubborn." Yet, as Swedenborg says at one point, "I have never understood *one* human destiny, not even my own insignificant one." *Charles XII* is the historical play that serves as counterpart to the Damascus plays: Just as the Stranger remains unknown even though the author has learned much about him, King Charles remains a stranger and an unknown even to himself.

X   *Gustav III*

Gustav III, the eighteenth-century charmer, did more than any other to set cultural patterns for Stockholm and Swedish cultural life. Founder of the Swedish Academy, the Royal Opera, and the Royal Dramatic Theater, and an enthusiastic disciple of both Voltaire and Rousseau, Gustav III has been admired by many and detested by others. Strindberg, native of Stockholm and in many ways one who benefited from what Gustav had done positively, nevertheless fixed his primary attention on Gustav as an actor — quite justifiably, too, because he wrote plays, acted in some dramas in his court theaters at Drottningholm and Gripsholm Castles, and deliberately created roles for himself in everyday life as a matter of self-defence and of preference.

Strindberg chose the artificial form of the well-made play just as he had for *Queen Christina* even though King Gustav III knew very well that he was acting and Strindberg's Queen Christina had become a sleepwalker:

The enlightened despot, who carries through the French Revolution at home in Sweden — that is to say, crushes the aristocrats with the help of the third estate. That is a paradox that is hard to deal with. And as a character, he is full of contradictions, a tragedian who plays comedy in life, a hero and a dancing master, an absolute monarch who is a friend of liberty, a man who strives for humanitarian [reforms], a disciple of Fredrik the Great, Joseph II, and Voltaire. Almost sympathetic, he, the Revolutionist, falls at the hands of the Revolutionists [*Open Letters to the Intimate Theater*, 258-59].

The play resembles the Scribean historical comedy with its intrigues and conspiracies, its figurative and literal fencing, its neatly arranged "scenes," and its atmosphere of superficiality.

Yet this four-act play is anything but superficial. By the time one has seen it in performance or considered it in the study one has gained insight into the king, his court, and his period. Critics and reviewers did not think the play amounted to anything as literature or theater when it first appeared in print, but, when it was produced for the first time in 1916, it was clear to the audiences throughout its long initial run that it is great theater. It is great literature as well.

XI *Plays about World History*

In addition to the twelve great historical plays, Strindberg had written some earlier pieces that have at least historical elements in them. The most notable are the two plays he wrote for his first wife, *The Secret of the Guild* and *Lord Bengt's Wife*, which have been considered in an earlier chapter. According to letters to Emil Schering, his German translator, and to notes in the Strindberg Collection, he had still more ambitious plans by way of a cycle of historical plays: "This trilogy, which has also been called *Moses-Socrates-Christ*, are the first three parts of a larger, yet unfinished, cycle of dramas about the history of the world in which *The Nightingale of Wittenberg* is the eleventh." The cycle, he assured Schering, was to consist of twenty plays, *independent*, but with the "invisible thread [the Conscious Will] which makes the necklace!" The cycle was never completed, and, if the four plays he did complete for such a cycle indicate what he would have done, it is probably good that he devoted his energies to the writing of other works.

The three plays — *Moses, or From the Wilderness to the Promised Land*; *Socrates, or Hellas*; and *Christ, or the Lamb and the Wild Beast* — are like none of his other plays. They are essentially a series of tableaux (twenty-one for *Moses*, nineteen for *Socrates*, and fifteen for *Christ*) apparently designed to illustrate significant episodes in history and to point out the divinely designated roles of the Hebrews, the Greeks, and the Christians (the latter primarily in their struggles with Caligula, Claudius, and Nero). The plays do clarify Strindberg's view of history as controlled by the Conscious Will; they might do as imaginary conversations or dialogs to be read against backdrops of pageantry, but they lack the great Strindbergian skills in making the historic dead come alive in superbly conceived and composed dramas.

The Nightingale of Wittenberg (1903) is a chronicle play, a series of episodes or tableaux divided into five acts. Its merits lie in Strindberg's interpretation of Martin Luther and his treatment of Dr. Faust.

But interesting as the trilogy and the play about Luther may be to scholars in search of minute knowledge of Strindberg and his works, they do not begin to compare with the twelve great plays about Swedish history. Those are structurally and substantially among the best plays in world literature. Taken together, they are an astonishingly effective revelation — in dramatic form — of the development of an important Western culture's ideas, values, and goals and a means of bringing into visible and audible form representations of men and women who played key roles in the development of that culture. Eleven of them have proved suitable for the Swedish stage; the twelfth — *Gustav Adolf* — could be easily adapted without doing injury to Strindberg; and all twelve would be ideal for the screen. At least seven — *Master Olof, The Saga of the Folkungs, Gustav Vasa, Erik XIV, Queen Christina, Charles XII,* and *Gustav III* — would be excellent theater abroad as well as at home.

CHAPTER 11

Assessment

S TRINDBERG tried his hand at many things and occupations
besides creative writing: He was at one or more times a reporter,
a feature writer, a reviewer, a critic, an editor, a telegrapher, a
tutor, a teacher, an actor, a translator, a librarian, a scholar, a
"scientist," a photographer, a painter, a sculptor, a composer, and
a director. Most of these roles were brief and temporary, some were
not, but all of them provided him with material for his creative
writing.

In some of the areas he made notable contributions. Take, for
example, his work as a librarian at the Royal Library; his learning
Chinese and Japanese in order to classify and catalog important
holdings led to scholarly activities far beyond his duties as a
cataloger: He produced scholarly studies that brought him
recognition abroad for substantial contributions to knowledge. His
years in the Royal Library obviously stood him in good stead in
preparing his numerous contributions to cultural and social history
and criticism as well as in his scrutiny of and participation in debate
about Sweden, past, present, and future.

How great an impact his analyses and suggestions may have had
on the very great changes that have taken place in Sweden can most
likely never be estimated with any great degree of accuracy. But
take, for example, his extensive consideration of the whole
educational system. Based on his own exposure to the system from
elementary schools through the university, his experiences as a
tutor and a teacher, his "program" was not merely negative but
highly constructive, thoughtful rather than petulant. He advocated
coeducation, giving girls and boys equal opportunities that would
prepare them for rewarding and useful roles in the community, a
revamping of the whole higher educational system so as to give the
student direction through closer contact with the professors and

other faculty members, setting up carefully planned curricula, and establishing a full-fledged university in Stockholm. Swedes interested in education can hardly have escaped exposure to what Strindberg had to say about the schools and the university system.

In some areas his achievements were great enough to have gained him some degree of recognition. His work as a sculptor was slight, his photography an interesting source of information about him, but his painting is something else. He was active as a painter especially in the late 1870s, the 1890s, and the early 1900s, the three periods during which he produced the well over one hundred paintings that have in recent years been examined by experts, viewed by large numbers of people at exhibitions, and praised by critics as important seminal contributions to art. There are, moreover, innumerable sketches in his manuscripts and in some of his letters, drawings that are always interesting if not always excellent.

He wrote a great many items about art and artists: *The Red Room* is appreciably a novel about artists and their concepts of art; his letter to Paul Gauguin (1895), used by Gauguin as an introduction to an exhibition of Gauguin paintings, is an indication of his perceptiveness; if *Directions for Becoming an Art Expert in Sixty Minutes* (*Anvisning att på 60 minuter bliva konstkännare*, 1877) is indeed his, it demonstrates his ability to strip expertise of all pretence and to do so humorously and goodnaturedly. Strindberg knew artists, major and minor, and commented pointedly and persuasively about many of them, including his one-time friends, Edvard Munch and Carl Larsson.

For those who would like to get some idea of Strindberg as the painter now hailed as the founder of the school of spontaneity and the forerunner of symbolic, expressionistic, and surrealistic painting, *Strindbergs måleri* (edited by Torsten Måtte Schmidt and Göran Söderström) is particularly useful: It has a great many reproductions in color of Strindberg paintings. His naïvely realistic landscapes from the 1870s, his symbolic "spontaneous" paintings from the 1890s, and his impressionistic ones from the early 1900s are worth noting; "My Child's First Cradle" (pregnant Siri bathing in the sea), "Jealousy" (a night of torment during his courtship of Frida), and a gray sea in storm are among the best known.

From all areas he gained material for his creative writing; from some he gained a great deal of personal pleasure as well as practical

Universal and timeless themes of great significance, segments that might very well be segments of actual life, the ultimate elimination of distracting factors such as intermissions until the ideal one-act form had been achieved, the concept of the characterless character, and simplification of staging are the major factors in what he considered his contribution through these pre-Inferno plays.

Open Letters to the Intimate Theater has a two-fold importance. The volume is devoted to one of his most rewarding undertakings, working for a theater in which only his own plays were presented from December 5, 1907, to December 11, 1910, and it contains the gist of his thinking about drama and theater toward the end of his most productive period.

The five letters contain a fascinating account of one of the most important chapters in the history of the Swedish theater. While it did undoubtedly give him a great deal of pleasure to have his plays presented under the direction of his admirer and friend August Falck and performed by actors enthusiastic about his plays and while the Intimate Theater's esthetic and financial well being called for his active participation, its greatest importance probably lies in its awakening a great many key people in and out of the Swedish theater to the superb contributions he had made to drama and theater. The Intimate Theater played a substantial role, moreover, in making the Swedish theater of the twentieth century deserve worldwide attention and admiration.

These letters contain several other matters of importance to an understanding of Strindberg's contributions to drama and theater: his appreciation of Shakespeare and his interpretation of several Shakespeare plays, his fullest and final statements about the composition of historical dramas and particularly about his own, a great deal about his theories of acting and staging, and some pertinent discussion of the state of the Swedish theater at that time. He acknowledges here and elsewhere his gratitude to Shakespeare — and to others — but very carefully indicates his own originality: "I substituted prose for verse [in the 1872 *Master Olof*], and instead of the opera-like blank verse drama with solo and special numbers, I composed polyphonically, a symphony, in which all the voices were interwoven (major and minor characters were treated equally), and in which no one accompanied the soloist" [*Open Letters to the Intimate Theater,* 18]. Even out of context this excerpt indicates the wealth of substantial matter.

The impact of his works in the areas of social and cultural history, social criticism, and satire on later writers has been very great. Vilhelm Moberg (1898 - 1973), one of Sweden's greatest twentieth-century writers and well known in the English-speaking world for his emigrant tetralogy on which the films, *The Emigrants* and *The New Land*, were based testified at various times to his debt to Strindberg: "So I read my first book by Strindberg and I was amazed that an author could write in that way. That he dared! He used words I had never before seen in print, brazen, dirty words. I had heard them, many belonged to common people's spoken language in the farm community where I lived. A person could say those words, but I had never believed anybody could print them" [*Berättelser ur min levnad*, 248-49]. It was not only Strindberg's tremendous influence on Swedish vocabulary that helped shape Moberg's career: Strindberg's folk dramas and prose fiction gave him the impulse to write a whole series of folk dramas that made him unsurpassed in that genre; Strindberg's greatest satire *The New Nation* has its recent parallel in Moberg's *The Old Nation* (*Det gamla riket*, 1953); there are links between all Moberg's novels, dramas, social criticism, social and critical historical works and Strindberg's. When Moberg died in 1973, his history of the Swedish people was not complete; the two volumes that were are remarkably original but remarkably parallel in intention and approach to *The Swedish People*.

Although Strindberg was always actively engaged with social and cultural matters and affected Swedish thinking about them, he considered his most important contributions his achievements in creative writing, that is, in the composition of works that are belles lettres.

While Strindberg produced a great quantity of verse, his verse is hardly comparable to that composed by such great contemporaries of his as Viktor Rydberg (1828 - 1895), Gustaf Fröding (1860 - 1911), Verner von Heidenstam (1859 - 1940), and Erik Axel Karlfeldt (1864 - 1931). Strindberg's verse is competent and some of his post-Inferno free verse, particularly some of the passages in his dramas, is very good. But the importance of his verse lies primarily in substance rather than in form, and the substance is largely identical to what he had to say in prose.

If one has to single out one matter that is primary in what he had to say, it will have to be his penetrating analyses and evocative presentations of human individuals. Deliberately studying psychology and every other available source of printed knowledge and deliberately using himself and other human beings more or less available to him as objects of close study, he considered the human individual from every point of view he could conceive and in every way he could imagine. He did on occasion injure others and on more than one occasion he may have been on the verge of destroying himself. In presenting the results of his probing, he produced works that have been extremely useful to psychologists and psychiatrists.

In two literary areas he ranks with the very best and most influential in world literature: autobiography and drama.

As the author of several very good novels such as *The Red Room, The People of Hemsö, The Scapegoat,* and *The Roofing Celebration,* several excellent novellas, and a great many very good short stories, Strindberg deserves high rank as a writer of prose fiction, but what raises him to the very top are the novels that are admittedly autobiographical.

He is unsurpassed as an autobiographer. His own classification of his autobiographical works (1. closing accounts and 2. confessions) is highly pertinent. To the first group belong all his autobiographical works before the Inferno period, to the second all those from *Inferno* on. (Four plays, the Damascus trilogy and *The Great Highway* are definitely autobiographical). *The Son of a Servant, Time of Ferment, In the Red Room, The Author,* and *A Madman's Defence* are models of realistic analysis within the limits imposed by finite senses; they are remarkably objective reports on one highly sensitive human being's development and on his confrontation with extremely personal dilemmas.

But Strindberg wanted it understood that the volumes in the second group were very different from those in the first: "The great crisis at fifty years of age; revolutions in my psychic life, wanderings in the desert, desolation, Swedenborg's Hells and Heavens. Not influenced by Huysman's *En Route,* but based on personal experiences" [*SS, XIX, 119*]. Informative and essentially persuasive as the pre-Inferno autobiographical volumes are, it is probably the post-Inferno ones that have the greatest impact on professionally trained experts in human psychology as well as on laymen today. Be that as it may, few if any other writers have examined themselves as thoroughly or, with admission of limitations, reported their findings as frankly as Strindberg.

Of the approximately seventy plays some are important only to the scholar, but those that are among the best in modern literature comprise a body of belles lettres that rivals his achievements as an autobiographer — many would say surpasses them.

There are twelve historical dramas that Swedes should with good reason treasure — they give Sweden a cycle that compares nicely with Shakespeare's histories. Several of the twelve could be stimulating additions to the repertories of theaters abroad: *Erik XIV* and *Queen Christina* have already demonstrated that. Strindberg enjoyed history, and his insights, interpretations, and presentations can give nonSwedes as well as Swedes an understanding of a rich variety of humanity in fascinating historical settings.

Strindberg was undoubtedly justified in insisting that he had contributed not only great plays such as *The Father*, *Lady Julie*, *Creditors*, and *The Bond* to the realistic-naturalistic theater and that he had contributed something substantially new structurally to the theater in his ever tightening compression of the segments from life from *The Father* to the very good one-act and one-scene plays of the early 1890s. These plays have been seminal in world theater; some of the shorter ones have been decidedly rewarding for student and little theaters.

His post-Inferno dramas have played and are playing important roles in post-Strindberg drama and theater. His dreamplays — particularly *A Dream Play*, *The Ghost Sonata*, and the Damascus trilogy — have suggested matter to probe and forms to exploit to Impressionists and Expressionists, Surrealists and Absurdists. *The Dance of Death* I and II have parented such notable offspring as Eugene O'Neill's *A Long Day's Journey into Night* and Edward Albee's *Who's Afraid of Virginia Wolf?* The Strindberg plays and autobiographical volumes together have played a striking role in the modern drama, modern literature in general, and in the cinema: He had a great deal to say about human beings in their rich variety and tangled webs of experience, and he said it on every conceivable level of expression from the naïve and the tender through dark humor and the grotesque to the extremely frank and brutal. And his variety of structure and form is equally great.

In Sweden and even in the rest of Scandinavia it is extremely doubtful that a single writer has escaped the impact of Strindberg.

Take, as examples, the three twentieth-century Swedish writers who are very probably the best known in the English-speaking world: Pär Lagerkvist, Vilhelm Moberg, and Ingmar Bergman. A Scandinavianist can read few if any Lagerkvist works, in verse or prose, without constantly being reminded of Strindberg and can surely never forget Lagerkvist's evaluation of Strindberg in the essay, *Modern Theatre*. But few will have seen the copy of the telegram Lagerkvist sent Strindberg on the latter's sixtieth birthday; it is preserved in the Strindberg Collection at the Royal Library:

A thank you to the fighter and the victor, the bringer of light, whose torch has lighted me on unbeaten paths, and the thinker who has met me with all his mystic mythical light when his soul has been dreaming in passionate longing.

Thank you! The memory of your struggles and dreams has etched your image in my soul.

Pär Lagerkvist
Växjö

Lagerkvist was only eighteen at the time. Ingmar Bergman has admitted his debt to Strindberg time and again; the debt can be easily discerned both in his handful of written plays and in his remarkable films. As I have said, Vilhelm Moberg disturbed the Swedes and particularly certain elements in the Swedish establishment much as Strindberg had done and in the process contributed major original works in several genres parallel to Strindberg's.

The impact of Strindberg on world literature has been very great: Scores of writers have paid tribute to him in one way or another, for example, Ibsen and O'Neill. Any scholar who visits the Ibsen room in the Oslo museum is not likely to forget the Christian Krohg portrait of Strindberg that hangs above Ibsen's desk and is likely to recall Ibsen's words that he could not write a word unless those eyes were staring down at him. A close look at the Ibsen plays from *Hedda Gabler* (1890) on is highly rewarding.

O'Neill asserted in the Provincetown Playhouse program (1923): "Strindberg still remains among the most modern of the moderns, the greatest interpreter in the theatre of the characteristic spiritual conflicts which constitute the drama, the life-blood of our lives today. ... It is only by means of some form of 'super-naturalism' that we may express to the theatre what we comprehend intuitively of that self-obsession which is the particular discount we moderns have to pay for the loan of life." The tribute is still valid.

Notes and References

Chapter One

1. Oscar II (1829-1907) reigned from 1872 to 1907.
2. *Strindbergs systrar berätta,* pp. 13-16.
3. *August Strindberg: Ungdom och mannaår,* pp. 18-19.
4. Wallin is remembered particularly for his lyric poetry, among the best of the Swedish Romantic period, and his very many psalms, among the finest in the Church of Sweden's psalmbook. In his own day and in decades after his death, his published sermons were highly admired for their emphasis on stoical moral duty and their exquisite, even poetic prose.
5. The Swedish term for *pietist* is *läsare,* which literally means *reader* because of such a serious Christian's insistence on reading the Bible and other religious material himself and theoretically coming into direct communion with Deity through His word and, of course, through prayer, and serving God through public testimony and keeping a watchful eye on fellow human beings. In many of his works Strindberg presents pietists who have missed the point of "joy in salvation" and have become sour unhappy creatures.
6. *To Damascus,* III, Scene 6.
7. Axel Johan Uppvall. *August Strindberg: A Psychoanalytic Study with Special Reference to the Oedipus Complex.*
8. *Strindbergs systrar berätta,* pp. 31-32.
9. The struggle for Swedish women's liberation began long before Strindberg's day. Writers such as Carl Jonas Love Almqvist (1793 - 1866) and Fredrika Bremer (1801 - 1865) were only two but, without doubt, the most widely known writers who had brought the problems involved in women's humiliating status into public Swedish and even Scandinavian debate in the first half of the nineteenth century. Almqvist's most important contribution, the novel *Det går an* (1839) is available in American translation as *Sara Videbeck.* Cf. Bertil Romberg: *C.J.L. Almqvist,* TWAS No. 401, New York, 1976. Bremer was as popular in the English-speaking countries as she was at home. The best American introduction is Signe Rooth's *Seeress of the Northland: Fredrika Bremer's American Journey 1849-1851* (Philadelphia: American Swedish Historical Foundation, 1955).
10. See, for example, Mary Sandbach's translation of Strindberg's preface to *Giftas* I in her *Getting Married* (New York: Viking Press, 1972).

199

Classifying Strindberg merely as a woman hater is an unfortunate distortion of the truth.

11. Quoted in "Bergman Speaks on Bergman" in *The American-Scandinavian Review,* 62:4 (December, 1974), p. 388.

12. *Strindbergs systrar berätta,* p. 63.

13. Strindberg's difficulties in gaining popularity and approval among critics and other key figures in Swedish society stemmed not only from his frankness about sex but from many other factors as well. His lack of reticence about revealing intimate details of his own life and those in others' and his blurting out what he believed was the truth about almost every conceivable subject may have been the two dominant factors.

14. The restaurant (*Berns salonger*) is still there, but its Red Room, originally a chess room and meeting place for bachelors, no longer exists. Strindberg's 1904 novel *Götiska rummen* (*The Gothic Rooms*) has its setting in the same restaurant which had been renovated in 1885 to provide an Old Scandinavian (*götisk,* i.e., Gothic) atmosphere.

15. Strindberg's favorite composer was Ludwig van Beethoven (1770 - 1827), whose works were to influence some of his post-Inferno plays and were the core of his so-called Beethoven evenings from December, 1900, on,with his brother Axel (pianist, cellist, and composer), Tor Aulin (composer), Richard Bergh (artist), Carl Eldh (sculptor), and Vilhelm Carlheim-Gyllensköld (physicist and, later on, a Strindberg editor) among the most regular attendants at usually monthly gatherings in Strindberg's home.

16. *August Strindberg, Ungdom och mannaår,* pp. 57-58.

17. *Four Plays by Hjalmar Bergman* (Seattle: University of Washington Press, 1968), p. 14. Cf. Erik Hjalmar Linder's *Hjalmar Bergman,* TWAS, No. 356, New York, 1975.

18. *An Essay on Man,* Epistle II, verses 1-2.

19. See my translation "Psychic Murder (Apropos *Rosmersholm*)" in *TDR: The drama review,* 13:2 (T42, Winter 1968), pp. 113-118.

20. *August Strindberg. Mannaår och ålderdom,* pp. 281-282.

21. *Ibid.,* p. 240.

22. See C. E. W. L. Dahlström's "August Strindberg — 1849 - 1912 — Between Two Eras," *Scandinavian Studies,* 21, 1-18, for an illuminating discussion of this point.

Chapter Two

1. Unless otherwise indicated, reference to Strindberg's letters will be to them as they appear in the Strindberg Society's *August Strindbergs brev.* Thus, *Brev,* IV, 993 will signify that series, volume IV, number 993.

2. References to the Landquist edition will be, for example, *SS,* XVII, 27-28. That is, *Samlade skrifter,* Volume XVII, pages 27-28.

3. The two Bonniers were Albert Bonnier and his son Karl Otto Bonnier.

4. Strindberg's extensive readings in contemporary psychologists is more than suggested by Strindberg scholars but a specialized in-depth study of the matter and its impact on Strindberg and his works has not yet been made.

5. Jules Vallès' autobiography, *Jacques Vingtras* (*L'Enfant* [1879], *Le Bachelier* [1881], and *L'Insurgé* [1882]), has many affinities with *The Son of a Servant*. How well Strindberg knew Vallès' work has not yet been determined.

6. Ina Forstén, the Finland Swedish fiancée of Strindberg's friend, the opera singer Algot Lange, had brought the manuscript of *Master Olof* to the Wrangels and may have arranged for Siri's meeting Strindberg as if by chance.

7. *Så var det i verkligheten*, 205.

8. *Ibid.*, 200.

9. *Strindbergs-litteraturen och osedligheten bland skolungdomen*, 50.

10. *Ibid.*, 62.

11. On November 2, 1898 [*Brev*, XIII, 3924], Strindberg sent to Gustaf af Geijerstam the first part of *Klostret*, a novel about his second marriage, with the comment, "The one who wants to know the story of my life can read it in the following order. *The Son of a Servant, Time of Ferment, In the Red Room, A Madman's Defence, The Cloister* I, *Inferno, Legends, The Cloister* II. That is a lot!" *The Cloister* was never completed; Strindberg used the material, however, in writing *The Quarantine-Master's Second Story* in 1902 (See pages 57-59). The fragment called *Klostret* was published, however, on pages 75-97 of *Samlade otryckta berättelser och dikter* (1919) and is particularly interesting because of its rather detailed account of bohemian life at the café labelled "Zum schwarzen Ferkel" and elsewhere in Berlin. In 1966 Bonniers published C. G. Bjurström's reconstruction of the novel by following leads in the manuscripts of *Klostret* and *Karantänmästarens andra berättelse* (*Klostret*, Utgiven med kommentarer, 1966. Pp. 178).

12. *Ur ockulta dagboken*, 155-156.

13. *Ibid.*, 131.

Chapter Three

1. Gustaf Fredrik Steffen (1864-1929), who became a prominent sociologist and politician, had studied chemistry and mineralogy in Berlin when Strindberg engaged him as an assistant on the trip to study French farmers; Steffen was also a correspondent for a Göteborg daily.

2. The "journeys" are far more than mere travel books; they are the results of scientific, economic, agricultural, and folklore surveys of the provinces of Öland, Gotland, Västergötland, Skåne, Dalarna, and Lapp-

land. Linné dealt with other parts of Sweden in other writings including his diaries. Strindberg knew these and many others of "the flower king's" works including *Nemesis divina* and his appreciations of nature.

3. See Alrik Gustafson's *A History of Swedish Literature* for accounts of these writers. Cf. Bertil Romberg, *C.J.L. Almqvist*, TWAS No. 401, New York, 1976.

4. Kymmendö, an island in the Stockholm Archipelago, is now a tourist attraction largely because of the popularity of *The People of Hemsö* in both its printed and TV forms and because of its role in Strindberg's life.

5. The Bonniers, a Jewish publishing family, have become the leading publishers of Swedish books and among the most powerful in other areas of cultural life as well. The first Bonnier came to Sweden in 1827.

6. Among his friends were such people as Hjalmar Branting (1860-1925), the first Social Democrat prime minister, and among his admirers and benefactors was Nathan Söderblom (1866-1931), the archbishop of Sweden who played a major role in the development of the ecumenical movement. The list of prominent Swedes exposed to Strindberg as a stimulant is inexhaustible.

7. Carl David af Wirsén (1842 - 1912), a minor poet and secretary of the Swedish Academy from 1884 until his death, served as a reviewer and critic for various Swedish newspapers, opposed naturalism and neo-Romanticism, and his enmity was a major reason why Strindberg never received the Nobel Prize that the Academy awards annually.

8. Probably the best illustration of his effectiveness in participating in debate about improving society is the still untranslated *August Strindberg's Little Cathechism for the Lower Class* (*August Strindbergs Lilla katekes för Underklassen*, *SS*, XVI, 175-99), a devastating attack on conditions in the mid-1880s. Imitating the form of the Lutheran cathechism all Swedes (i.e., members of the Church of Sweden) supposedly memorized before confirmation, Strindberg in turn considers the community, the means by which the upper class controls the lower class (religion, politics, laws, sciences, arts, and moral standards), the upper class ways of talking in order to fool the lower class ("reform yourself before you reform others," for example). Anyone who reads the "cathechism" and his many other journalistic contributions from the 1870s on must be amazed by his awareness of social and political ills and his proposals for improvement, many of which have been realized.

9. No one has yet ventured on a thorough study of Strindberg's development as a religious being. His own autobiographical volumes are the best sources of information and Brandell's *Strindberg in Inferno* the best secondary help for those who do not read Swedish.

Chapter Four

1. How thoroughly he knew the many languages he cited in the

philological studies mentioned in this chapter has never been determined and probably never can be.

2. Strindberg was a voracious reader and apparently delighted in recording what he had read, what he thought of the writer and his work, how it affected him, and what general significance the writer had. His letters as well as his autobiographical volumes have innumerable leads.

3. Studies of individual authors' influence on Strindberg are few. Harold Borland's *Nietzsche's Influence on Swedish Literature with Special Reference to Strindberg, Ola Hansson, Heidenstam and Fröding* is a particularly fine study of this kind and probably will have many parallels.

4. P. 25.

5. While there are many short studies of Strindberg's great influence in these areas, only Karl-Åke Kärnell's *Strindbergs bildspråk: En studie i prosastil*, a study of Strindberg's use of imagery, has a fairly detailed summary in English. For those who read Swedish *Strindbergs språk och stil* is a particularly useful introduction (in the form of articles by several scholars) to various aspects of Strindberg's literary art.

6. Birger Mörner, *Den Strindberg jag känt,* 189. Mörner includes Hjalmar Öhrvall's informative and amusing "P.M. Angående Strindbergs kväveproducerande ko" ["P.M. Concerning Strindberg's Nitrogen-Producing Cow"] as an appendix. Öhrvall was a professor of physiology at the University of Uppsala and a friend of Strindberg.

Chapter Five

1. Sweden and Norway were united from 1814 to 1905. Strindberg, who frequently commented on the unhappy union, favored independence for the Norwegians.

2. Strindberg, who spent three autumn weeks in Paris in 1876, visited theaters, museums, and galleries. From 1883 on until the late 1890s he spent extended periods in France. Regrettably, Stellan Ahlström's *Strindbergs erövring av Paris* [*Strindberg's Conquest of Paris.* Stockholm: Almqvist & Wiksell, 1956] and Gunnar Brandell's *På Strindbergs vägar genom Frankrike* [*On Strindberg's Journeys through France.* Stockholm: Wahlström & Widstrand, 1949] are not available in English.

3. Visby on the island of Gotland with its many medieval church ruins is a popular vacation center.

4. Alfred Nobel (1833 - 1896) was able largely to found the Nobel Prizes (1896) because of his fortune based on inventions and improvements of inventions including that of dynamite.

5. Loki was the evil power, a sort of devil, among the pagan Scandinavian gods. See any edition of Peter Munch's *Norse Mythology.*

6. The French community in which he associated with literary figures as well as painters and sculptors, some of them friends of Strindberg's such as Carl Larsson and Richard Bergh.

7. Strindberg's play, *Midsommar*, is only one of his many literary treatments of the thoroughly celebrated holiday. *Lady Julie* is undoubtedly the most famous.

8. See, as a starter, any list of Lagerkvist's complete works. See also Robert Donald Spector's *Pär Lagerkvist*, TWAS, No. 267, New York, 1973.

9. See *The Father*.

10. Skansen, the open air museum in Stockholm, was opened October 11, 1891, and was designed to preserve mementoes of Swedish cultural life from all periods.

Chapter Six

1. The term *giftas* has been translated *married* and *getting married*. Both the word and the substance of the stories suggest that *being married* is the accurate translation.

2. *Fjärdingen* ("the quarter") and *Svartbäcken* are sections of Upp-sala. The city, seat of the oldest university in Scandinavia, has for centuries had the sort of relationship between townspeople and students conveyed by the expression *town and gown*. Strindberg's emphasis is on student life.

3. The provincial house (*nationsförening* or *landskapsförening*) has been a prominent feature of university life in Uppsala and even at Lund and Helsingfors for many generations. The *nation* plays a role in the student's life beyond that of the merely social.

4. What Strindberg emphasizes in this story is the striking difference in attitudes and behavior between student generations.

5. Dickens and Andersen were among his favorite writers; he acknowledged his debt to both in letters and autobiographical volumes. A subtitle reads *Stories of Life among Artists and Authors* (*Skildringar ur artist- och författarlivet*).

6. See Harold Borland's *Nietzsche's Influence on Swedish Literature*.

7. Queen Sophia (1830 - 1913), born Princess Sophie Vilhelmina Mariana Henrietta of Nassau, married Prince Oscar in 1857. They were crowned in 1872. The queen was known particularly for her strictly pietistic religious views and her philanthropic activities.

8. Sten Linder's *Ibsen och Strindberg: en litteraturpsykologisk parallel* deals with the matter but is not available in English. By the time he wrote *Hedda Gabler*, Ibsen knew *The Father*, *Lady Julie*, and *Creditors* as well.

9. The novel has the subtitle *Släktöden från sekelskiftet* (*Family Situations about the Turn of the Century*).

10. A great deal of commentary on *Black Banners* appears in *En blå bok* (*A Blue Book*). As noted elsewhere, the *Blue Book* has as part of the title "Delivered to Those Concerned and Comprising a Commentary on *Black Banners*."

Chapter Seven

1. See *Open Letters to the Intimate Theater* for translations and introductions for more detailed information about Strindberg's theories of dramatic composition, staging, and theater arts in general.

2. The details of his frustration and bitterness appear in his letters as well as in his autobiographical volumes, *The Son of a Servant.*

3. Strindberg contributed the sections called "A Walk in Stockholm in the 1730s," "Christmas and Easter," "Street Music and Folk Entertainments," "Children and Young People," "Guilds, Crafts, and Journeymen Groups," "Slang and Folk Variants," "Fairy Tales and Superstition," "Flora and Fauna" to *Old Stockholm* (1880-82). Claes Lundin (1825 - 1908), a journalist and minor writer, was his collaborator.

4. There is no definitive account of Swedish women's struggles for equality, but they were among the first to organize, set up definite programs, and then proceed to realize them.

5. See note 7, page 202.

Chapter Eight

1. For a detailed account, see Børge Madsen's *Strindberg's Naturalistic Theatre: Its Relation to French Naturalism*.

2. *The Father.*

3. For my detailed discussion of *The Father, Lady Julie, Creditors, The Stronger,* and *The Bond,* see my introductions to those plays in *Pre-Inferno Plays* (Seattle: University of Washington Press, 1970).

4. Herbert Grevenius (born 1901), dramatist and critic, reviewer and translator, is quoted in the Blanche Theater program of February 2, 1938: "Det är en bra otäck pjäs, men den är otäckt bra."

5. At the extreme southern tip of Gotland is Hoburgen, a cliff part of which resembles a human head. Swedes have been exposed to a tale about a rich troll who lived in the cliff.

Chapter Nine

1. On March 10, 1898, Strindberg wrote to his friend Axel Herrlin (1870 - 1937): "I seem to have rewon the gift of being able to write for the theater, and have recently completed a major play [*To Damascus*, I]. I feel grateful for having been allowed to do so. I thereby admit that that is a gift which can be taken away if I misuse it. ... My former fatalism has thus been changed into providentialism, and I fully understand that I have nothing and can do nothing of myself. But I'll not become absolutely humble, because I haven't the conscience to let my self commit suicide" [*Brev*, XII, 3763].

2. See Carl Enoch William Leonard Dahlström's *Strindberg's Dramatic Expressionism* (Ann Arbor: University of Michigan, 1930) for the earliest

detailed consideration of Strindberg's dreamplays as Expressionistic. The volume has since been republished together with a recent article updating the material.

3. See Acts 9.

4. See my detailed discussion of *Advent, Easter, There are Crimes and Crimes*, and *The Dance of Death* I and II in *Dramas of Testimony* (Seattle: University of Washington Press, 1975).

5. See *A Dream Play and Four Chamber Plays* (Seattle: University of Washington Press, 1973) for my detailed discussion of the five plays.

6. When the Intimate Theater opened in 1907, Strindberg had a copy of Arnold Böcklin's famous painting hung on either side of the proscenium.

7. Verner von Heidenstam (1859 - 1940), winner of the Nobel Prize in literature in 1916, was a neo-Romantic poet and a novelist. He and Strindberg had been friends; Strindberg particularly objected to Heidenstam's glorification of Charles XII in *The Charles Men* (*Karolinerna*, 1897 - 98). Axel Klinckowström (born, 1867) wrote a minor tragedy, *Olof Trätälja*, which, to Strindberg's horror, was awarded the Great Prize of the Swedish Academy and produced at a time when Strindberg's great historical plays were not receiving much recognition.

Chapter Ten

1. "People have undoubtedly for a long time thought they could detect laws governing the march of history resembling those which control nature. In history men have detected traces of the physical law of balance (European balance), the power of attraction (larger nations' inclination to assimilate smaller ones), elective affinity, substitution and so on. And from the organic world men have borrowed the concepts of the splitting of cells, segmentation, struggle, and selection and the like. But the march of history shows such a union of freedom and necessity that on the one hand *one has to admit freedom of the human will to a certain degree*, on the other *admit the existence of a necessity, which in keeping with circumstances limits the efforts of the individual and brings about synthesis.* The great synthesist who unites antitheses, resolves incompatibles, maintains the balance, is no human being and can be no one but the invisible lawgiver, who in freedom changes the laws according to changed conditions: the creator, the solver, and the preserver he may then be called — whatever you like" [*SS,* LIV, 398].

2. Strindberg has acknowledged his admiration for and debt to Shakespeare, particularly in his early biographical volumes and in *Open Letters to the Intimate Theater.*

3. See my *Strindberg and the Historical Drama* and my introductions to translations of the major historical plays.

4. Compare Ingvar Andersson's interpretations in his *A History of Sweden* with Strindberg's, for example.

Selected Bibliography

PRIMARY SOURCES

A. Editions of Strindberg's Works

Samlade skrifter. Edited by John Landquist. 55 volumes. Stockholm: Bonniers, 1912-1920. The standard edition.
Samlade otryckta skrifter. 2 vols. Edited by Vilhelm Carlheim-Gyllensköld. Stockholm: Bonniers, 1918-1919. Supplements the Landquist edition; includes the world-historical plays and the drama fragments (*Holländarn, Homunculus, Starkodder skald, Toten-Insel*).
Skrifter. 14 vols. Selected and edited by Gunnar Brandell. Stockholm: Bonniers, 1945-1946.
August Strindbergs brev. Edited by Torsten Eklund for the Strindberg Society. Stockholm: Bonniers, 1947 to date. His letters plus a wealth of information.
August Strindbergs dramer. 3 vols. (1: *Fritänkaren, Hermione, I Rom, Den fredlöse, Anno fyrtioåtta, Gillets hemlighet*; 2: *Mäster Olof, LyckoPers resa*; 3: *Herr Bengts hustru, Kamraterna, Fadren, Fröken Julie, Fordringsägare*). Edited by Carl Reinhold Smedmark with introductions and notes. Stockholm: Bonniers, 1962-1964.
Strindbergs brev till Harriet Bosse. Stockholm: Natur och Kultur, 1932. Letters to his third wife plus her comments.
En dåres försvarstal. Translated from the French by Tage Aurell. Stockholm: Bonniers, 1962.
Ur Ockulta dagboken: Äktenskapet med Harriet Bosse. Edited by Torsten Eklund. Stockholm: Bonniers, 1963. Excerpts from *The Occult Diary* concerning his third marriage.
Det sjunkande Hellas. Edited by Erik Gamby. Uppsala: Bokgillet, 1960. Early version of *Hermione.*

B. English translations

See Gustafson's *A History of Swedish Literature*, 651-654, for a fairly complete list of pre-1961 translations. See the annual bibliographies in *Scandinavian Studies, The Publications of the Modern Language Association*, and *Samlaren* for more recent translations as well as studies of Strindberg and his works.

By the Open Sea. Translated by Ellie Schleussner. London: Rider, 1913. [*At the Edge of the Sea*]

The Chamber Plays (*Storm Weather, The Burned House, The Ghost Sonata, The Pelican*). Translated with an introduction by Evert Sprinchorn, Seabury Quinn, and Kenneth Petersen. New York: Dutton, 1962.

Dramas of Testimony (*The Dance of Death* I and II, *Advent, Easter, There Are Crimes and Crimes*). Seattle: University of Washington Press, 1975. Translations and introductions by Walter Johnson.

A Dream Play and Four Chamber Plays (*A Dream Play, Stormy Weather, The House That Burned, The Ghost Sonata, The Pelican*). Seattle: University of Washington Press, 1973. Translations and introductions by Walter Johnson.

Eight Expressionistic Plays (*Lucky Per's Journey, The Keys to Heaven, To Damascus I, II, III, A Dream Play, The Great Highway, The Ghost Sonata*). Translated by Arvid Paulson. New York: Bantam, 1965.

Five Plays of Strindberg (*Creditors, Crime and Crime, The Dance of Death, Swanwhite, The Great Highway*). Translated by Elizabeth Sprigge. New York: Doubleday, 1960.

From an Occult Diary: Marriage with Harriet Bosse. Translated by Mary Sandbach. Edited by Torsten Eklund. New York: Hill and Wang, 1965.

Getting Married. Edited and introduced by Mary Sandbach. New York: Viking, 1972. [*Married*]

The Growth of a Soul. Translated by Claude Field. London: Rider, 1914. [*Time of Ferment*]

Gustav Adolf. Translation and introduction by Walter Johnson. Seattle: University of Washington Press, 1957.

Inferno, Alone and Other Writings ("The New Arts, or The Role of Chance in Artistic Creation," "Graveyard Reveries," *Jacob Wrestles*). Edited and introduced by Evert Sprinchorn. Garden City: Doubleday, 1968.

The Last of the Knights, The Regent, Earl Birger of Bjälbo. Translations and introductions by Walter Johnson. Seattle: University of Washington Press, 1956.

Letters of Strindberg to Harriet Bosse. Edited and translated by Arvid Paulson. New York: Nelson, 1959.

A Madman's Defense. Translation (based on Ellie Schleussner's 1912 translation *Confession of a Fool*) and introduction by Evert Sprinchorn. New York: Doubleday, 1967.

The Natives of Hemsö and *The Scapegoat.* Translated by Arvid Paulson with an introduction by Richard B. Vowles. New York: Bantam, 1967.

Open Letters to the Intimate Theater. Translations and introductions by Walter Johnson. Seattle: University of Washington Press, 1959.

Pre-Inferno Plays (*The Father, Lady Julie, Creditors, The Stronger, The Bond*). Translations and introductions by Walter Johnson. Seattle: University of Washington Press, 1970.

"Psychic Murder (Apropos *Rosmersholm*)," *Tulane Drama Review* 13:2, 113-118. Translated by Walter Johnson.

Queen Christina, Charles XII, Gustav III. Translations and introductions by Walter Johnson. Seattle: University of Washington Press, 1955.

The Red Room. Translated by Ellie Schleussner. London: Howard Latimer, 1913. New translation by Elizabeth Sprigge. London: Dent; New York: Dutton; Everyman's Library, 1967.

The Road to Damascus. Translated by Graham Rawson. New York: Grove, 1960.

The Saga of the Folkungs; Engelbrekt. Translations and introductions by Walter Johnson. Seattle: University of Washington Press, 1959.

Seven Plays (*The Father, Miss Julie, Comrades, The Stronger, The Bond, Crimes and Crimes, Easter*). Translated by Arvid Paulson and introduced by John Gassner. New York: Bantam, 1960.

Six Plays (*The Father, Miss Julie, The Stronger, Easter, A Dream Play, The Ghost Sonata*). Translated by Elizabeth Sprigge. Garden City: Doubleday, 1955.

The Son of a Servant. Translated by Evert Sprinchorn. Garden City: Doubleday, 1966.

Strindberg's One-Act Plays. Translated by Arvid Paulson. New York: Washington Square, 1969.

The Vasa Trilogy: Master Olof, Gustav Vasa, Erik XIV. Translations and introductions by Walter Johnson. Seattle: University of Washington Press, 1959.

World Historical Plays (*The Nightingale of Wittenberg, Through Deserts to Ancestral Lands, Hellas,* and *The Lamb and the Beast*). Translated by Arvid Paulson. New York: American-Scandinavian Foundation, 1970.

Zones of the Spirit: A Book of Thoughts. Excerpts from the *Blue Books* translated by Claude Field. London: Allen, 1913.

SECONDARY SOURCES

C. Books in English

ANDERSON, CARL. *Poe in Northlight: The Scandinavian Response to His Life and Work*. Durham: Duke University Press, 1973.

ANDERSSON, HANS. *Strindberg's Master Olof and Shakespeare*. Uppsala: Almqvist & Wiksell, 1952.

ANDERSSON, INGVAR. *A History of Sweden*. Translated by Carolyn Hannay. London: Weidenfeld and Nicolson, 1956.

BENTLEY, ERIC. *The Playwright as Thinker*. New York: Meridian, 1960.
———.*In Search of Theater*. New York: Vintage, 1954.
BORLAND, HAROLD. *Nietzsche's Influence on Swedish Literature with Special Reference to Strindberg, Ola Hansson, Heidenstam and Fröding*. Göteborg: Wettergren & Kerber, 1956.
BRANDELL, GUNNAR. *Strindberg in Inferno*. Translation of *Strindbergs Infernokris* (1950) by Barry Jacobs. Cambridge: Harvard University Press, 1974.
BRUSTEIN, ROBERT. *The Theatre of Revolt*. Boston: Little, Brown, 1964.
BULMAN, JOAN. *Strindberg and Shakespeare*. London: Jonathan Cape, 1933.
DAHLSTRÖM, CARL E.W.L. *Strindberg's Dramatic Expressionism*. Second edition. New York: Blom, 1965. First edition, Ann Arbor: University of Michigan Press, 1930.
ESSLIN, MARTIN. *The Theatre of the Absurd*. Garden City: Doubleday, 1961.
GASSNER, JOHN. *Masters of the Drama*. New York: Dover, 1945.
GUSTAFSON, ALRIK. *A History of Swedish Literature*. Minneapolis: University of Minnesota Press, 1961. Strindberg bibliography, 601-610; list of translations of Strindberg works, 651-654.
JOHANNESSON, ERIC. *The Novels of August Strindberg: A Study in Theme and Structure*. Berkeley: University of California Press, 1968.
JOHNSON, WALTER. *Strindberg and the Historical Drama*. Seattle: University of Washington Press, 1963.
KLAF, FRANKLIN. *Strindberg, The Origin of Psychology in Modern Drama*. Introduction by John Gassner. New York: Citadel Press, 1963.
LAMM, MARTIN. *August Strindberg*. Translated and edited by Harry G. Carlson. New York: Blom, 1971.
———.*Modern Drama*. Translated by Karin Elliott. New York: Philosophical Library, 1953.
MADSEN, BØRGE GEDSØ. *Strindberg's Naturalistic Theatre: Its Relation to French Naturalism*. Copenhagen: Munksgaard and Seattle: University of Washington Press, 1962.
MORTENSEN, BRITA, and DOWNS, BRIAN. *Strindberg: An Introduction to His Life and Work*. Cambridge, England: University Press, 1949.
OLLÉN, GUNNAR. *August Strindberg*. Translated from German by Peter Tirner. New York: Ungar, 1972. Thumbnail sketches of the plays with some attention to their production.
PALMBLAD, HARRY. *Strindberg's Conception of History*. New York: Columbia University Press, 1927.
SPRIGGE, ELIZABETH. *The Strange Life of August Strindberg*. London: Chatto & Windus, 1949.

STEENE, BIRGITTA. *The Greatest Fire: A Study of August Strindberg.* Carbondale: Southern Illinois University Press, 1973.

UPPVALL, AXEL JOHAN. *August Strindberg: A Psychoanalytic Study with Special Reference to the Oedipus Complex.* Boston: Gorham, 1920.

VALENCY, MAURICE. *The Flower and the Castle: An Introduction to Modern Drama.* New York: Macmillan, 1963. Strindberg and his influence on modern drama.

D. Articles in English

ANDERSON, CARL. "Strindberg's Translations of American Humor," *Scandinavian-American Interrelations.* Oslo: Universitetsforlaget, 1971. Pp. 153-194.

BERENDSOHN, WALTER. "Strindberg's *Ensam*: A Study in Structure and Style," *Scandinavian Studies* 31: 4, 168-179.

BERGHOLZ, HARRY. "Strindberg's Anthologies of American Humorists, Bibliographically Identified," *Scandinavian Studies* 43: 4, 335-343 (1971). *Amerikanska humorister* (1879) and *Lustiga historier från Danbury* (1879): Artemus Ward, Mark Twain, Charles Dudley Warner, Thomas Bailey Aldrich, James Bailey.

―――."Toward an Authentic Text of Strindberg's *Fröken Julie*," *Orbis Litterarum*, IX (1954), 167-192.

DAHLSTRÖM, CARL E.W.L. "August Strindberg ― 1849-1912 ― Between Two Eras," *Scandinavian Studies*, 21, 1-18 (1949).

―――."Strindberg and Naturalistic Tragedy," *Scandinavian Studies,* 30: 1, 1-18.

ELOVSON, HARALD. "August Strindberg and Emigration to America Until ca. 1890," *Scandinavian-American Interrelations.* Oslo: Universitetsforlaget, 1971. Pp. 129-152. Considers Strindberg's great interest in America and a play he intended to write about emigration and its causes.

Essays on Strindberg. Edited by Carl Reinhold Smedmark. Stockholm: Beckmans, 1966.
Raymond Williams' "Strindberg and Modern Tragedy"; Evert Sprinchorn's "Julie's End"; Brian Rothwell's "The Chamber Plays"; J. R. Northam's "Strindberg's Spook Sonata"; Göran Lindström's "Strindberg's Chamber Plays, Opus 2 'After the Fire' "; Michael Meyer's "Strindberg in England"; Walter Johnson's "Strindberg and the Swedes: Past and Present"; Rune Waldekranz' "Strindberg and the silent cinema"; Elie Poulenard's "Among French peasants."

JARVI, RAYMOND. *"Ett drömspel:* A Symphony for the Stage," *Scandinavian Studies* 44: 1, 28-42.

————."Strindberg's *The Ghost Sonata* and Sonata Form," *Mosaic* 5: 4, 69-84.

JOHANNESSON, ERIC. "The Problem of Identity in Strindberg's Novels," *Scandinavian Studies*, 24: 1, 1-35.

————."*Syndabocken*: Strindberg's Last Novel," *Scandinavian Studies* 35: 1, 1-28.

————."*Taklagsöl*: An Early Experiment in the Psychological Novel," *Scandinavian Studies* 35: 3, 223-238.

JOHNSON, WALTER. "*Gustav Adolf* Revised," *Scandinavian Studies: Essays Presented to Dr. Henry Goddard Leach.* Seattle: University of Washington Press, 1965. Pp. 236-246.

LAMM, MARTIN. "Strindberg and the Theatre," *Tulane Drama Review* 6: 2, 132-139.

LEWIS, LETA JANE. "Alchemy and the Orient in Strindberg's *Dream Play*," *Scandinavian Studies* 35: 3, 208-232.

MADSEN, BØRGE GEDSØ. "Strindberg as a Naturalistic Theorist: The Essay 'Om modernt drama och modern teater'," *Scandinavian Studies* 30: 2, 83-92.

Modern Drama, V: 3 (1962).
Richard Vowles' "A Cook's Tour of Strindberg Scholarship"; Jackson Bryer's "Strindberg 1951-1962: A Bibliography"; Hans Alin's "August Strindberg—Reminiscences of a Protégé"; Walter Johnson's "*Creditors* Reexamined"; Børge Gedsø Madsen's "Naturalism in Transition: Strindberg's 'Cynical' Tragedy, *The Bond* (1892)"; Harold Borland's "The Dramatic Quality of Strindberg's Novels"; John Milton's "A Restless Pilgrim: Strindberg in *The Inferno*"; Haskell Block's "Strindberg and the Symbolist Drama"; Kenneth White's "Visions of a Transfigured Humanity: Strindberg and Lenormand"; Bernard Dukore's "Strindberg's The Real and the Unreal"; Sister M. Vinsentia's "Wagnerism in Strindberg's *The Road to Damascus*"; David Scanlan's "*The Road to Damascus*, Part One: A Skeptic's *Everyman*"; Evert Sprinchorn's "The Logic of *A Dream Play*"; Richard Vowles' "Strindberg's *Isle of the Dead*."

RAPHAEL, ROBERT. "Strindberg and Wagner," *Scandinavian Studies: Essays Presented to Dr. Henry Goddard Leach.* Seattle: University of Washington Press, 1965. Pp. 260-268.

Strindberg: A Collection of Critical Essays. Edited and introduced by Otto Reinert. Englewood Cliffs: Prentice-Hall, 1971. Robert Brustein's "August Strindberg"; Raymond Williams' "Private Tragedy: Strindberg"; R. J. Kaufmann's "Strindberg: The Absence of Irony"; Victor Svanberg's "The Strindberg Cult"; Maurice Gravier's "The Character and the Soul"; Pär Lagerkvist's "Strindberg and the Theater of Tomorrow"; Eric Bentley's "Strindberg, the One and the Many"; Martin Lamm's "*Miss Julie*"; Walter Johnson's "Strindberg and the Danse Macabre"; Birgitta Steene's "Shakespearean Elements in Historical Plays of Strindberg"; Evert Sprinchorn's "The Logic of A Dream Play"; Brian Rothwell's "The Chamber Plays."

Strindberg and Modern Theatre. Stockholm: The Strindberg Society, 1975. Papers read at the Strindberg Symposium, 1973. Luciano Codignola's "Two ideas of dramatic structure; Strindberg's last period and Pirandello's third period, a confrontation"; Timo Tiusanen's "Strindmatt or Dürrenberg? Dürrenmatt's Play Strindberg"; Walter Johnson's "Strindberg and the American University Audience"; Irena Slawinska's "Strindberg and early expressionism in Poland"; Ileana Berlogea's "Strindberg and the Romanian Modern Theatre"; Evert Sprinchorn's "The Zola of the occult"; Egil Törnqvist's "Strindberg and the drama of half-reality. An analysis of *To Damascus* I"; plus Maurice Gravier's "Strindberg et Ionesco" and Marian Lewko's "Rezeption der theatralischen Theorie Strindbergs in Polen."

T D R: The Drama Review, 13: 2 (T42, 1968).
Martin Esslin's "Naturalism in Context"; Brooks McNamara's "Scene Design, 1876-1965"; Strindberg's "Psychic Murder" (translated by Walter Johnson); Evert Sprinchorn's "Strindberg and the Greater Naturalism."

UPPVALL, AXEL JOHAN. "Strindberg in the Light of Psychoanalysis," *Scandinavian Studies*, 21: 3, 135-150.

VOWLES, RICHARD B. "Strindberg and Beethoven," *Växelverkan mellan skönlitteraturen och andra konstarter.* Uppsala, 1967. Pp. 163-182.

———. "Strindberg and the Symbolic Mill," *Scandinavian Studies*, 34: 111-119.

WINTHER, SOPHUS. "Strindberg and O'Neill," *Scandinavian Studies*, 31: 103-120.

World Theatre, XI (Spring, 1962). Edited by René Hainaux. Brussels: International Theatre Institute, 1962.
Gunnar Ollén's "Strindberg, 1962"; John Gassner's "The Influence of Strindberg in the United States"; Siegfried Melchinger's "German Theatre People Face to Face with Strindberg"; Maurice Gravier's "Strindberg and French Drama"; Raymond Williams' "Strindberg and the New Drama in Britain"; Claes Hoogland's "How to Produce Strindberg?"

E. Bibliographies

Annual bibliographies of Strindberg items appear in *Scandinavian Studies, The Publication of the Modern Language Association*, and *Samlaren.* See also the bibliographies in Gustafson's *A History of Swedish Literature* and Tigerstedt's *Svensk litteraturhistoria* (Stockholm: Natur och Kultur, 1948) and for bibliographical information about Strindberg's works in languages other than English, see also *Suecana extranea*.

BRYER, J. R. "Strindberg 1951-62. A Bibliography," *Modern Drama*, V (1963).

GUSTAFSON, ALRIK. "Some Early English and American Strindberg Criticism," *Scandinavian Studies Presented to George T. Flom*. Urbana: University of Illinois Press, 1942.

LINDSTRÖM, GÖRAN. "Strindberg Studies, 1915 - 1962," *Scandinavica*, II (1963).

RAPP, ESTHER. *Strindberg in England and America. Scandinavian Studies,* 23 (1951): 1-22, 49-59, 109-137.

F. Books in Swedish

The scholarly literature about Strindberg is extremely rich as the Gustafson and Tigerstedt bibliographies mentioned above indicate. Listed below are only those books which have been quoted in this volume and a few that touch on matters of popular interest.

FALCK, AUGUST. *Fem år med Strindberg*. Stockholm: Wahlström & Widstrand, 1935. Falck's account of the Intimate Theater.

HEMMINGSSON, PER. *August Strindberg som fotograf*. Stockholm: Bonniers, 1963. Strindberg as a photographer.

KÄRNELL, KARL-ÅKE. *Strindbergslexikon*. Stockholm: Almqvist & Wiksell, 1970. A useful guide to characters, titles, etc. in Strindberg's works.

LINDER, STEN. *Ibsen, Strindberg och andra*. Stockholm: Bonniers, 1936. Possible Strindberg influence on Ibsen.

MÖRNER, BIRGER. *Den Strindberg jag känt*. Stockholm: Bonniers, 1924. A friend's account.

Ögonvittnen: I, *August Strindberg, Ungdom och mannaår,*II, *August Strindberg, Mannaår och ålderdom*. Edited by Stellan Ahlström and Torsten Eklund. Stockholm: Wahlström & Widstrand, 1959, 1961. Testimony about Strindberg by people who knew him.

OLLÉN, GUNNAR. *Strindberg i TV*. Stockholm: Sveriges Radio, 1971. Productions on Swedish and foreign television, 1951-71.

Släkten Strindberg från Strinne. Strindberg's family tree—a booklet obtainable from the Strindberg Museum, Stockholm.

SMIRNOFF, KARIN. *Strindbergs första hustru*. Stockholm: Bonniers, 1926. Her oldest daughter's defence of Siri Strindberg.

————.*Så var det i verkligheten*. Stockholm: Bonniers, 1956 "That's how it really was" in reply to David Norrman's *Strindbergs skilsmässa från Siri von Essen* (1953; Strindberg's divorce from Siri von Essen).

SÖDERSTRÖM, GÖRAN. *Strindberg och bildkonsten*. Stockholm: Forum, 1972. A dissertation on Strindberg's life and painting with an English summary. Illustrated.

SOMMAR, CARL OLOV. *Stockholms promenad med Strindberg.* Stockholm: Bokvännerna, 1972. A pleasant guide to places in Stockholm important to Strindberg.

Strindberg i Blå Tornet: Ögonvittnesskildringar 1908-1912. Excerpted from *Mannaår och ålderdom* by Torsten Eklund. Stockholm: Wahlström & Widstrand, 1961. Contemporaries' accounts of Strindberg in his last Stockholm home, The Blue Tower (Drottninggatan 85).

Strindbergs måleri. Collected and edited by Torsten Måtte Schmidt and Göran Söderström. Malmö: Allhem, 1972. Reproductions in color of Strindberg paintings.

Strindbergsfejden. Two volumes. Foreword by John Landquist. Edited by Harry Järv. Uddevalla: Bo Cavefors, 1968. Excerpts from many hands in the Strindberg Controversy, April 29, 1910, to August 28, 1911.

Strindbergs systrar berätta om barndomshemmet och om bror August. Stockholm: Norstedt, 1926. Anna von Philp's and Nora Hartzell's recollections of their childhood home and of their brother August.

If you do read Swedish, by all means consult studies listed in the bibliographies (annual as well as Tigerstedt's and Gustafson's) by such scholars as Gunnar Ahlström, Stellan Ahlström, Walter Berendsohn, Ulf Boëthius, Gunnar Brandell, Lars Dahlbäck, Sven-Gustav Edqvist, Torsten Eklund, Allan Hagsten, Erik Hedin, Lennart Josephson, Martin Lamm, Göran Lindblad, Hans Lindström, Johan Mortensen, Nils Norman, David Norrman, Gunnar Ollén, Henry Olsson, Sven Rinman, Carl Reinhold Smedmark, and Göran Stockenström. There are, moreover, major studies by the Danes Vagn Børge and Harry Jacobsen, the Frenchmen Maurice Gravier, A. Jolivet, and Elie Poulenard, and by the Germans Karl Jaspers and Carl-Ludvig Schleich. Thérèse Dubois Janni's *August Strindberg: En biografi i text och bild* (Stockholm: Bonniers, 1970) is particularly interesting because of its photographs of persons, places, and other things important in Strindberg's biography.

Index

216